Public Transport
Its planning, management and operation

THIRD EDITION

Peter White
University of Westminster

UCL
PRESS

Third edition, first published in 1995 by UCL Press.
Second edition 1986.
First edition 1976.

UCL Press Limited
University College London
Gower Street
London WC1E 6BT

The name of University College London (UCL) is a registered
trade mark used by UCL Press with the consent of the owner.

ISBN:
1-85728-159-4 PB

British Library Cataloguing in Publication Data
A catalogue record for this book is available from the British Library.

Typeset in Optima and Times.
Printed and bound by
Biddles Ltd, Guildford and King's Lynn, England.

Contents

List of tables

Preface

This volume succeeds the second edition, published in 1986 by Hutchinson. The broad structure of the first two editions has been retained, but material has been extensively updated and revised to reflect the current institutional structure in Britain, and research findings in recent years.

The institutional framework is that applying as at April 1994, following passage of the Railways Act 1993, which aims to privatize the passenger and freight operations (although the full implications of this change have yet to become evident). London is discussed in the context of the government's decision not to press ahead with bus deregulation, announced in November 1993. Subject to any radical political developments, this structure is likely to continue in effect for the immediate future, although further change in the form of local government is currently proposed.

The impacts of radical change in the local bus industry following deregulation under the 1985 Transport Act are examined, notably in Chapter 10.

Use has been made of the latest national surveys – principally the 1991 Census and 1989/91 National Travel Survey – to illustrate the current rôle of public transport.

Chapters 1–9 provide a description of various aspects of public transport. A broader approach has been taken in the final chapter, giving viewpoints on current and future policy.

Since 1971 I have been based at the Transport Studies Group of the University of Westminster (until 1992 known as the Polytechnic of Central London). Work on all three editions of this book has been undertaken during that period, drawing on the expertise and support of colleagues, notably research staff who have worked directly with me on specific projects, including Stephen Williams, Paul Heels, Martin Higginson, Stephen Holt, Andrew Mellor, Tony Kent, Roy Turner, Neil Anderson, Derek Robbins and Steven Cassidy. Assistance has also been provided by teaching and research staff primarily concerned with other modes within the Transport Studies Group, notably Nigel Dennis in respect of air transport. Work undertaken at other academic institutions is also quoted extensively, notably the many studies in the public transport field at the Institute of Transport Studies, University of Leeds. Originals for Figures 2.1 and 2.2 were supplied by London Transport.

The area covered in terms of organisational structure and statistical evidence in this volume is that of the United Kingdom of Great Britain and Northern Ireland, but reference is also made to experience elsewhere, notably in other west European countries, where relevant.

Within the constraints of length imposed by the need to provide a compact textbook at a reasonable price, it has not been possible to go in to the depth that one would wish on many topics – indeed, to have written a longer book would have been easier than making the sometimes difficult selection of material to be included. However, the references given at the end of each chapter will hopefully provide opportunities for readers to examine certain aspects in greater depth.

PRW, spring 1994

CHAPTER 1

Organization and control of transport in Britain

Within this chapter the organizations and legislation relevant to public transport in Britain and Northern Ireland are outlined, with brief reference made to circumstances in other countries for purposes of comparison. The situation described is that applying from April 1994.

Central government

Overall responsibility for transport policy lies with the Department of Transport (DOT), whose scope has expanded in recent years to cover all modes, including shipping and aviation, the sole exception being inland waterways, which fall under the Department of Environment (DOE). The latter also has influence on transport policy through its rôle in control of local government expenditure and approval of land-use plans. Joint DOT/DOE regional offices appraise local authority transport plans.

Both departments are headed by a Secretary of State, with cabinet rank, assisted by several Ministers of State. Their power is exercised directly in England, and within Wales through the Welsh Office, although generally under identical legislation. Within Scotland, the Scottish Development Department (SDD), under the Secretary of State for Scotland, takes the rôle of both DOT and DOE, sometimes under different legislation, as described below. Within Northern Ireland, the Northern Ireland Office administers the province on behalf of central government; here also different legislation may apply. The self-governing Channel Islands and Isle of Man determine their own local policies, but are strongly influenced by central government in aviation and shipping policy.

The Department of Transport had until recently a direct rôle in the construction and maintenance of the trunk road and motorway network – a situation not matched by so immediate an involvement in any other modes, which tend to be regulated through separate statutory bodies (such as the Traffic Commissioners), or operated by State-owned industries (such as Railtrack and London Regional Transport), or by local authorities.

Within the Department of Transport, several Ministers and Under-Secretaries assist the Secretary of State. In 1985, for the first time, one of them was specifically designated as Minister for Public Transport. This was followed by a Minister with specific responsibility for transport in London from April 1992. Other ministerial responsibilities include national policy on roads and traffic, aviation, and shipping. The Civil Service staff of the Department is headed by a Permanent Secretary, responsible to whom are various Deputy Secretaries, each in turn responsible for a specialist sector (whose definitions and responsibilities change from time to time).

Some activities previously under the direct control of the Department of Transport are now the responsibilities of specific executive agencies (which have greater power in determining their own policy, especially in relation to staffing). These include the Vehicle Inspectorate, responsible for annual inspection and other safety controls on road vehicles, and the Transport Research Laboratory (TRL), which undertakes research into highways and public transport. The largest such agency is the Highways Agency, established on 1 April 1994, with responsibility for the management, maintenance and planning of trunk roads and motorways.

Two other government departments also have substantial influence on transport policy. The Department of Trade and Industry (DTI) is involved in certain aspects of industrial strategy and the operation of competition policy, exercised through the Office of Fair Trading (OFT) and the Monopolies and Mergers Commission (MMC). This aspect has gained increasing importance in the transport sector since deregulation of local bus services. The Treasury is responsible for overall allocation of expenditures between departments, and fiscal policy such as fuel duty, and taxation of company car benefits. The rôle of financial control has become particularly strong in the transport sector in recent years, and it tends to determine other aspects of policy.

Local government

Most parts of England and Wales are placed under county councils (sometimes known as "the shires"), numbering 47 in all. Their extent and structure dates from the local government re-organization of 1974. They are highway and transportation authorities, being directly responsible for local road maintenance and construction (and sometimes likewise for motorways and trunk roads, as agents of the Department of Transport). In the field of public transport, they do not operate services directly (except, in a few cases, some school buses), but provide support for non-commercial bus services through seeking tenders for such operations. They retain a rôle in the promotion of public transport (until the 1985 Transport Act one of "co-ordination") which may involve provision of comprehensive timetable information, etc. As education authorities, they may spend large sums on school transport (often exceeding direct support to public transport). A positive rôle in stimulating rail use is often adopted, albeit rarely with major responsibility for meeting operating losses, but including, for example, re-opening of rural stations.

A two-tier system of local government exists within the counties, the lower tier being the districts, typically of 50,000 to 200,000 population and each based on a small to medium-size town, but including some larger cities such as Nottingham. There are 333 district councils in England and Wales, of which about 20 own companies operating bus services; these are the former "municipal" undertakings, until 1986 directly controlled by local authority committees. Districts are usually responsible for setting concessionary fares for elderly, disabled and children, although in some counties a common county-wide scheme has been established. Some districts – typically larger urban areas such as Southampton – also undertake highway maintenance and traffic management, under powers delegated by the county council. Parking is generally managed at district level. Under the Road Traffic Act (1991), districts may also create Special Parking Areas (SPAs), in which they take over responsibility for on-street parking control from wardens controlled by the police. From July 1994, this power has been used by all London boroughs and may be applied in some cities other than London. Districts are also the licensing bodies for taxis and private hire cars.

Within Scotland, local government was re-organized in 1975. There are nine regions, each based on a major city such as Aberdeen (Grampian), and three island councils. They are the highway and public transport authorities. One bus operating company remains in public ownership (Lothian Region). The 53 district councils in Scotland are smaller than those farther south, and they have very limited transport functions, except in respect of taxi licensing.

Within the major conurbations in England, a one-tier system of local government exists. In the six metropolitan regions (West Midlands, Merseyside, Greater Manchester, South Yorkshire, West Yorkshire, Tyne & Wear) local government is provided through metropolitan district councils (about six in each area, 36 in all), undertaking almost all transport and planning functions, with some *ad hoc* co-ordinating bodies covering each metropolitan area as a whole. In London, some 32 boroughs (plus the City of London Corporation) function similarly, although with greater central government involvement in co-ordinating London-wide activities (notably the rôle of the Traffic Director, responsible for Red Routes). The Metropolitan Police also plays a significant rôle in London, both in traffic policy and (through the Public Carriage Office) as the licensing body for taxis.

Under the Transport Act 1968, Passenger Transport Authorities (PTAs) were set up in four conurbations (West Midlands, Merseyside, Greater Manchester, and Tyne & Wear). These took over the existing municipal bus operators, and also acquired a general responsibility for the integration and planning of public transport as a whole in their areas. The PTAs as such consisted of elected members of local authorities in their area. Until 1974, they were special-purpose

3

authorities, but on creation of the six metropolitan counties, the four areas above being slightly re-defined and joined by West and South Yorkshire, they effectively became the public transport committees of the metropolitan counties. Following abolition of the metropolitan counties in 1986, the PTAs reverted to being bodies composed of elected members from district councils in their areas, and are also dependent upon transfers from district budgets for their financing.

Within each PTA area, day-to-day responsibility for its public transport rôle is placed under the Passenger Transport Executive (PTE), a body of professional managers. The PTEs are responsible for agreements with railway operators (under section 20 of the 1968 Act), and provision of tendered bus services and concessionary fares (under the 1985 Transport Act). They also play a major rôle in providing comprehensive passenger information systems, provision of school transport, co-ordinated ticketing arrangements (such as multi-operator travel-cards), and the planning, construction and financing of light rail systems such as those in Manchester and Sheffield.

A Passenger Transport Authority and Executive also functions in Strathclyde, the largest of the Scottish regions, covering the Glasgow area. It also operates a small underground railway. One other PTE, Tyne and Wear, runs a larger system, the local Metro.

Within London, London Transport reverted to central government control (from that of the former Greater London Council) in 1984, under the London Regional Transport Act, and was re-named London Regional Transport (LRT). However, its area of coverage remained the same, and for public purposes it has reverted since 1990 to the familiar "London Transport" title.

In Northern Ireland, some 26 district councils exist, but have a very limited rôle in transport. The only municipal bus undertaking, Belfast, was absorbed by the nationalized Ulsterbus fleet some years ago, and it operates as its Citybus subsidiary.

Public finance

Although the majority of expenditure on transport is that incurred by private individuals in running cars, and in paying fares to operators, public finance plays a major rôle. The principal categories of expenditure in 1992–3 are identified in Table 1.1

In practice, much of the expenditure handled through local authorities is covered through central government grants: Rate Support Grant (RSG) supporting local authority expenditure in general, and the Transport Supplementary Grant (TSG) covering certain transport items, principally capital spending on road schemes of more than local importance. However, most transport expenditure (such as that on tendered bus services) comes from the local authority's budget as a whole, rather than specific grants for transport purposes. Central govern-

Table 1.1 Public expenditure on transport in Great Britain, 1992–3 (£ million).

Through central government:	
National roads system (capital and current)	2,409
British Rail:	
Public Service Obligation (PSO) grant	900
Level crossings grant	27
Pensions grant	68
Bus fuel duty rebate	189
London Regional Transport:	
Concessionary fares compensation	113
Bus service revenue support (including capital)	159
Other grants (mostly Underground investment)	487
Other central government spending (administration, research, vehicle licensing, freight, shipping, etc.)	544
Local transport (excluding London Regional Transport):	
Roads and car parks (capital and current)	3,404
Public transport – capital	184
Public transport – revenue support	373
(of which, PTE payments to BR)	(116)
Concessionary fares compensation	327
Ports and airports – capital	94
Education transport	397

Source: derived from tables 1.17 and 1.18 in *Transport statistics Great Britain* (London: HMSO, 1993).

Notes:

The "local transport" element is principally that handled through local authority budgets, but also includes some central government grants (Transport Supplementary Grant for roads, and Section 56 Grant for rail schemes).

Total support to BR comprised the PSO, pensions, and level crossings grants, plus PTE payments.

The "revenue support" element of local transport relates primarily to bus services, and includes costs incurred by local authorities and PTEs, in addition to payments (for tendered services) passed onto the bus operators as such.

The fuel duty rebate payable to London Regional Transport is included in the national fuel duty rebate total.

The revenue support to bus services in London includes a large element for depreciation and renewal: no equivalent grants apply elsewhere.

Local public transport capital spending related mainly to the South Yorkshire Supertram scheme.

Education transport spending is from *Education statistics for the United Kingdom* (London: HMSO, 1992), table 6.

ment funding to local authorities is determined by the Standard Spending Assessment (SSA), which takes account of factors such as total population, density of the area, and so on. The proportion of revenue received directly from the tax on local households (the council tax) is relatively small. Rates levied on business (the National Non-domestic Rate, NNDR) are collected by central government and reallocated to local authorities through the SSA and RSG mechanisms.

Each London borough, metropolitan district council, and county (or region, in Scotland), prepares an annual Transport Policies and Programme (TPP) document, covering in detail the forthcoming financial year, with an outline programme for capital spending over five years. This is assessed for grant purposes by the Department of Transport, with an approved total spending, and level of TSG, announced around the end of the calendar year, effective for the next financial year. The development of the system is discussed further in Chapter 10. TSG is limited largely to capital spending on road schemes (and some related aspects, such as traffic safety measures and bus priorities/park-and ride affecting major roads; Department of Transport 1993). However, grants for major public transport capital schemes can still be made under Section 56 of the 1968 Transport Act, under which (subject to a complex economic evaluation) central government may contribute a grant of 50% of the capital cost (Department of Transport 1989). TSG never applied in Scotland, the TPPs being used only to determine approved total expenditure and RSG contribution.

A more comprehensive package-approach to TPP preparation, including public transport projects, is now being encouraged, under Department of Transport Circular 2/93, but as yet TSG remains largely limited to road schemes (further comment is made in Ch. 10). Local government spending in total is also strictly limited by recent legislation, which enables government to limit the level of council tax, as well as to control grants paid to local authorities.

The operating industries

The bus and coach industry

The bus and coach industry comprises five main segments:

The independent operators
These are firms that have always been in private ownership, generally running small fleets, except for some of the larger coach operators. The typical fleet size is around 1 to 10 vehicles. It is also clear from Table 1.2 that this sector is concentrated mainly in the "other" services market (primarily contract and private hire work) although the opportunities to enter scheduled services were substantially enlarged by the Transport Act of 1985.

Regional bus companies
Under the Transport Act 1985, the National Bus Company (a state-owned holding company, controlling about 40 regional operating companies in England and Wales) was privatized through the sale of each company as a separate business. This process was completed in 1988, and was followed by the sale of subsidiaries of the similar Scottish Bus Group (SBG) between 1989 and 1991, under the Transport (Scotland) Act of 1989.

Many companies were purchased by management buy-outs, sometimes with employee shareholdings. Others were purchased by new holding companies which have in some cases grown through purchase of some of the earlier independent management buy-outs. The largest is the Stagecoach Group, followed by Badgerline Holdings, both floated in 1993. These regional companies typically provide a mix of rural, inter-urban and urban services, and in some cases

6

have also replaced or taken over local authority bus fleets. In Northern Ireland, Ulsterbus Ltd took over the bus interests of the Ulster Transport Authority (UTA), under the Transport (NI) Act of 1969, and it remains wholly in state ownership.

London Transport

Bus services, largely confined to the Greater London area, were operated by London Buses Ltd (LBL), through ten subsidiaries covering specified areas within London, all of which were privatized during autumn 1994. London Underground Ltd controls the rail interests. Through its rôle as provider of a comprehensive bus network, London Transport had placed about half the network out to competitive tendering on a route-by-route basis by autumn 1993. Both LBL companies and other operators were able to bid, and each gained about half the services thus tendered. The remaining half of the overall network was operated directly by LBL subsidiaries under a negotiated contract, but has not yet been subject to route-by-route tendering. LT's bus responsibilities are now grouped under London Transport Buses (LTB), responsible for overall planning and co-ordination of the bus network which, following privatization of the LBL companies, will be operated entirely by companies in the private sector. LTB handles all bus-related matters within LT, including service tendering.

Local authority fleets

Following the Transport Act of 1985, fleets owned by local authorities and PTEs were restructured as "arm's length" Passenger Transport Companies (PTCs). Privatization is not mandatory, but has been strongly encouraged by central government. All seven ex-PTE companies have been privatized, and about half of those owned by district or regional councils have ceased trading or been privatized. One of the remaining local-authority-owned companies, Blackpool, also runs a tramway. Their operations remain predominantly in local, scheduled services, but many have diversified into coach operation, in some cases setting up separate subsidiaries for this purpose.

Express coach services

Although opened to competition under the Transport Act of 1980, the express coach network is dominated by one operator, National Express Ltd, originally a part of the National Bus Company, and initially privatized through a management buy-out in 1988. Subsequently it was floated as a plc in 1992, and has expanded into other activities, notably through the purchase of East Midlands Airport in 1993. It took over the similar Scottish-based Citylink network in 1993. Very few vehicles are owned by National Express as such, as almost all are hired in from other companies (mostly former NBC/SBG regional companies, or smaller independents).

The internal structure of bus and coach companies, apart from informal structures found in the very smallest concerns, has been traditionally based on a

7

Table 1.2 Structure of the bus and coach industry, by fleet size and vehicle-kilometres run, 1991/2.

Type and size of operator	Local bus vehicle-km (% of GB total)	"Other" bus and coach vehicle-km (% of GB total)
London Buses Ltd	10.6	*
PTCs and private sector operators, by fleet size:		
Under 10 vehicles	3.1	33.9
10–19 vehicles	3.7	24.5
20–99 vehicles	15.4	26.6
100–249 vehicles	16.9	5.0
Over 250 vehicles	50.5	10.0
GB total km (millions)	2,487 (100.1%)	1,386 (100.0%)

Sources: Bus and coach statistics 1991/2 (London: HMSO, 1992), table 10.3; London Transport annual report 1992/3, p. 54.

Notes:

*All LBL kilometres assumed to fall in "local" category, although in practice a very small part might be classified as "other".

Of the local bus service vehicle-km in 1991/2, 32% was handled by public sector operators (i.e. LBL and the remaining PTCs) (Bus and coach statistics 1991/2, table 10.4). This fell to 28% in 1992/3 (ibid. 1992/3, table 9.1).

In addition to the totals shown for Great Britain, Ulsterbus and its Citybus subsidiary operated 56 million vehicle-km, mostly on local services in calendar year 1992 (data from Ulsterbus).

separation of "traffic" and "engineering" functions, the former encompassing the planning and operation of services, the latter provision of vehicles to operate them. This was also associated with a centralized structure in which the two functions were only brought together at the level of senior management. A much more decentralized approach is now taken, with greater power given to managers of subsidiary companies, and to area or depot managers within those companies.

Outside London and Northern Ireland, companies determine which services they will operate on a commercial basis. Other services may then be provided by the local authority under contract, following a competitive bidding procedure. Typically, these are for parts of the day and week (e.g. evening and Sunday services) rather than entire routes throughout the week, in contrast to the situation within London where contracts normally apply to the entire operation throughout the week of the services concerned.

The railways

The British Railways Board (BRB), a nationalized industry, is responsible for the national passenger network, most public freight services and the great majority of passenger traffic by rail. In addition to railways as such, there are several subsidiary companies. The British Railways Property Board handles the sale and letting of non-operational property.

At autumn 1993, the railway operations as such were organized on the principle of sector management, i.e. according to the market sectors served rather than on the territorial structure previously found. This structure dated in essence from 1982, but had been modified on several occasions. The sectors comprised:

- InterCity, covering the principal main lines from London to other cities, and the cross-country Newcastle–Bristol and Birmingham–Poole corridors
- Network South East (NSE), covering the London commuter network and other services in the South East region, extending as far as Exeter, Northampton and King's Lynn
- Regional Railways, comprising all other passenger services, including local services within the PTEs under Section 20 agreements, rural services, and major non-InterCity routes such as Liverpool–Leeds–Newcastle
- Trainload Freight, handling trainload movements such as coal, oil and aggregates
- Railfreight Distribution, handling container traffic, etc.
- Parcels.

Freight, Parcels and InterCity sectors were required to meet their attributed costs from user revenues and attain a real return on current assets, whereas the NSE and Regional sectors relied for a substantial part of their income upon the Public Service Obligation (PSO) grant.

The establishment of sector management enabled BR to gear its policies more specifically to customers in specific sectors, and to set investment programmes (for example, in purchase of rolling stock) to meet them more appropriately. The process was completed in 1992 with the introduction of Organizing for Quality (OfQ) in which previous conflicting management structures arising from the former territorial pattern of responsibilities were abolished, and sectors took direct responsibility for track and other overhead costs.

Other major activities are the responsibility of subsidiary companies:

- European Passenger Services Ltd (EPS), responsible for the current international traffic, and development of services to operate through the Channel Tunnel from autumn 1994
- Union Railways Ltd, responsible for planning the proposed high-speed line from London to the Channel Tunnel.

From May 1994 EPS was transferred from the BRB to direct central government control. When the winning private sector consortium for the Channel Tunnel Rail Link (CTRL) is selected, EPS and Union Railways will be handed over to that body.

- British Rail Maintenance Ltd (BRML), responsible for repair of locomotives and rolling stock
- BR Telecommunications Ltd (BRT), responsible for the existing railway telecommunications systems, and its development as public operation

- British Rail Property Board, responsible for sale and letting of property, and development schemes at stations
- British Rail Infrastructure Services (BRIS), responsible for track and signalling maintenance on contract to Railtrack.

It is planned to privatize these businesses, probably starting with BRIS, BRML and BRT.

Under the Railways Act 1974, the Secretary of State for Transport could give the Railways Board policy directives. The first of these merely required the Board to provide a service "generally comparable" with that offered in 1974 (in effect, no major route closures). More specific directives have been given recently, notably in setting financial targets for each Sector. The PSO Grant enabled the railways to offer a very much more extensive passenger network than would otherwise be the case, especially for local and cross-country routes. As most track and signalling costs were allocated to the passenger services under the "prime user" cost convention (see Ch. 6), freight and parcels traffic bore a relatively modest share of total costs, in addition to those clearly specific to it. The PSO payment replaced specific grants for passenger services, which had been introduced under the Transport Act 1968. The 1974 Act also provided compensation for the pensions burden faced by the railways, and half the cost of operating level crossings.

Within the seven PTA areas, BR services rely on local support paid through the PTEs, under Section 20 of the 1968 Act. These enable the PTEs to establish common fares and service-level policies for BR and tendered bus services, but also result in a substantial financial burden on local budgets (see above) which is not felt by local authorities elsewhere. It is not surprising that some of the greatest pressures to reduce costs and improve efficiency are coming in areas covered by PTEs. Conversely, funding for BR services in the London area came through the PSO Grant. Both BR and London Underground systems are effectively controlled by central government, and some greater co-ordination is now evident, such as the common travelcard introduced in 1986, and planning of the CrossRail scheme.

The rather limited rail network in Northern Ireland – on a slightly wider gauge than mainland Britain – is operated by Northern Ireland Railways (NIR), which took over rail services from the former Ulster Transport Authority.

Many preserved steam railways are operated by private companies and voluntary organizations, generally providing seasonal tourist services. Preserved steam and electric lines on the Isle of Man are owned by its government.

Under the Railways Act of 1993, British Rail is to be privatized. The recently finalized sector management structure has been replaced from April 1994 by a reversion to a territorial structure. Individual groups of services are being offered to franchisees, the London–Gatwick service (previously part of Inter-City) being operated on a "shadow franchise" to test the concept from October 1993. Passenger services are now operated by 25 Train Operating Units (TOUs), of which five joined Gatwick Express as shadow franchises from April 1994 (e.g. South West Trains, operating the network of services from London Waterloo). When franchised, these will be run by Train Operating Companies (TOCs), many of which are likely to be management buy-out companies. The possibility of "micro-franchising" (of individual services, or much smaller groups of services) has also been raised

The allocation of franchises, and the financial support most or all of them will need from central government, will be handled by the Office of Passenger Rail Franchising (OPRAF) under its Franchising Director, appointed by the Secretary of State for Transport.

Track, signalling and certain major stations are now the responsibility of Railtrack plc. Currently, most of the track maintenance work is carried out by BRIS (see above), but contracting-in from private sector companies is likely to grow in importance. Railtrack's costs are covered by charges made to train operators (see Ch. 6).

From 1 April 1994 the passenger rolling stock fleet was transferred to three rolling stock leasing companies (ROSCOs), who charge the train operating units for the provision of stock.

The previous Trainload Freight sector management structure was replaced by three territorial groupings. Rail Express Systems (RES) handles Post Office contract traffic. The Freightliner and Red Star Parcel businesses currently remain in the public sector, with major responsibility for developing freight services through the Channel Tunnel.

Some limited private operation has already been attempted on the BR network, although with little success in the case of overnight passenger services (by the Stagecoach company) and a public freight service (by Charterail). Of greater importance has been the precedent set by the operation of stone and aggregate bulk traffic by the quarrying companies concerned (Yeomans and ARC – now merged as "Mendip Rail"), using their own locomotives and wagons on BR tracks. A similar pattern may be followed by major power generators for movement of coal. An increased rôle for the private sector is also evident in rolling stock and infrastructure maintenance, and is likely to expand further under Railtrack. Rolling stock manufacture was privatized several years ago.

Sea and air transport

Sea

Following privatization policies in the early 1980s, all marine operations are in the private sector, except for many smaller airports, and Caledonian MacBrayne (Calmac) – the remaining component of the Scottish Transport Group (the greater part having been the former Scottish Bus Group), operating many of the Scottish island seryices. The largest ferry operators are Sealink Stena and P&O,

whose services compete strongly in the cross-Channel market. Both operators have shifted towards roll-on/roll-off services for cars, coaches and lorries as their major activity, but also remain important for foot-passengers interchanging from rail and bus services. Other ferries are operated by many private companies, some very small.

Air

Trunk domestic air services are provided by the two largest UK-based carriers, British Airways and British Midland, competing directly on major routes to Scotland. British Midland also plays a wider rôle in operating many secondary services. Another major operator in this sector is Air UK. Regional services may be operated by local "third-level" carriers such as Manx Airways, and Aurigny in the Channel Islands. BA also provides some local services through its Scottish network and Scilly Isles helicopter service. Although the UK domestic air scene has experienced the arrival of many new small operators under increasingly liberal regulatory policy in recent years, the market has grown slowly on the minor services (see Ch. 9), resulting in a large turnover of small operators on marginal routes.

Major international airports, including Heathrow, Gatwick, Stansted, Glasgow, Edinburgh and Aberdeen are operated by BAA plc, formerly a nationalized industry. Many other airports are operated through local authority companies, such as Humberside, or have now been privatized through individual sales, such as that of East Midlands. Minor airports in Scotland, which have little hope of functioning commercially, are run directly by the Civil Aviation Authority (CAA), a body that also provides the national air-traffic control system.

Regulation

Regulation may be considered in three aspects: quality, quantity and price. In many countries they are closely linked, but in Britain very little quantity and price regulation remains, apart from the effective control over BR and LT services by central government.

Quality

Quality control of bus and coach operators is exercised through the regional Traffic Commissioners (of which there are eight) under the Public Passenger Vehicles Act 1981. This established a system of "operator licensing", under which a person or company seeking to operate public services has to establish good repute, adequate financial support and satisfactory maintenance facilities.

The term "public service vehicle" (PSV) largely corresponds to the everyday definition of a bus or coach (there is virtually no legal distinction as such between them), except that certain small vehicles of 16 seats or fewer, and those used other than for public service (such as school buses owned and operated by a local education authority), are excluded. A licensed taxi "plying for hire" may have up to 8 seats, but a vehicle of 9 to 16 seats used in public service (other than with a Minibus Permit, or as a community bus; see Ch. 8) requires a PSV licence.

The number of buses and coaches that the holder of an operator licence is permitted to run (which may vary according to the quality of maintenance, financial resources, etc.) is specified by the Traffic Commissioner. For each vehicle permitted, a disc is issued, which it must display. The commissioners have the power to revoke or (at present) curtail the duration of an operator's licence, or change the number of vehicles it covers.

Each PSV is subject to strict annual inspections, following which a new licence is issued. A Certificate of Initial Fitness is issued to a new vehicle, provided that it meets the standard regulations regarding dimensions, etc. (see Ch. 3). Each driver is required to hold a passenger carrying vehicle (PCV) driver's licence, issued following a specialized driving test and medical examination.

The Traffic Commissioners formerly enjoyed a much wider rôle. Under the Road Traffic Act 1930 (whose principles applied largely unchanged until 1980) they also regulated the quantity and price of bus services. Apart from hire and contract markets, which have not been subject to price and quantity regulation in Britain (unlike, for example, the USA), all scheduled services, excursions and tours required a road service licence, specifying the route followed, timetable, and, generally speaking, the fares charged. Even the size of vehicle or extent of duplication could be controlled by attaching conditions to the licence. Some minor changes aimed largely at innovative services in rural areas (see Ch. 8) were introduced in the late 1970s, but the first major change came in the Transport Act 1980, which removed the need for road services licences for express services and tours carrying passengers over 30 miles or more, measured in a straight line. For express services, a simple notification to the Commissioner of the proposed route and starting date (in practice, a very nominal requirement) was all that was required. The 1980 Act also effectively removed the control of fares from the commissioners.

The Public Passenger Vehicles Act 1981 is a piece of consolidating legislation, incorporating the regulatory changes of the 1980 Act and those of the late 1970s (such as the Minibus Act 1977), and continues to form the basis of bus and coach "quality" regulation.

The 1985 Act took the process of deregulation one stage further by removing the need to obtain a road service licence for a stage carriage service. A distinction is now drawn between a local service – one carrying some or all passengers distances of less than 15 miles – and all others (thus changing once again the definition of "express"). For the local service, the proposed route must be registered with the Traffic Commissioners at least 42 days before operation is due –

for others, not even this process is required. Provided that the person registering the service is the holder of an operator licence, the process is automatic, and objections from other parties are not accepted. The only restriction on operation is through Traffic Regulation Conditions, which may, for example, prevent buses from using certain streets, or picking up at some points, but may not discriminate between operators.

Taxi regulation was also changed under the 1985 Act, although not to the same extent. Quality and quantity control is handled by district councils, all of whom now exercise powers to licence hackney carriages (taxis, i.e. vehicles permitted to pick up in the street or at ranks, for separate fares). Most authorities also exercise their powers to licence "private hire vehicles", i.e. those hired by prior arrangement (such as a telephone request, or through an office). In London, the Metropolitan Police licence the hackney carriages (commonly known as black cabs), through a strict system of quality regulation (both for vehicle and driver), but quantity limits have never applied. However, private hire vehicles (locally known as minicabs) remain almost totally uncontrolled. A general review of taxi and private hire vehicle regulation was announced by the government in October 1993.

Regulation of rail safety is exercised through the Railways Inspectorate of the Health and Safety Executive (transferred from the Department of Transport), which is empowered to approve new installations, and carries out a very thorough investigation of all major accidents.

Under the Railways Act (1993), the Office of the Rail Regulator (ORR) was created, responsible for regulating the privatized passenger railway, including matters such as open access arrangements, and promotion of the use and development of the railway network.

Quantity and price

Road

The 1985 Act also discouraged the application of quantity restrictions on taxi services (i.e. limiting the total number of taxis, or "plates" in each district's area), but some district councils do retain this power, subject to showing that "no significant unmet need" would remain as a result. Powers to set fares for taxis remain. Shared taxi operation (splitting the costs of a hired journey between individual passengers), and "taxibus" operation (running a vehicle of 8 seats or less on a timetabled service at advertised individual fares) were also legalized, but with little impact nationally.

The local bus deregulation of the 1985 Act does not apply to the London area (i.e. that covered by the former GLC), or to Northern Ireland. The London Regional Transport Act of 1984 removed London Transport's combined rôle of operator and licensing authority. Applications to operate local bus services may be made to the South Eastern and Metropolitan Traffic Commissioner, operating in the same rôle generally adopted by the Traffic Commissioners elsewhere until 1986. However, services in London may also be operated through an agreement with LT, and London Transport Buses themselves do not need to obtain local service licences.

Air

Both quality and quantity control of civil air transport are exercised through the Civil Aviation Authority (CAA), a nominally independent body. The general framework of regulation was set out in the Civil Aviation Act 1971, and modified in subsequent Acts. However, much of the regulatory policy has been determined by government directives to the CAA, and the Authority's own policy statements. From September 1985, the controls over domestic air fares were largely removed, with the CAA intervening only in exceptional circumstances. Fares are simply notified ten days in advance. However, a proposal to remove capacity control for an experimental period of two years was not proceeded with.

Domestic air service regulation thus became increasingly liberalized, although not to the same extent as road transport. International services, within Europe gradually became subject to a more competitive regime, under EC policy.

From 1 January 1993 previous domestic and EC regulation was replaced by EC regulations 2407/92, which covers operator licensing of air carriers; 2408/92 (access to intra-Community air routes), and 2409/92 (fares and rates). These largely remove previous restrictions, although member states retain some powers in respect of domestic and cabotage traffic. Simplified procedures apply to operation of aircraft under 20 seats.

Other organizations

Other organizations involved in the public transport industry include trade unions, user groups and professional institutions.

Trade unions

Road

The largest trade union is the Transport and General Workers Union (T&GWU), covering many aspects of public transport, including bus and coach drivers, and airport and seaport staff. Some bus and coach drivers in district council companies are represented by the General and Municipal Workers. The Rail Maritime and Transport (RMT) Union (incorporating the former National Union of Railwaymen) also represents some drivers in regional bus companies, a legacy of railway holdings in earlier regional groups. Engineering workers in the bus

15

industry are represented by a wide range of craft unions, who co-operate in bargaining procedures.

Following deregulation and substantial privatization of the bus and coach industry, and parallel changes in labour legislation, the former pattern of national negotiations over wages and conditions has been replaced by local bargaining.

Rail

In the railways, there has traditionally been a sharp demarcation between the manual, skilled, and clerical staff. The majority of staff are represented by the RMT, including guards, station staff and signalmen. Clerical and supervisory staff are represented by the Transport Salaried Staffs Association (TSSA). Drivers are represented by the Associated Society of Locomotive Engineers and Firemen (ASLEF). Until 1993, negotiations over wages and conditions were carried out nationally with British Rail, but a pattern of local bargaining is likely to emerge following the creation of franchises, and privatization (see above).

User groups

Passengers' interests are represented by both statutory and independent groups. Rail users are represented by the Central Rail Users' Consultative Committee (CRUCC), which submits an annual report to the Secretary of State, but has little effective power.

In the London region, the London Regional Passengers' Committee (LRPC) represents the interests of users of London Transport, and British Rail services. Its members are appointed by the Secretary of State for Trade and Industry. It is the only statutory consumers' committee with responsibility for bus, as well as rail, services.

Local consumers' committees and user groups have been set up, in some cases as a result of encouragement under the Transport Act 1978, such as that in Merseyside. Others arise from spontaneous action by consumers themselves, notably rail users' associations on routes to London. Ironically, these may support some of the more prosperous and well served users. However, a National Federation of Bus Users was set up in 1985. The most poorly served, those in rural areas, find it difficult to organize, in part because facilities are so thin already. More enlightened operators have sought to consult the public on matters such as extensive service revisions, sometimes by calling public meetings.

External effects of transport modes have received increasing attention, together with concern about the need to encourage ecologically efficient modes. Nationally based pressure groups may combine this interest with a support for public transport and its users – for example, in seeking to encourage use of public transport rather than cars in congested cities. They include groups such as the Friends of the Earth (FOE) and the Council for the Protection of Rural England

(CPRE). The organization Transport 2000 is supported by a range of such organizations, together with the rail trade unions, in seeking to encourage a national policy more favourable to public transport, especially rail.

Industry associations and professional institutions

Interests of local public transport operators (other than British Rail and London Underground) are represented nationally by the Confederation of Passenger Transport UK (CPT), incorporating the former Bus and Coach Council (BCC). Most members are bus and coach operators – from both the private and public sectors – covered in two sections (Section 1 for operators with fewer than 50 vehicles, section 2 for all others). Another section comprises urban rail operators such as Sheffield Supertram. Its rôle within the independent bus and coach sector has become greater in recent years, although many small operators are not members. Local coach operators' associations also represent the interests of the independent sector.

Local government associations concerned with transport matters include Association of District Councils (ADC), the Association of Metropolitan Authorities (AMA, covering the metropolitan districts), and the Association of County Councils (ACC). Anticipating planned restructuring of local government into a single-tier pattern, a merger between them is now proposed. Within Scotland, the Convention of Scottish Local Authorities (COSLA) plays a similar rôle.

The major professional body is the Chartered Institute of Transport (CIT), whose Membership grade (MCIT) is the main qualification specific to the transport operating industry. Transport co-ordinating officers in the county and regional councils are represented by the Association of Transport Co-ordinating Officers (ATCO), which liaises with the ACC, and the County Surveyors Society (CSS) on policy issues. Economists practising in transport may often join the Transport Economists' Group (TEG). Academic teaching and research in transport is co-ordinated through the Universities Transport Studies Group (UTSG) and Organization of Teachers in Transport Studies (OTTS).

References and suggested further reading

Department of Transport 1989. Circular 3/89.
— 1993. Circular 2/93: *Transport policies and programme submission for 1994–5.*
— 1994. Local Authority Circular 2/94: *Transport policies and programme submissions for 1995–6.*
An annual review of the Department of Transport's activities and spending plans is published each year, as part of the government's overall expenditure plans for the next three years. The most recent is *Transport report 1994: the Government's expenditure*

17

plans 1994–5 to 1996–7 (Cm 2506, London: HMSO, 1994)

The law regarding bus and coach operations is extensively described in *Croner's coach and bus operations* (New Malden, Surrey: Croner) in loose-leaf form, updated quarterly.

CHAPTER 2
The rôle of public transport

The overall pattern

The rôle played by public transport in Britain has changed considerably in recent decades, from a semi-monopoly in the late 1940s – under somewhat artificial conditions – to a small share of the market in the early 1990s. In the case of bus travel, this has been associated with an absolute decline in the volume of travel; for rail an approximately stable absolute volume but a fall as a percentage of a growing total market. The overall share of motorized domestic passenger-kilometres (km) taken by public transport – 13% in 1992 – is fairly typical of Western Europe, but the absolute decline is highly untypical. In most other European countries, the volume of passenger-km on local public transport, as well as rail, has often remained roughly stable, or increased, despite similar or higher levels of car ownership.

Table 2.1 summarizes some of the main aspects of motorized transport use in Britain in 1992.

No estimates are available for domestic passenger ferries, but these probably represent a very small share of passenger-km. Estimates of total passenger-km by private road transport are included to complete the picture, together with household expenditure (including taxes paid in purchasing transport).

It can be seen from Table 2.1 that BR and the urban rail networks are of similar size in terms of passenger trips, but that the former is much greater in terms of passenger-km, owing to the higher average length of journey (about 43 km, compared with 8 km). The average trip length by bus and coach is likewise short at about 8 km: substantially less for local bus journeys as such, at about 5 km.

Within the total 31,700 million passenger-km on BR in 1992/3, about 12,100 were made on InterCity sector services, 13,600 on Network South East (mostly commuting into London), and 5,900 on Regional Railways services. In terms of passenger trips, about 500 million per year were made on Network South East, 150 million on PTE-supported services (the most intensively used networks being in Merseyside and Strathclyde), and 65 million on InterCity. Rail use is thus highly concentrated in and around the major urban areas, especially London, and on the InterCity flows.

Within the bus and coach industry, the local trips (i.e. those on public local

Table 2.1 Motorized transport used in Britain, 1992.

Mode/sector		Passenger trips (millions)	Passenger-km (millions)	Passenger-km (%)	Revenue (£ millions)
Railways:					
British Railways[a]		745	31,700		2,150
LUL, DLR[b]		735	5,790		590
Tyne & Wear, Glasgow,					
Manchester[c]		61	365		40
	Total	1,541	37,855	6[g]	2,780
Buses & coaches:					
Local		4,669[d]			2,109[h]
Other		619[e]			857[h]
	Total		43,000[g]	6[g]	2,966
Domestic air		12[f]	4,800[g]	1[g]	800[i]
Private road					
Car, van, taxi			585,000[g]	86[g]	
Motor cycles			6,000[g]	1[g]	
Pedal cycles			5,000[g]	1[g]	
	Private road total		596,000[g]	88[g]	40,450[j]
ALL MODES			681,000[g]	100[g]	47,000[i]

All data (except notes e and i) are derived from *Transport statistics Great Britain* (*TSGB*) (London: HMSO, 1993). Since sources and definitions for individual modes may differ slightly, totals may not correspond exactly for the table as a whole.

a. 1992/3 totals from tables 5.1 and 5.11.
b. 1992/3 totals from tables 5.22 and 5.25.
c. 1992/3 data from tables 5.26–28.
d. Local bus data for 1991/2 from table 5.2
e. "Other" bus and coach service ridership for 1990/1 (data not subsequently collected) in *Bus and coach statistics 1990/1* (London: HMSO, 1992), table 2.2
f. 1991 data, table 2.2b.
g. 1992 calendar year estimates for total passenger-km from table 1.1.
h. 1991/2 data, from table 5.3.
i. Approximate estimate, Transport Studies Group, University of Westminster, 1993.
j. Estimated from weekly household expenditure in 1991, derived from the Family Expenditure Survey, for "motoring" and "all transport and travel" (table 1.15), multiplied by the number of household in Britain and by 52 weeks per year. (NB This may also include some spending on international travel by British residents, but excludes that on domestic passenger modes by foreign visitors.)

scheduled services) are handled largely by the current and former public sector urban, and regional, operators, while the independent sector has predominated in the "other" market, as discussed in Chapter 1. The latter totals around 600 million trips per annum, largely composed of school and works services. The express service category – based on the Transport Act 1985 definition of those carrying all their passengers a distance of at least 15 miles measured in a straight line – is a fairly small one, around 15 million trips. In practice, many long-distance and commuter coach services also carry intermediate traffic, and are therefore registered in the local service category. Total passenger-km for the whole bus and coach industry are shown in Table 2.1. Estimates for specific sectors or operators are not available, except for London Transport, which recorded a total of 3,900 million passenger-km in 1992/3.

Within this chapter, attention will now be focused on local movement, especially in urban areas. The rural market is treated separately in Chapter 8 and long-distance in Chapter 9.

Measures of use

At this point it is important to define more precisely the measures of use that are available, and the dangers of bias in their composition.

Passenger trip

The simple term "passenger trip" appears unambiguous, but is subject to distortion, especially in large urban areas. From the passenger's point of view, a trip consists of movement from one activity to another, such as home to work. This typically consists of several links, e.g. walk to bus, ride in bus, and walk to final destination (implications of this for journey time are considered in Ch. 5). Within the National Travel Survey (NTS), the term "journey" is used for a trip from one activity to another, and "stage" for each transport mode used (where use is made of the same mode more than once in succession within the same stage, e.g. use of two buses, the stage may be divided into "boardings"). Note that the term "stage" as used in the NTS is not the same as the "stage" concept in setting fare scales (see Ch. 7).

Most bus operators simply count as a passenger trip each ride in one of their vehicles, this being the definition implicitly adopted for bus services in Table 2.1. Where only one vehicular ride is involved, as in most small towns and rural areas, the distortion is not serious (except insofar as the non-motorized links are concerned), but in larger cities, with their more extensive networks, more than one ride in a public transport vehicle may be needed to reach the destination activity.

Even in all-bus systems, some interchange occurs as a result of a through service not being available (or passengers reducing travel time by taking the first bus to arrive and interchanging where necessary, rather than waiting for a less frequent through service) and where integrated bus/rail systems are operated, a very large difference may exist between totals for unlinked trips (i.e. rides in each vehicle counted separately) and linked trips (where only one public transport trip is counted, even if two or more rides are involved). A good example may be found in the Tyne and Wear system, where the introduction of an integrated bus/metro network made it necessary to monitor carefully the extent of such trips. In 1983–4, a total of 371.4 million passenger boardings took place (on all public transport modes, including buses, ferries and the Metro). These corresponded to 311.1 million linked passenger trips (a ratio of 1:1.19). For the

21

Metro in particular, linked trips were very important: of the 49.5 million passenger boardings in that year, only 13.8 million (or 28%) consisted simply of a metro ride (with walk links), all the others being linked trips which also involved use of bus, ferry, etc.

Most bus operators traditionally issued a separate ticket each time a passenger boarded a bus, the number of tickets sold thus being equated with the number of trips. Even where through tickets are offered, such as travelcards, annual statistics are usually based on the number of passenger boardings. Several sources of bias exist in bus operators' estimates, even on this basis. With the spread of electronic ticketing systems (ETS), this problem is now much less serious, but distortions arise in historic data series, which may have overstated past years' totals, leading to exaggeration of the decline in bus use.

Changes in network structure may also affect the ratio of linked to unlinked trips. For example, in 1977, the chain ferry across the River Itchen at Southampton was replaced by a bridge, over which through-bus services were operated, instead of terminating at either side. As only one ticket would be needed for the through journey, an improvement in service produced an apparent decline in passenger numbers.

Where season tickets, travelcards or concessionary passes are in use, a separate record is not normally made of each trip. Estimates of total use may be made by multiplying the number on issue by a trip rate derived from a sample survey, or from continuous on-vehicle surveys, as currently used for estimating pensioner concessionary travel in London. A shift to contactless smart-card format for travelcards will enable data on boardings to be collected automatically as tickets are validated. Estimates of trips per holder may need periodic adjustment in the light of changing market penetration, reduction in the number of working days per year, and so on.

On railways and long-distance coaches, through tickets to the final destination have generally been issued, at any rate within the network of the same operator (double-counting thus occurs between London Underground and BR services in London), making the unlinked/linked trip distinction less critical. However, the high proportion of season or travelcard use on rail makes accurate assessment of trip rates by their holders especially important. The traditional British Rail ticket issuing system based on sale at stations, with destination station named on the ticket, makes derivation of a station-to-station matrix from ticket sales data possible, subject to some qualifications. This is now provided by CAPRI (Computer Analysis of Passenger Receipts and Information), replacing the less sophisticated NPAAS (National Passenger Analysis and Accounting System).

Passenger-kilometres

Passenger kilometres (passenger-km) may be defined as the total distance travelled (or paid for) by users. They may be derived from an estimate of trips (subject to bias as discussed previously) multiplied by the average length of trip, or an estimate of average vehicle occupancy, multiplied by estimated total vehicle-km, the latter being the basis of national totals for road transport in Table 2.1. On railways, station-to-station ticket sales have enabled estimates to be made for many years. On buses, the ticketing system is less suitable for this purpose, but, where a finely graduated fare scale is applied, the number of fare stages paid for can be estimated, or estimates can be made from passenger surveys of average trip length. In many respects, passenger-km is a better measure of the use made of public transport, in that bias attributable to the definition of trip may be avoided, and a meaningful estimate made of vehicle occupancy by dividing its volume by total vehicle-km.

Note that this figure is not the same as the "passengers boarding per km" figure obtained by dividing passenger trips by vehicle-km. For example, if a bus runs 50 km, and is boarded by 100 passengers, with an average trip length of 4 km, then total passenger-km travelled will be 400 (4×100), and average occupancy 8 (400/50), whereas passengers boarding per km is 2 (100 divided by 50). This distortion becomes greater as trip length increases. The "passengers boarding per km" indicator is particularly inappropriate as a means of comparing use of routes within the same network, between which average trip length may differ substantially. However, it may be of value in comparing trends over time (for example, in average bus occupancy since deregulation), in the absence of any specific evidence in respect of change in average trip length.

Revenue

Revenue may also be used as a indicator of usage. Apart from its obvious financial importance, it may also act as a proxy for the utility derived by consumers. Thus, users of taxis pay substantially higher fares than on buses, which reflect the speed and convenience offered. In the intercity market, first-class fares likewise represent higher product quality. User spending may also be measured nationally as a means of indicating the different sums spent on each mode. If subsidies to operators are added, and the transfer element of taxes paid deducted, these then become estimates of resources used.

Clearly, the money that users are willing to pay indicates the minimal valuation of the service they obtain. However, it does not indicate the consumer surplus and, for relatively inelastic markets in particular, this may be very large. An operator may increase total revenue through raising fares, but this would not be a good indication of utility obtained (for a given quality of product), since not only would those who had ceased to travel lose the benefit from so doing, but consumer surplus of remaining users would be reduced. Given that urban and short-distance travel is generally inelastic, the revenue measure is thus of limited value in this context (see Fig. 7.4).

23

Major characteristics of the urban and short-distance market

Sources of data

In addition to data from the operators themselves, several other sources enable a fairly comprehensive picture to be built up. The ten-yearly Census, the latest in 1991, gives estimates of household car availability and, for a 10% sample, the mode of travel between home and workplace. It can also give a zonal population base for trip rate estimates using operators' data, as shown below.

Comprehensive Land Use Transportation Studies (LUTS) were carried out in many towns and cities from the mid-1960s to the late 1970s. These typically provide a great deal of household survey data on the use of all motorized modes, which enable the public transport share to be estimated for specific markets. However, few have been repeated (the only significant case being the Greater London Transportation Survey (GLTS) in 1962, 1971, and 1981, and its successor, the London Area Transport Survey (LATS) in 1991). Some studies have also been carried out in other towns relatively recently, for example Hemel Hempstead. Hence they may be used for cross-sectional comparisons, but rarely for trends over time.

In addition, a new generation of "integrated transport studies" (ITS) has appeared, pioneered by that in Birmingham. These follow an approach broadly similar to that of the LUTS, but with a greater emphasis on testing major policy options, and less on construction of the very detailed zone-to-zone trip matrices characteristic of the earlier studies (May 1991).

Surveys by operators themselves for network planning methods such as MAP, VIPS and BODS (see Ch. 5) provide data similar to LUTS, but normally within the public transport mode only, and not indicating market share. MAP studies covered many of the rural areas and smaller towns during the late 1970s, with more recent and continuing urban studies. Other operator surveys amplify the picture: for example, London Transport's annual cordon count of all modes for peak travel into the central area, and its trip diaries compiled by travelcard holders.

Panel surveys (longitudinal surveys) have been adopted in some areas as a means of monitoring changes over time, through a panel of respondents, notably in London and South Yorkshire. They are particularly useful for assessing the rates of turnover in the market. The panel is composed of the same individuals, who are repeatedly contacted, so that a picture is obtained of how, and perhaps why, individuals change their travel patterns over a given period.

The National Travel Survey (NTS) is the most comprehensive source, although care has to be taken in applying it to specific zones, owing to the small sample size in any one area. It has been conducted on six occasions since 1965–6, the latest in 1989–91. Use is made of this below to analyze market structure, with some additional data drawn from the previous (1985/86) survey. All modes are covered, with increasingly comprehensive coverage of non-motorized modes in the recent surveys.

24

The General Household Survey (GHS) provides some supplementary information on a larger and more frequent sample than NTS, especially car and bus use among the population as a whole, and distribution of household expenditure. The Family Expenditure Survey (FES), whose primary rôle is in calibration of the Retail Price Index (RPI), provides a further source in terms of household spending on transport.

The journey to work

Table 2.2 Modal shares for the journey to work: overall average percentages, 1991.

	Walk	Pedal cycle	Car driver	Car passenger	Motor cycle	Bus or coach	Rail	Other / at home
NTS	12.2	3.5	52.4	10.4	1.6	9.6	5.0	5.3
Census	12.0	3.0	54.1	7.8	1.5	10.1	5.8	5.6

Notes: Derived from the comparison between the 1989/91 NTS and 1991 Census results, as shown in the main report of the *National travel survey 1989/91* (London: HMSO, 1993), table D8, p. 142. The Census definition is based on "usual means of travel to work". In general, a very similar pattern is shown at national levels by both surveys.

Table 2.3 Usual means of travel to work by usual place of work, 1989/91 (%), rounded to nearest whole number).

Area	Walk	Pedal/ motor cycle	Car driver	Car passenger	Bus or coach	British Rail	London U'ground	Other
London								
Central	8	4	16	2	11	32	27	1
Outer	13	4	49	6	13	8	7	–
Conurbation								
centre	9	3	46	11	22	7	n/a	2
Other urban	14	6	57	12	10	1	n/a	1
Not urban	20	7	53	12	5	1	n/a	1

Source: National travel survey 1989/91, table 8.6.

Tables 2.2 and 2.3 show the shares of the journey-to-work market by different modes, from the 1991 census and 1989–91 NTS. Note that the principal mode of transport used is shown – for example, if someone commutes to central London by British Rail, and then makes a shorter ride on the Underground to reach their final destination, only British Rail will be shown as the mode used.

Overall, buses account for about 10% of all journeys to work, and rail about 5% (or, as shares of the motorised market, about 13% and 6% respectively). As one would expect, the public transport mode share is greater for central London, with 59% of journeys to work by BR or Underground, and 11% by bus. Note that these figures are for the whole day: during the morning peak (0700–1000), the rail share is substantially greater at about 74%. Elsewhere, the rail share is generally small, and varies substantially between different parts of outer London

25

(Croydon is well served, for example) and between the conurbation centres. The greatest shares handled by bus and coach are for outer London (13%) and conurbation centres (22%). Note that over five times as many car commuters travelled as drivers than passengers, giving an average car occupancy for this purpose of only 1.2.

Other journey purposes

Although public transport's rôle tends to be associated mainly with the work journey, it is evident that this is not necessarily where bus takes the greatest share. As Table 2.4 shows, local bus took 9% of all trips in 1989–91, a figure virtually identical to its share in the journey-to-work market (Table 2.2). Of the shopping/personal business market, bus took 16%. The largest share taken by local bus is within the education trip market, at 19%, (and it is likely that a good deal of the 18% "other" for this journey purpose is by contract school bus) which varies little with size of area served. This in turn comprises mainly trips to and from school, plus an important further and higher education market in some areas. As many school trips are above walking distance, a major demand for public transport is created, especially in rural areas, as discussed further in Chapter 8.

Table 2.4 Shares by each mode within major journey purposes.

Purpose	Walk	Car driver	Car passenger	Local bus	Rail	Other	All
Business	2	80	11	3	3	3	102
Education	18	6	32	21	3	18	98
Shopping	10	43	27	16	1	2	99
Personal business	7	52	31	6	1	3	100
Leisure	12	37	37	6	2	6	102
ALL	9	46	28	9	2	6	102

Notes: Derived from table 8.4 (Journeys per person per year by journey purpose and main mode of travel) in National travel survey 1989/91 (London: HMSO, 1993). Percentages sum across rows, and may not sum exactly to 100, because of rounding.

The rôle of rail is generally small for non-work purposes, so that estimates are often unreliable.

Car occupancy levels are often much higher for non-work purposes – averaging 2.0 for leisure, and 1.6 for shopping. Hence for these purposes, perceived cost per person by public transport may compare unfavourably where car running and parking costs are split.

The proportion of public transport trips – both for all purposes, and work – falls gradually with size of urban area, associated with absence of rail services, lower levels of bus service, higher car ownership and less constraint on car use. These factors are considered further below.

It will be noted that the proportions of motorized trips by mode quoted from the NTS in Table 2.3 differ considerably from the proportions of passenger-km in Table 2.1, bus taking 10% of all motorised trips (and if school contract and long-distance services were included, somewhat more) but only 6% of passenger-km – a reflection of its very short average trip length, below that by car. For rail, the respective proportions were 2.5% and 6%, giving the opposite outcome.

Table 2.5 Composition of the market for each mode, by journey purpose, 1989–91.

Purpose	Local bus	Rail	All modes
Work (commuting)	22	46	20
Business	1	5	5
Education	10	5	5
Shopping	33	11	23
Personal business	15	11	23
Leisure	19	22	29
TOTAL	100	100	101

Notes: Derived from table 8.4 in *National travel survey 1989/91* (London: HMSO, 1993). Percentages sum down the columns and may not total exactly to 100, because of rounding.

We can also divide the market served by each mode according to journey purpose, as shown in Table 2.5. For local bus, shopping represents the single most important journey purpose, some 33% of all trips, whereas rail is clearly dominated by work (46%). In comparison with the all modes average, public transport is less strongly associated with the leisure market and personal business travel, as would be expected. If work and education trips are taken as a proxy for peak period demand, this forms 32% of all bus journeys, and 51% of all rail journeys, compared with 25% for the all modes average. Hence, demand by time of day is much more sharply peaked for rail travel.

Taxis

The total number of taxis and private hire cars has grown rapidly in recent years, associated with legislative changes (Ch. 1), and increasing unemployment stimulating more entry into the trade. Licensed taxis as such grew from 32,700 in 1985 to 48,300 in 1991, by 48% (TSGB93, Table 5.9). Use of taxis and private hire vehicles grew by a very similar 55% between 1985/6 and 1989/91 (NTS Table 5.1). While representing only 11% of all public transport journeys in 1989/91 (and hence just over 1% of all motorised trips), they accounted for about 25% of all personal expenditure on public transport, due to the very much higher cost per trip.

In some respects, the rôles of taxis/private hire vehicles and other public transport could be seen as complementary: they are used particularly for late-night travel. Some of the growth since 1985 may have been associated with reduced quality of bus services since deregulation. However, London displays

27

both a high level of conventional (bus and rail) public transport use, and the highest taxi/minicab mileage per person per year within Britain (NTS, Table 5.8).

Variations by time of day, and day of week

The internal structure of the public transport market may also be examined in terms of trip length distribution, and split by time of day and day of week. Within the Monday to Friday working day, work and education trips tend to be concentrated at peak periods (around 0800–0930, and 1600–1730). However, they do not usually coincide in both peaks, since the school day is generally shorter than the adult working day. Where service industry employment predominates, working hours are typically around 0900–1700, causing the morning school and work peaks to coincide, but with a spread in the late afternoon, as schools finish around 1530–1600. Conversely, where traditional manual employment remains significant, with its earlier start around 0730–0800, it is the afternoon peak which coincides, around 1600. The pattern is often a regional one, with older towns in Wales, Scotland and northern England displaying the latter pattern.

Figure 2.1 shows the pattern of bus demand in London in 1992 – the effect of the higher morning peak is clear. In considering the economics of peak operation – discussed further in Chapter 6 – one thus has to bear in mind that some vehicles may perform only one loaded trip per day.

In many areas, it is the school peak which causes almost the entire additional peak vehicle demand above a base level from 0800 to 1800. This is evident in almost all smaller towns, and in most cities up to about 200,000 population, such as Plymouth and Southampton. Although journeys to work by public transport are substantial, they do not necessarily require more vehicular capacity (given the higher load factors accepted in the peak) than for shopping, and other trips between the peaks. Even in the largest conurbation bus networks, it is only on the radial routes to the central area that journeys to work create sharp peaks, school travel causing the peak within suburban areas.

Rail networks display a very different peaking ratio, however, being oriented almost entirely to the centres of large cities, and thus the adult work journey. For example, in the West Midlands in 1984–85, 62% of the passenger trips on the rail network on Mondays to Fridays occurred in the peak periods (start of day to 0929, and 1530 to 1759), compared with 45% of bus trips. In London, this contrast is also marked. The Greater London Travel Survey of 1981 showed that 53% of the passenger trips on the underground on Mondays to Fridays by Greater London residents were for work purposes, and hence highly peaked, compared with 29% of the trips on the bus network.

Within large conurbations, the ratio of peak to base demand may be somewhat greater in terms of passenger-km than passenger trips, since the journeys to work in the centre are much longer than local shopping and personal business trips within the suburban areas. The 1989–91 NTS shows that for all modes, work trips

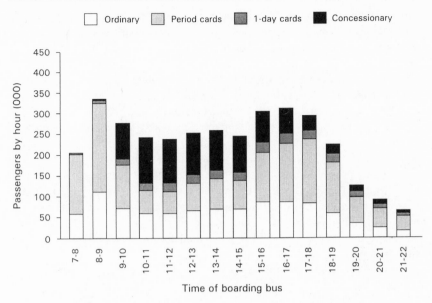

Figure 2.1 Distribution of London Transport passenger journeys by hour of day an ticket type (Monday–Friday average 1992); buses above, Underground below.

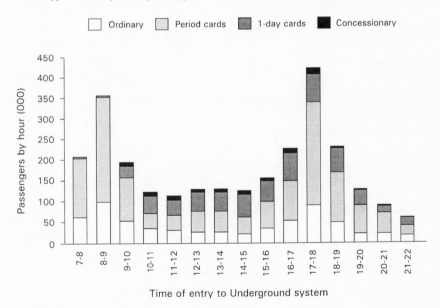

tend to be longer (at 13.1 km average) than those for education (7.2 km) or shopping (7.8 km). Conversely, in smaller towns employment and shopping may show a similar degree of concentration, leading to similar trip lengths, and hence a good balance of demand during the base period. This is particularly noticeable

29

in towns of about 50,000 to 150,000 people, such as Oxford, or Grimsby. Many work trips are by car, and much school travel within walking or cycling distance. Shopping is fairly concentrated in town centres, generating good levels of demand on radial networks.

In recent years, a similar flattening out of the public transport demand ratio between peak and inter-peak periods (the latter being the shopping hours from about 0930 to 1600) has been observed, as work trips have shifted to the private car, or, more recently, declined owing to rising unemployment. The inter-peak demand has often held up better, owing to the rising proportion of pensioners in the population, often without cars, whose use of public transport is further encouraged by concessionary fares at such times. The availability of cars within the car-owning household during this period is also limited by the use of cars for the work trip, creating a potential public transport market among those based at home during the day, perhaps stimulated by lower off-peak fares. The growth of high-frequency minibus services has also stimulated non-work travel to a greater extent than peak demand, aiding this process.

In the West Midlands, for example, the proportion of peak period trips (defined as above) fell from 50% of the Monday to Friday total in 1978–79, to 45% in 1984–85, while the inter-peak demand grew from 36% to 42%, also rising in absolute terms.

This flattening out, while occurring within an overall decline, has thus enabled some improvement in vehicle and crew utilization through more efficient scheduling, whose cost implications are considered in Chapter 6.

A sharper decline has occurred in early morning, evening and Sunday travel, car availability to the household as a whole being much greater in the last two periods, and the first affected by loss of work journeys and changes in working hours. Evening travel has also been hit by the long-term drop in cinema attendance (albeit recently reversed), and a reluctance in some areas to go out in the dark for fear of assault. However, very late evening and all-night bus travel has grown in London following the revamped network introduced during the 1980s.

Since deregulation of local bus services outside London, it has been common to find that a Monday-Saturday service is registered to run commercially from about 0800 to 1800 (even in some low-density areas), while early morning, evening and Sunday services become the responsibility of local authority tendered operations. Operators may also be unwilling to register additional peak-period journeys required largely for school travel.

Within the week as a whole, Mondays to Fridays display similar demand patterns, although Friday is often busier for shopping, and has an earlier afternoon peak, especially where the working week has been shortened by shorter hours on this day. In long-distance travel, a marked peak occurs on Friday evening, for weekend trips.

Saturday continues to be a busy day for shopping trips, especially where car ownership is low, but has suffered a marked decline in high car-ownership areas, owing to use of the car by the family as a whole on that day.

30

Within larger conurbations, the shopping activity is often concentrated in the secondary centres. Thus central Manchester is relatively quiet, while heavy traffic is carried to shopping centres in Stockport, Bolton, and other surrounding towns.

Where such centres are located in well established towns, then good bus access is normally provided. For example, in 1987 some 46% of all shopping trips into central Bolton were by bus. However, the rôle of rail is much weaker. The main contrast is between shopping activity located within existing urban centres, and that at "out of town" locations, usually dependent on car access.

Trip chaining

Patterns of travel during the day may be best understood in terms of trip chains. Just as individual journeys are better analyzed as linked trips from one activity to another, the day's travel can be seen as a chain of such links, starting at home, then via various activities and destinations until home is reached again. The simplest consists of "home – one activity (for example, work) – home", but more complex patterns may be found, such as returning home for lunch (mainly in smaller towns), or returning in the evening via the shops, or place of entertainment. Analysis of travel diaries from the 1985/86 NTS enables us to understand such chains more clearly (White et al. 1991).

In analysing such data, short walk links must also be considered. For example, someone working in a city centre might walk to a shopping street open in the evening, then return home by public transport: although only two public transport journeys would be recorded, the trip chain is nonetheless a complex one in terms of individual behaviour.

Complex public transport-based trip chains are found mainly in larger cities, often associated with the use of tickets such as the travelcard which permit additional linking trips at zero money cost.

Trip chain analysis also enables us to understand how trips made by the same individual are linked by time of day – for example, a substantial proportion (around 40%) of one-way trips made on bus services after 1800 are in reality the return leg of trip chains which began earlier in the same day, rather than new home-based trips. Hence, cutting out a poorly loaded evening service has implications for ridership on daytime services, should the inability to make the return leg of the trip result in the user switching to another mode for the whole trip chain. This has implications for the extent to which evening services are in fact cross-subsidized by profitable daytime operation (see Ch. 7).

The more complex chains may explain why cars are used sometimes for the peak work journey into large cities even when public transport may appear more convenient, as the car is available for indirect homeward journeys in the evenings, or business trips during the day. To capture a high share of the work market, public transport may need to offer good evening services, and facilities such as travelcards which permit complex trip patterns without financial penalty or the inconvenience of checking fares for occasional journeys.

Trip length distribution

Having examined variations in trips by time, their distribution by length may now be assessed.

For this purpose, the NTS also provides useful illustrations. However, it should be borne in mind that most NTS data (as quoted earlier in this chapter, for example) excludes very short trips (those under one mile, or 1.6km, largely made on foot). The effect of including all journeys (defined as links between activities) is shown in Table 2.6. The analysis of trip chaining described above is also sensitive to this difference in definition, where such short links are critical to the categorisation of chains as complex or simple.

Table 2.6 Composition of journeys by length (all modes), 1989/91.

Journey length (km)	Excluding journeys under 1.6km (%)	All lengths included (%)
Under 1.6	n/a	29
1.6–3.2		18
3.2–4.8		11
4.8–15.5		28
1.6–15.5 (sum)	81	57
15.6–80.0	17	12
Over 80.0	2	2

Sources: National travel survey 1989/91 (London: HMSO, 1991), table 9.1 (for data excluding journeys under 1.6km) and table 6.1 (all lengths data).

Table 2.6 shows the distribution for all purposes, by all modes (including non-motorized). A sharp fall in trip frequency as length rises can be seen, as one would expect from the gravity model (i.e. trip rate is inversely proportional to square of distance). Note that this distribution only follows a consistent trend if the non-motorized trips are included, since motorized trips peak at about 2–3km. Shopping and education trips tend to be shorter than average, and hence associated particularly with walking and cycling, especially for younger schoolchildren.

The distributions in Figure 2.2 reflect those of all journey lengths shown in Table 2.6, with a modal average of about 2–3km. Rail trips, oriented to work in the central area, have much higher mean length of 10km. Trip length distributions tend to vary by passenger type, with a marked skew to shorter trips by pensioners, but a less peaked pattern for travelcard use, associated with the journey to work.

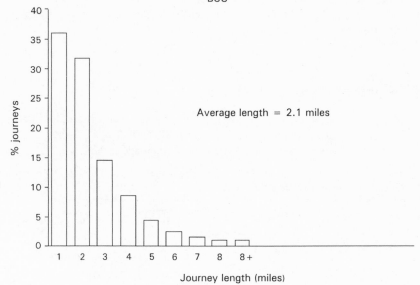

BUS

Average length = 2.1 miles

% journeys

Journey length (miles)

Figure 2.2 The distribution of trip lengths for London Transport passengers in London, 1992/3; buses above, Underground below. Note that each bus ride is counted as a separate trip, whereas each Underground trip is counted only once, including interchanges within the network.

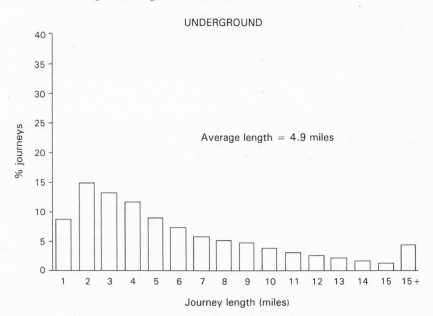

UNDERGROUND

Average length = 4.9 miles

% journeys

Journey length (miles)

Hence, there is a substantial overlap between bus and non-motorised modes for shorter journeys, which may be more sensitive than bus travel as a whole to cost and time factors.

Variations by type of person

So far, this analysis has concentrated mainly on types of trip, but a fuller understanding requires the individual traveller to be considered. Table 2.7 shows some variations in frequency of bus and rail use by sex and age in 1989/91.

Table 2.7 Variations in bus and rail use by age, sex and household car ownership; journey stages per person per year, 1989/91.

	Children 0–15	Men 16–29	Women 16–29	Men 30–59	Women 30–59	60 and over
Local bus						
Main driver in household with car	n/a	14	29	10	13	23
All persons in car-owning households	50	58	104	17	53	38
All persons in households without cars	117	202	236	173	234	166
Rail						
Main drivers	n/a	23	37	23	12	10
All in car-owning households	7	34	43	29	13	9
All in households without cars	11	78	72	46	40	11

Sources: National travel survey 1989/91 (London: HMSO, 1993), tables 4.3 and 4.10.

It can be seen that bus use is greatest among the youngest and oldest groups, associated mainly with car availability. Young adults and those still in education are the most dependent, averaging 80 to 130 stages per person per year. Among the oldest groups, there is also high bus dependence, although the most common frequency of use is about 80 stages per year (i.e. about two trips per week), associated with shopping and personal business, rather than work or education trips. Among the middle-aged, especially males, bus use is relatively low, owing to greater car availability. However, many females use the bus 2–4 days per week, typically for shopping.

Rail use follows a very different pattern. Whereas bus use is associated mainly with living in low-income households and with limited car availability, rail use, especially of British Rail services, is associated with higher-income households. There is also a correlation with regional income levels, bus use being highest in the older industrial conurbations, while rail use is concentrated in London and the South East. In 1989–91, persons in the lowest quintile of households (i.e. the bottom 20%) defined by income made 113 bus journeys per year, but for the highest quintile this figure was only 35. In terms of rail use, persons in the lowest quintile made 7 journeys a year, but those in the highest made 41 (NTS 1989/91, Table 4.2). This difference by social class and income is also reflected in the political and media attention devoted to rail matters, as compared with bus issues. Differences between those in car-owning and non-car-owning households are much less marked in the case of rail use than local bus travel.

Amongst pensioners, bus use is relatively high in the age range 60–75, but falls thereafter as greater difficulty is experienced in using any mode of transport. This is associated largely with getting on and off the vehicle: implications for vehicle design are considered in Chapter 3.

Trip rates per person per year

The NTS provides overall estimates of trip rates per person per year. In 1989/91, each resident in Britain made on average about 1090 journeys per year (if all lengths are included), or 771 journeys if only those over 1.6km are included. For public transport use as such the national average journey stages per person per year was 80 by all types of bus and coach service, 22 by rail (all operators), and 13 by taxi (Table 5.2), a total of 115 trips, or slightly over two per week.

These rates vary substantially by area of residence, with London residents averaging about 114 local bus, 98 rail and 16 taxi/private hire car stages, a total of about 230 stages per year (from Tables 4.8, 4.12 and 5.7). On the same basis, those in the English metropolitan areas averaged about 127 bus, 10 rail and 13 by taxi, a total of 150 per year. South East England excluding London displays a low overall public transport use but within this, a marked tendency toward use of rail (37 local bus, 30 rail and 9 taxi, a total of 76). Similar overall averages are found in other parts of England, but with a greater stress on bus use.

Data from operators may also be used to estimate average trip rates per person, and to some extent by person type. These permit more detailed local comparisons to be made within Britain than the NTS sample permits, and for international comparisons to be readily produced. However, the absolute figures are usually based on rides recorded by the operator, which will give a higher figure than the stages recorded in NTS, especially in large cities where more interchange between routes and modes arises. Trips by non-residents may also increase the total vis a vis estimates produced for residents only – these include frequent trips by residents of other areas (for example a British Rail commuter into London who uses the Underground for the last leg of their trip), and business or tourist visits by residents of other parts of the same country, or by foreigners.

Local estimates, updated annually, may be produced, as long as operators disclose their data and the population catchment served by an operator can be defined from census data (annual updating may be accomplished by using the intermediate population estimates from OPCS).

On this basis, the average trip rate for London Transport (bus and Underground) was about 285 in 1992/3 – adding around 40 for trips on BR services gives an overall public transport trip rate of about 325 (excluding taxis). The BR estimate is based on the fact that about 240 million trips per year were made on NSE services within London, of the 500 million per year total on NSE.

In the West Midlands in 1978–79, an average public transport (bus and rail) unlinked trip rate of 207 per head was observed. This ranged from 94 for those under 16, to 231 for pensioners and 223 for working-age adults. These are, of course, crude averages, and within each market a gearing may be observed (i.e. proportion of all trips accounted for by a certain proportion of individuals). For example, in the working age adult category, travelcard holders made about 850 unlinked trips per year, some 15% of the working-age population thus accounting for about half of all the public transport boardings by that category. A fairly high gearing in the under 16 market may also be found, associated with those school children who use public transport every school day, but it is lower within the working-age users (for trips other than journey to work), and pensioner, sectors.

In terms of international comparisons, the overall average trip rate per head by public transport is similar in Britain to that in other European countries. London's 325 is comparable with that in Paris and other large cities. In smaller towns, the rate may even compare favourably where high-frequency minibuses have been successfully introduced. However, in the metropolitan conurbations (which correspond to the largest cities in most other European countries, excluding Paris) the current average of about 150 compares poorly with cases such as Amsterdam (320), Munich (300), Vienna (397), Hannover (230) and especially with Zurich (470), which has followed a strongly pro-public transport policy (Jones 1994). A striking feature is the dependence on bus services in such British conurbations, compared with the major rôle of rail systems offering higher quality services in the other European cities of similar size.

Time spent in travel

Irrespective of income, status or modes used all individuals ultimately face the same constraint in terms of time – 24 hours per day. Allowing for time spent in work, sleeping and household activities, the discretionary time in which travel and other activities may be fitted is fairly limited, especially within the Monday-Friday working week. Although the amount of time spent by individuals in travel obviously varies, the average time spent in travel per person per day is surprisingly constant. Increased travel may thus be seen as arising from faster modes being used within the same time budget to cover greater distances.

For example, the 1989/91 NTS shows that average distance per person per year, compared with that in 1975/6, rose by 37% (for all modes), while average speed rose by 19% – hence time spent in travel rose by only 15%. Over the same period journeys per person per year rose by 17%. Hence, the main change was in travelling greater distances rather than making more journeys.

A more detailed time-activity diary enables such trends to be examined in greater depth. Work by Brög (1993) in German cities indicates that for intra-urban travel the average time spent per person per day is very stable (at about 60 minutes), as is the number of activities outside the home. For example, in comparing surveys carried out in Essen and Hannover in 1976 and 1990 it was found that average travel time per person in Essen had changed from 60 minutes to 59 minutes, and in Hannover from 61 to 62. Activities per person per day like-wise changed very little (stable at 2.7, and from 2.9 to 2.8 respectively). One could see thus the urban transport market as a whole as a saturated market, with little scope for dramatic expansion. More substantial changes were seen in the mix of modes used, and total travel distance (a shift from non-motorised modes to car driver and public transport). However, in Hannover in particular, public transport did not decline as a share of total trips, but rose from 16 to 22% over this period.

Such time budget constraints are less likely to apply to weekend, leisure and long-distance travel.

Changes in individuals' travel over time

So far, although we have disaggregated the market into certain categories of per-son, we have not looked at individual behaviour. Individuals shift from one cat-egory to another, not simply as their ages change, but also their status – from child to student, to adult, to married person possibly with children, to pensioner, etc. These stages in the life-cycle are associated with changes in household size and structure, car availability and in trip purpose. Thus the work journey is a major factor determining household travel behaviour for certain stages, the need to get children to school at others.

Changes in travel behaviour are often associated with critical events in the life cycle, such as setting up a new home, or changing jobs. Many people may change their mode of travel for this reason, at least in the short run, rather than because of modal characteristics as such. This leads to a high turnover in the market, such that net changes between one year and the next are often small com-pared with the gross changes that produce them. For example, panel surveys in Tyne and Wear showed that a net reduction in the public transport share for the journey to work of 2 percentage points between 1982 and 1983 was the net result of 7% of respondents ceasing to be public transport users, while 5% became new users in that period. A net change of 2% thus involved about 12% of the sample in changing modes (Smart 1984).

These changes are likely to be particularly noticeable if an individual service is examined, since people may change routes used when changing homes and/or jobs, while remaining in the public transport market. Even in a zone of apparently stable land use and total population, such as a well established residential area, constant change is occurring. On a typical urban bus or rail route, as many as 20% of users may have begun to use that specific service within the last 12 months. Hence, if examining the impact of a recent change (such as conversion to high-frequency minibuses) it is important to distinguish users who have switched to a route for such personal reasons, as distinct from those attracted by service characteristics as such.

Patterns of individual behaviour may influence trip frequencies over a very long period. For example, based on work in South Yorkshire and elsewhere, Goodwin and others have suggested that trip rates developed in early adult life may strongly influence subsequent modal use.

The implication of this for transport operators and planners is that responses to changes in fares and service quality should be assessed not only in the short-run, but over long periods, since much short run change is caused primarily by non-transport factors, but in the long run transport characteristics will affect other choices. For example, individuals may be firmly committed to a specific mode of travel for their existing home to work trip, which may not be affected even by large changes in price or service quality, but when relocating, will have to re-consider the routing, and perhaps mode, of that trip. If a good public transport service is offered, then re-location may take account of access by that mode; if not, then car might be the inevitable choice.

However, public transport operators currently tend to take a very short-run view of the market, given financial constraints, and the philosophy behind the deregulation of local bus services. Hence, the short-run impact of a fares increase (which almost invariably raises total revenue) is likely to be basis for decision-making, rather than the greater sensitivity to price changes which exists in the longer run (this aspect is discussed further in Ch. 7).

Public transport and car use

As car ownership has grown, it has had a direct effect on public transport use. First, the individual having first choice in use of the car (usually corresponding to the main driver in the NTS, and typically the working head of household) will tend to use it, unless other specific factors apply (such as commuting into a large city centre, for which public transport may be more convenient). His or her trips will then be lost to public transport, except for occasional journeys. In addition, however, other members of the household may also transfer some of their trips to the car, as passengers – a child being given a lift to school, or the family travelling together at weekends. The loss of trips to public transport will thus be greater than those of one person alone, although this could depend upon price and quality of the service offered: if it is good, then other members of the household may be less inclined to arrange their trips so as to travel as passengers in the household car. Teenagers, for example, may prefer the greater independence of travel by public transport to being given lifts by their parents (and the latter appreciate the reduction in chauffeuring).

Overall, each new car may reduce local bus trips by about 200–300 per annum (see Table 2.7 for changes in individual trip rates). The effect is greater for the first car than the second, since the latter will be used in part to take trips that were being made as car passengers in the first (the children acquiring their first cars, for example). The effect on public transport use is that the members of a one-car household still make substantial numbers of public transport trips, although these are concentrated into categories such as school and Monday-Friday shopping trips, with much less evening and weekend public transport use. A two-car household may make very little use of public transport, except where comprising more individuals than average, or employing public transport for the work journey.

The majority of rail users come from car-owning households, and in many areas this is also true for bus use.

In 1992, 20.1 million private cars were licensed in Britain, corresponding to about 0.36 per head, or 0.88 per household. The most common category was the one-car household, some 44% of the total. Another 19% of households had two or more cars, thus leaving 33% without a car (TSGB93, Tables 3.1 and 3.14). The proportion of households with one or more cars has grown less rapidly than car ownership in total, as average household size has fallen. Its rate of growth has also declined. For example, between 1963 and 1973 this proportion rose from 36% to 54%, but by 1984 by only another 7 points to 61%, and a further 6 points to 67% in 1992. Marked variations occur by area. The 1991 Census indicates that Glasgow still has 66% of households with no car, while in parts of the South East this figure is below 18%. Some 39% or more of households in inner London boroughs were without cars (OPCS Census Monitor no 27, October 1993).

) The effect of unemployment

The sharp rise in unemployment in the late 1970s/early 1980s had a very damaging effect on public transport in certain areas, especially older cities with declining industries. The recession since 1990 has also had marked effects – notably on commuting to central London, reversing previous growth. It may be described in a fashion similar to that of car ownership: for each extra person unemployed, a certain number of public transport trips is lost, together with the knock-on effects of reduced household income causing a reduction in other trips. It has also been the case that those becoming unemployed are more likely to have been public transport users, given their status and income. In West Yorkshire, a loss of 18 bus trips/week per person becoming unemployed was estimated in the early 1980s.

More generally, this could be represented as a loss of about 1% in local bus patronage for each one percentage point rise in the unemployment rate, within the range currently experienced (around 5% to 20%). Car use is also affected, but perhaps less so, as the incomes of those still in work have continued to rise in real terms.

Variations in public transport use

The picture presented so far could be seen as a rather deterministic one, with public transport use influenced very strongly by external factors such as composition of the population and car ownership. However, while giving a broad background, this is by no means the whole story. Large variations may be found in public transport use associated with quality of service, urban structure and fares. These may all be influenced by transport operators and planners. Some operators have succeeded in retaining much higher trip rates per head than others.

For example, in assessing variations in the share of all motorized transport held by bus services from late 1960s' LUTS data, I found by that the share was about 14 percentage points higher in towns with their own municipal bus services than those covered by area companies (typified by those in NBC ownership from 1969 to the late 1980s), after allowing for the effect of car ownership (White 1976). This in turn was associated with the higher level of service, and lower fares, offered on the municipal systems, these being a consequence of greater financial support and avoidance of the burden of cross-subsidizing rural operations which has characterized area company urban services. Municipal fleets often attained much better levels of reliability than larger company systems, benefiting from locally based management.

Since local bus deregulation marked variations have been observed, with London and Northern Ireland (not subject to deregulation) retaining higher levels of use than the deregulated regions as a whole. However, individual towns benefiting from high-frequency minibus conversions have displayed substantial ridership growth as a result of frequency effects. Further consideration of the impacts of fares levels and structure is presented in Chapter 7.

A particularly worrying outcome since local bus deregulation (on which further commentary is given in Ch. 10) is the loss of ridership in the metropolitan areas – some 28% between 1985/6 and 1991/2. In terms of the mix of users on buses, the greatest drop nationally between 1985/6 and 1989/91 was in working age (16–59) males, of 25% (NTS 1989/91, Table 4.4), i.e. those most likely to have the choice of using a car. There is also evidence of a stimulus to car ownership rates in the metropolitan areas during this period, possibly as a result of declining bus service quality (Fairhurst 1991).

40

The London case

London is of importance in its own right as a part of the public transport market – the majority of rail travel and about 20% of all bus journeys in Britain – and also displays markedly different trends to public transport use elsewhere in Britain. Following a period of gradual decline from a peak of use around 1950, the Underground network saw very rapid growth in use during the 1980s, from 498 million trips in 1982 to 815 million in 1988/9, (by 64%) exceeding the previous peak around 1950 when car ownership was a fraction of the present level. British Rail peak period commuting into central London also rose by 21% during the same period (TSGB93, Table 1.3). Bus use, while not experiencing any dramatic growth, remained fairly stable at about 1100 million trips per year from 1982 to 1992 (TSGB93, Tables 5.2 and 5.22), in contrast to sharp drops elsewhere.

The growth in central area peak demand (concentrated wholly on rail) is explained by growth in central area employment, notably in the financial services sector. Off-peak underground ridership growth and the high level of bus use may be explained largely by the stimulus resulting from the Travelcard (see also Ch. 7), and, in the latter part of this period, improved bus service frequency and reliability.

The sharp growth in peak period demand resulted in several major rail schemes being put forward (see Ch. 4), although the fall since 1989 raises some doubts: is it simply a short-term impact of the current recession, or a longer-term effect reasserting itself?

Forecasting techniques

Analysis of variations in patronage, establishing statistical links between them and causal factors, enables us to produce forecasts of the likely effect of change in variables such as real fares, or frequency, and of external factors such as unemployment.

The LUTS approach is based largely on predicting peak demands for motorized transport, and hence the infrastructure and rolling stock which may be required to meet it. Early studies in particular, focused largely on road network planning, despite the major rôle of public transport which was evident from the related surveys. LUTS forecasting begins with estimation of zonal populations and activities for a design year-typically 15 to 20 years after the survey date – to which trip rates (per head, or per household) are applied to estimate total trip generation. Both public and private travel modes may be estimated in this way, using different trip rates according to car ownership.

The spatial distribution of these generated trips is then modelled using techniques such as the gravity model, in order to predict zone-to-zone flows. The trip rate falls as distance increases (as illustrated in Table 2.6). The deterrent effect

41

of this may be represented most simply by including distance itself as the variable in the model. However, it is time and cost which deter travel, rather than distance as such. These variables may be used instead, often combined into a single measure: generalized cost (the perceived monetary cost of a trip, such as the bus fare or parking charge, plus the value of time spent making it).

On some flows, those with cars available may be encouraged to use public transport – for example, trips terminating in city centres where high parking charges may be levied – and this modal choice is also modelled, taking account of factors such as generalized cost, the assumed pattern of car availability, etc. These techniques have been refined recently by the development of disaggregate models, and stated preference techniques, which describe more accurately individual behaviour, although requiring more sophisticated data than the traditional aggregate forms. A good general description of the LUTS technique is given by Bruton (1985).

The forecasts produced by late 1960s LUTS models for public transport appear in retrospect to have been rather optimistic. Although decline had already occurred from the early 1950s, they often predicted fairly stable levels of demand, despite rising car ownership. This was largely because fairly stable public transport trip rates per household were assumed: although account was taken of anticipated growth in car ownership, no allowance was made for reductions in level of service, or increases in real fares which public transport operators might have to make to meet financial targets. In addition, the overall assumptions regarding economic growth, population and employment often proved very optimistic, especially in older industrial areas.

A study by Mackinder & Evans (1981) examined some of the earlier LUTS forecasts 10 years after they had been produced. Overall, an increase in motorized trips of 32% had been suggested (taking public and private modes together), whereas in reality the total was little changed – a net rise of only about 5%. Within this, public transport use had declined and car use risen (but considerably less than forecast). In addition, zonal populations and employment levels had been over-stated. Subsequently, even greater discrepancies may have developed, owing to the effect of unemployment and population loss in some areas. The overstatement of public transport use was associated mainly with a failure to allow for effects of fare and service level changes. In addition, confusion in earlier studies between household car ownership and car availability to individuals may have led to calibration of modal choice models which over-estimated the number of "choice" public transport users.

One should not, however, dismiss the LUTS approach entirely. The picture presented from the initial surveys may be a very useful one, and of value for short-to-medium term planning. Certain projects, such as major railway schemes, inevitably involve looking 15 to 20 years ahead owing to the time taken for construction and period over which such investments are evaluated. Although imperfect, some long-term forecasts have to be made. The 1981 GLTS data and modelling framework has been used extensively for testing alternative rail options in London, for example. For bus networks, however, much more short-run change is likely. Certain elements of the LUTS approach have been incorporated in bus network planning methods, as described in Chapter 5, notably the Volvo planning system (VIPS), which includes zone-to-zone demand models. However, they are based on much more detailed and up-to-date surveys, based solely on public transport users.

The major alternative to the LUTS approach has been the development of time-series models for bus use, typically of the form:

$$\Delta T = a\Delta RF + b\Delta BM + C$$

in which ΔT represents the percentage change in bus trips in a given area from one period to the next (typically one year, but shorter periods may also be used), ΔRF the change in real revenue per passenger trip (crudely described as average "real fare"), ΔBM the change in bus kilometres run – a surrogate for service levels – and C a trend factor. The last-named is usually negative, i.e. representing a decline owing to external conditions, such as rising car ownership and a more dispersed pattern of land use. The coefficients a and b represent elasticities applied to the percentage changes in RF and BM, respectively. In more recent years, a fourth variable has been added, to represent the effect of changing unemployment, for which a coefficient may be similarly calibrated.

Such models have been found to give a reasonably good fit with observed data, and enable the effects of some policy changes to be assessed, such as a decision to reduce real fares, or change the level of service. An average elasticity for real revenue per trip of –0.3 has been found remarkably robust for cash-paid fares: price elasticities are discussed further in Chapter 7. For the bus-km effect, the elasticity is less certain, since separating cause and effect in observed data becomes more difficult. An average of about +0.4 may be assumed, as illustrated in case studies of minibus conversion (Watts et al. 1990). However, where initial frequencies are relatively high the value is likely to be smaller: the most recent work in London suggests an average value for the whole network of about +0.18 (London Transport 1993). For the trend factor, a value of about –1.0% to –1.5% per annum, excluding population change, may be assumed in most cases.

Since deregulation, such models have fitted overall behaviour less well than before. Effects of instability and poor passenger information have offset the growth in ridership that would otherwise be expected due to the substantial growth in bus-km run (for further commentary, see Ch. 10).

Where total population is changing significantly, it may be better to redefine the dependent variable in this model as trips per head of population (the trip rate then being affected by fare and service quality), rather than subsume this effect in the residual "trend factor", which already incorporates several variables.

This form of model represents a considerable advance on the LUTS approach in several respects, giving a more accurate picture of short-to-medium run change. However, it is more appropriate for network-wide assessment of policies such as fare changes, than use on individual links or routes. Modal split is not predicted directly, but is in effect incorporated in the model, since the factors which would cause total trips to be generated or suppressed are also those likely to encourage diversion between modes, e.g. a lower real fare may encourage some car users to switch to public transport, as well as extra public transport trips to be generated. Indeed, much of the change in bus use may reflect modal choice, not so much between car and public transport, but between non-motorized modes and public transport, especially for shorter trips.

Other aspects of perceived quality of service may also be critical to the user, such as helpfulness of staff, ease of boarding and alighting, or convenience of ticket purchase. As in other models, the time-series technique should not be seen as giving a totally deterministic prediction, but a general guide as to the likely effect of certain changes.

In both LUTS and time-series models, good quality data are vital, with due allowance made for bias in definitions of passenger trip discussed earlier in this chapter.

References and suggested further reading

Extensive use has been made of two recent national reports, abbreviated as follows:
NTS: *National travel survey 1989/91*. London: HMSO, September 1993.
TSGB93: *Transport statistics Great Britain 1993*. London: HMSO, September 1993.
Subsequently the 1994 edition of *Transport statistics Great Britain* has been published, and the NTS is now carried out on a "rolling" basis. Latest results are described in the "National travel survey 1991–1993"; HMSO 1994.
Mention has also been made of data from OPCS (Office of Population Census and Surveys).
Use has also been made of the annual reports of the British Railways Board, and London Regional Transport.

Brög, W. (Socialdata, Munich) 1993. Behaviour begins in the mind – possibilities and limits of marketing activities in urban public transport. Paper presented at ECMT (European Conference of Ministers of Transport) Round Table 92, "Marketing and Service Quality in Public Transport", Paris, December 1991.
Bruton, M. 1985. *Introduction to transportation planning,* 3rd edn. London: Hutchinson.
Fairhurst, M. H. 1991. *An analysis of bus passenger traffic trends in England since 1982*. Research Report R272, London Transport Planning Department.
Jones, P. 1994. *Study of policies in overseas cities for traffic and transport (SPOTT)*. Transport Studies Group, University of Westminster, for Traffic Policy Division, Department of Transport.
London Research Centre 1994. *Travel in London* [London Area Transport Survey, 1991]. London: HMSO.
London Transport 1993 (February). *London Transport traffic trends 1971–90*. Research Report R273, London Transport Planning Department.
Mackinder, I. H. & S. E. Evans 1981. *The predictive accuracy of British transport studies in urban areas*. Research Report SR699, Transport Research Laboratory, Crowthorne, Berks.

May, A. D. 1991. *Integrated transport strategies: a new initiative or a return to the 1960s?* Discussion Paper 21, Transport and Society Project, Rees Jeffreys Road Fund/ Transport Studies Unit, University of Oxford.

Smart, H. E. 1984. The dynamics of change – application of the panel survey technique to transportation surveys in Tyne and Wear. *Traffic Engineering and Control* **25** (December), 595–8.

Watts, P. F. et al. 1990. *Urban minibuses in Britain: development, user response, operations and finances.* Report RR269, Transport Research Laboratory, Crowthorne, Berkshire.

White, P. R. 1976. *Planning for public transport* (Ch. 2). London: Hutchinson.

— R. P. Turner, N. P Dennis 1991. Understanding the behaviour of public transport users through the trip chain concept. Proceedings of Seminar H (pp. 15–30), PTRC Summer Annual Meeting, September.

CHAPTER 3

The technology of bus and coach systems

Design of the vehicle

In this section, general principles will be described, together with conditions specific to the UK market. Most references are to local bus requirements, with coach design issues identified where applicable.

The designer has to produce a compromise between many conflicting requirements: to minimize fuel consumption, maintenance and purchase costs; to maximize passenger capacity within certain comfort limits; to permit ease of boarding and alighting; to provide a smooth ride through use of appropriate transmission and suspension systems. Some of these may be quantified more easily than others. In particular, fuel, maintenance and capital costs can be combined in a single measure, whole life cost. Forecast fuel consumption and maintenance costs – for a given service pattern – may be discounted over the proposed life of the vehicle and added to capital cost to identify the vehicle which is cheapest overall. This enables trade-offs to be identified, such as the purchase of a heavy-duty vehicle – with its higher initial cost – to give subsequent maintenance cost savings, and hence a lower overall whole life cost.

Such trade-offs will depend partly on the local circumstances. For example, in Western Europe and North America, labour-intensive maintenance costs have risen rapidly in recent years, making these a major factor in vehicle choice, whereas fuel costs represents only about 5% of total costs. In many developing countries, where labour costs are low, fuel costs may form up to 20% of total costs, and thus become a critical factor.

The designer is also constrained by the legal limits on length, width, height, gross vehicle weight, and maximum weight on any one axle. In Britain, for two-axle vehicles these are:

length	12.0 m
width	2.5 m
gross vehicle weight	17.0 tonnes
maximum axle load	10.5 tonnes

A rigid three-axle variant is also permitted (used mostly for long-distance coach work) with a gross weight of up to 25 tonnes within the same length.

Unlike most other countries, Britain has traditionally not imposed a maximum height limit as such, but a "tilt test" is applied, in which a single-decker must be tilted to 35° from the horizontal before toppling over (for a double-decker 28° applies). Under harmonization of standards within the EU, a height limit of 4.57m applies to all newly constructed vehicles, some versions being slightly lower than this where bridge clearances are limited. In many other countries more severe constraints may apply, making double-deckers largely impracticable.

The unladen weight is defined as the weight of vehicle structure. The term "kerbside weight" is also employed to describe the vehicle as ready for service (including fuel, driver, etc.). The effective payload is thus the gross weight minus kerbside weight. An average weight per passenger of 65kg is generally assumed (hence, for example, a vehicle of 17.0 tonnes gross with a kerbside weight of 10.5 tonnes could carry 100 passengers). In practice, for a two-axle double-decker, the typical maximum capacity is about 85–90 (75 seated plus 10–15 standing). The gross weight constraint is more likely to cause difficulties in coach operation, when passengers are carrying heavy luggage or duty-free goods.

Legal constraints have changed over time. For example, not until 1981 did the articulated single-decker become legal for regular service, with a maximum length of 18m and gross weight of 27 tonnes. Today, maximum dimensions are about as large as the designer would wish, and smaller limits may often be imposed by road network conditions: the 12-metre maximum length, for example, is generally confined to long-distance work.

Types of buses and coaches

Major types of bus and coach found today include:

Minibuses

The term "minibus" has a specific legal meaning in Britain, being a vehicle of 9 to 16 seats, constructed and used for work other than public local bus services (for example, vehicles operated under minibus permits by voluntary groups). These are typically mass-produced vehicles based on integral van designs, modified to incorporate passenger seating. More specialized designs, often fitted with wheelchair lifts, are used for dial-a-ride operations in many urban areas. It should also be noted that the term "taxi" applies to a vehicle of up to 8 seats (i.e. a small minibus), used for public service.

However, the term "minibus" is also widely used to cover the smaller of the vehicles used in public service, especially following their rapid expansion in Britain from 1984. These are typically vehicles of 16 to about 30 seats, usually based on mass-produced van chassis with a purpose-built body (such as the Ford Transit, or Mercedes 709 series), or vehicles of a similar layout, with front engine, built as integral minibuses (notably the Optare Metrorider). The earlier, smaller, models such as the Transit are now being replaced by larger models offering slightly greater seating capacity, wider passenger doorways and more luggage space. Improved suspension and transmission systems are now incorporated to improve comfort and reduce maintenance costs. However, the benefits of low-priced spares through commonality with light goods vehicle models remain.

Midibuses

This term has no specific legal meaning, but typically applies either to the large front-engine minibuses (such as the Mercedes 811 series), or in effect a shorter version of a conventional single-deck chassis, such as the Dennis Dart or Volvo B6 – a rear-engined vehicle typically seating around 30–35 which may be employed in a similar rôle to the smaller minibuses (i.e. replacing larger vehicles to offer a higher frequency, as in many parts of London), or to substitute on a 1-for-1 basis for larger vehicles where average loads have fallen since deregulation.

Standard single-deckers

These are typically 10–12m in length:
  (a) Front engine, forward of the front axle and alongside the driver. A simple, robust layout, but with a high floor and interior noise levels. Popular in many developing countries, where mechanical reliability is the major factor, but no longer purchased in Britain.
  (b) Underfloor engine, mounted centrally or at the rear. This permits a wide front entrance adjacent to the driver. The underfloor version (for example, the Volvo B10M) is common both as a coach (in which case high-floor bodies are often specified to increase luggage space and improve the passenger view), or as a local bus. However, to minimize floor height the rear engined layout is more common for local bus work (such as the Leyland Lynx, or Optare Delta), albeit requiring a sloped floor, or step towards the rear of the vehicle, in order to accommodate engine and transmission. To improve access further, notably for wheelchair users, very low floor models have been developed, such as the Neoplan N4014, or Dennis SLF.

The seating capacity of single-deckers varies with length and pitch. For local service work, 45 to 54 seats is typical, with some layouts using five-across seating (two persons one side of the gangway, three on the other) to give over 60, usually for school work. For intensive urban services, layouts with a high proportion of standing passengers may be used, such as 44 seats plus 20 standing. By further increasing the ratio of standing space, over 70 may be carried. For coaches, up to about 50 may be carried in the 12m length, with space for toilet, and a reasonable seat pitch.

Double-deckers

These are usually on two axles, typically about 10m long, seating about 75, of two configurations:

- Rear-mounted transverse engine. This permits low entrance and floor level. Current types include the Leyland/Volvo Olympian, Dennis Dominator, and Optare Spectra.
- Underfloor horizontally mounted engine (Volvo D10M Citybus). This has a slightly higher floor, but better weight distribution.

Articulated single-decker

This usually comprises a four-axle front section with steered two-axle rear section linked by flexible connection permitting through passenger movement, based either on underfloor-engined chassis (such as Volvo BIOM), or rear-mounted "pusher" design. Very popular elsewhere in Europe, with a high proportion of standing passengers to give a capacity of over 100, but rare in Britain, as a high proportion of seated capacity is usually preferred, and on this basis the traditional two-axle double-decker gives a similar capacity at lower cost.

It should be borne in mind that the above examples do not include some minor design variants, or types now becoming obsolete in Britain (such as the Routemaster in London – a front-engined, rear open-platform double-decker, with a roving conductor).

Some current issues in bus and coach design

Vehicle life and replacement policy

Assumptions regarding optimal vehicle life remain somewhat crude, being based on accounting conventions and engineers' judgement as much as precise calculation. In Britain, 15 years was typical on both criteria for full-size vehicles. This has tended to be revised upwards, especially for some of the types such as the Leyland National, following the abolition of the new bus grant – which until the early 1980s covered up to 50% of the cost of new vehicles – and the inability since deregulation of many operators to generate sufficient cash to meet full replacement costs. Up to 20–25 years may now be assumed, where vehicles are extensively refurbished and re-engined. The vehicle is required to pass a strict annual test, and the operator thus faces a trade-off between increasingly costly work to bring a vehicle up to the required standard as it ages, and complete replacement. The average life now found in Britain is now exceptionally high, and while refurbishment may enable some improvements to be incorporated, it does not, for example, provide the accessibility benefits now offered by very low-floor designs. The proportion of full-size buses 12 years old or more rose from 21% in 1986 to 44% in 1993 (Bus and Coach Statistics Great Britain 1992/3, table 2.2).

The increased complexity of modern vehicles has in many cases led to a rise in maintenance costs, both in real terms and as a proportion of total costs. Following local bus deregulation in Britain, sharp cuts in engineering staff reversed this trend, but this factor itself is now being offset by rising average vehicle life (see above). After driver costs, vehicle maintenance forms the second largest element within total costs. If real labour costs begin to rise, then a shift back toward a shorter vehicle-life may be justified, especially if newer designs offer significant improvements in reliability and ease of maintenance. As a reasonable target, one might expect fleet availability of 85% to 90% (i.e. the proportion of vehicles in a fleet available for peak-period service), but this may fall as average age rises.

Optimal life of minibuses and lightweight vehicles

Following extensive experience in Britain during the 1980s, a somewhat longer life than initially anticipated may be acceptable for minibuses, in the order of five to seven years for van-derived models, or up to about ten years for "midibus" vehicles such as the Metrorider or Dart. Nonetheless, the anticipated life is shorter than that for full-size heavyweight vehicles, and hence for intensive public service, low initial capital cost may thus be offset by a high annual depreciation charge. As a rule of thumb, the initial capital cost per seated passenger is about £1,500 at 1993 prices for a wide range of vehicles, from minibuses to double-deckers (slightly higher for some midibuses and articulated buses).

The rôle of mass-production

Bus and coach manufacture remains in many respects a craft industry, with small-scale production characteristic of both developed and developing countries. Although this has some advantages, in permitting many variations to meet users' requirements and local bodywork manufacture in countries not large enough to make chassis or engines, it results in high unit costs. Only one model in Britain has been made on a production-line basis, the Leyland National single-decker, manufactured on a large scale during the 1970s, but ceasing production in 1985.

Energy consumption

Typical consumption of derv for a large single-decker, or double-decker, is about 30–35 litres per 100 kilometres, or somewhat better for longer-distance services with fewer intermediate stops. As Figure 3.1 shows, this is strongly influenced by stop spacing. For minibuses around 20 litres per 100km may be consumed in urban service. At loads of about 15 passengers over the whole day (full-size vehicles) or 10 (minibuses), this is about half the energy consumed per passenger-km for private cars. Some opportunities for improvements exist, although less marked than in the case of urban rail (Ch. 4), as unladen weight per seated passenger space is already low (about 125 kg, compared with 250 kg for "heavy" urban rail systems). Regeneration – converting energy otherwise wastefully converted during the braking phase – may be incorporated, through flywheel storage, giving energy savings of up to 25%. However, at present fuel prices the necessary investment and added mechanical complexity is unlikely to be justifiable in financial terms. The main current problem in Britain is the low average load at which buses are operating since deregulation, reducing the relative energy advantage over private car previously displayed.

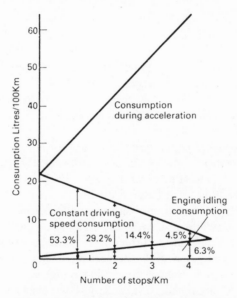

Figure 3.1 Energy consumption of an urban bus, related to stop spacing. Consumption during acceleration and engine idling increases with the number of stops per kilometre. (From *Motor Transport*, 27 October 1982.)

Electric vehicles

As in the case of long-distance rail (see Ch. 9), electric traction gives significant advantages over diesel in maintenance costs, availability, local pollution impacts and increased acceleration. Regenerative braking may also be incorporated more easily. Although often thought outdated, the trolleybus – using a pair of overhead wires mounted above the vehicle – offers all of these features. Re-design of the overhead equipment has reduced its capital cost and environmental intrusion. Bradford, the last of many trolleybus systems in Britain, closed in 1972, but following the oil cost increases from the following year, many elsewhere were renewed and extended, such as Seattle, Wellington and Lyon. Reintroduction in West Yorkshire has been proposed within Britain, but is currently deferred due to complexities arising from local bus deregulation, and the high unit capital costs of a small installation. A much smaller range of benefits is offered by battery buses, whose theoretical attractiveness is offset by limited range, high unladen weight and high cost of battery replacement, although an experiment using a battery-powered version of the Metrorider minibus began in Oxford in November 1993.

Noise levels and local pollution

Although buses generally emit less pollution per passenger-kilometre than private cars (notably in carbon monoxide, CO, and lead, Pb), localized concentrations in busy central area streets may result in pressures to remove buses, unless pollution and noise levels can be reduced. Acceptability within residential areas may also be critical.

Within the EU, tighter requirements now exist for both passenger and goods diesel vehicles, notably in emission of particulates (smoke). Under Euro 1 regulations, applying to new vehicles from October 1993, the maximum allowance for particulates is $0.36\,g/KWh$. Under Euro 2 from October 1996 this maximum will fall to $0.15\,g/kWH$. Lower limits are also set for nitrous oxides (NO_x), CO, and hydrocarbons. While new vehicles, and those fitted with replacement engines, will meet these criteria, current fleet replacement rates mean that up to twenty years may pass before all buses meet such standards. An exterior noise level is now specified according to power (in kW) for new vehicles with over 9 passenger seats – 81 dBA if under 75 kW; 83 dBA for vehicles of 75–150 kW; and 84 dBA for vehicles over 150 kW.

In some countries, experiments are currently taking place with alternative fuels, to reduce bus pollution impacts. These include liquified natural gas (LNG), compressed natural gas (CNG), and methanol. Another approach, adopted by Transit Holdings (whose minibuses serve the centres of Torquay, Oxford and Exeter via bus/pedestrian streets), is a dual-mode petrol–electric minibus, which can operate as a conventional diesel vehicle, or use the petrol engine to feed an accumulator. The vehicle operates under electric power in sensitive areas.

Structural strength

Coach accidents, where the collapse of the body in roll-over incidents has been a major cause of serious injuries and fatalities, have encouraged stricter requirements for the strength of bodywork, now incorporated in ECE regulations. Integral vehicles may offer significant advantages in this respect: designs such as the Leyland National also have much greater resistance to end-on collisions.

Safety of passengers

Most casualties in local service operation are associated not with vehicular accidents, but in boarding, alighting and movement within the vehicle by the passengers themselves, especially the elderly (White et al. 1993). Appropriate positioning and shape of grab rails, use of low step heights, and careful design of entry and exit, may all assist. Most new and refurbished vehicles now follow the guideline specifications produced by DPTAC (Disabled Persons Transport Advisory Committee). One commonly used technique is to create a split step in the front platform, so that three small steps replace two larger ones. Another feature is to ensure that stairs in double-deckers rise toward the front of the vehicle so that passengers are not thrown downwards should sharp braking occur. A particularly dangerous feature is the retention of open rear-platform vehicles in London (the Routemaster type). Alighting casualties have also been associated with the use of driver-controlled centre exit doors, to which stricter design criteria (to detect obstructions in closing) now apply. Many operators have reverted to a single entry layout, the time savings offered by simultaneous exit being marginal in most cases.

Provision for the disabled

Making boarding and alighting easier assists not only the elderly and the partially ambulant disabled, but also other types of passenger, such as those with heavy shopping. Those suffering more severe disabilities, and the rapidly growing numbers aged over 75, may not be able to use conventional systems. Provision of wheel-chair lifts on full-size buses is one solution, and some urban systems run such buses on specially selected routes and timings, able to carry both the disabled and non-disabled passengers. However, a more commonplace solution is the provision of special dial-a-ride services using minibuses, such as Readibus in Reading, and those in many parts of London. Another type of specialized service, often more cost-effective than dial-a-ride, is the Taxicard scheme in London, using standard taxis (now constructed to incorporate wheelchair access).

However, a better solution may be to adopt very low floor buses, operated in place of standard vehicles on all-day services, thus offering a wider choice of travel opportunities to elderly and disabled users, and improving access for all types of passengers. The first such services in Britain commenced in Liverpool in 1993, followed by London in 1994.

The rôle of European Union policy

As standard regulations are adopted for bus and coach design within the EU, this will affect policy in Britain. EU regulations already specify maximum emission levels (above), roll-over strength for coaches, and maximum coach speed (100km/h). It is likely that they will also affect access requirements for the elderly and disabled to standard vehicles, and possibly result in a sharper demarcation between coach and local bus designs in future, although this could have adverse effects, especially in rural areas, where the dual rôle of coaches provides useful economies in utilization (see Ch. 8).

Ticketing systems

One-person operation of buses is now almost universal in North America and Western Europe, apart from some busier routes in London. Two approaches to revenue collection and ticket issue may be taken:
(a) All passengers are required to pass the driver, to pay a cash fare, produce a return ticket, or display a pass/travelcard. This system is general in Britain, with a tradition of most fares being collected in cash (see Ch. 7), and ensures that almost all passengers are entitled to travel, but imposes the penalty of extra boarding time, ranging from about 2.5 seconds for passholders or those with the exact change, to about 6 seconds or more where many passengers pay in cash and require change. As a result average journey speeds are reduced, and greater variation occurs between successive runs on the same route, as boardings vary. Statistical data may be collected through the machine issuing a ticket for each cash fare, and the driver may record each pass holder as they board. Developments in magnetic card and smart card technology now make it practicable to validate passes automatically (without physical contact being required), enabling a higher degree of inspection, and a more comprehensive statistical record, to be obtained.
(b) Most passengers have purchased tickets off-vehicle, either as passes, travelcards or self-cancelling multi-ride tickets. Drivers only deal with a very small proportion still paying in cash, and other passengers may board by any entrance. This gives much more rapid boarding, especially useful on articulated buses or tramcars, but a significant risk of revenue loss, despite checks by groups of inspectors who have power to levy fines or

penalty fares. On the Dutch system, for example, virtually no cash fare collection on vehicles now takes place.

Most single cash fares are now handled by driver-operated electronic ticket machines (ETMs), such as the Wayfarer which can print extensive information on the ticket (such as time of issue) and store comprehensive data for management analysis (although its use in practice is very limited). They may be linked with payment of the exact cash fare into a farebox to speed boarding. However, these systems do not reduce boarding times if cash fares are still applicable.

The adoption of magnetic re-encodable, and smart card, technology offers a partial solution. Where a fixed decrement is made for each trip, then manual self-cancellation may be replaced by a card offering a fixed total value for travel, re-encoded by a contactless reader each time a trip is made (for example, in Greater Manchester, the concessionary flat fare is now handled in this manner). ETMs such as newer models of Wayfarer may incorporate card validators/encoders for this purpose. However, retention of the graduated (distance-based) fare scale in most parts of Britain makes such automation of cash-paid adult trips of little value in reducing boarding times on buses. The technology of fare collection cannot be divorced from the need for simplicity in fare structures (see Ch. 7).

On urban rail networks, however, with a closed system in which all stations are fitted with entry and exit barriers, re-encoding of tickets for variable sums per journey (by time of day, distance covered, etc.) is far more practicable, for example on the Hong Kong Mass Transit Railway, or the Washington Metro.

Control and supervision of bus services

Unlike railways, buses do not necessarily require any special control systems beyond those for road traffic in general. However, it is desirable that drivers can communicate with supervisors in emergencies, such as breakdown or assault. On denser urban routes measures are needed to cope effectively with frequent crew changeover and the irregularities caused by traffic congestion. Traditionally, inspectors at depots, stations and on-street stands have monitored buses and crews, using telephones and hand-held radios. However, this method is very labour-intensive and may give poor results if inspectors themselves do not work on a co-ordinated basis. A central control point is better able to detect overall patterns and take the most appropriate action to maintain regularity, while using fewer staff.

Cab radios

The simplest approach is to fit all vehicles with cab radios, for direct-voice contact. Most urban fleets are now fitted, and many coach operators also use such systems (or employ standard cellular mobile phones). Their value in emergencies is clear, but on large networks they are often limited through the small number of wavelengths allocated to operators. Around 100 drivers or more may be served by a single channel, making frequent reporting of position impracticable in the airtime available.

Cab radio may be supplemented by closed-circuit television cameras placed at strategic junctions and boarding points in the central area. In a medium-size town, most congestion can thus be monitored through one control room which is also linked to each driver. Examples include Leicester and Nottingham.

Automatic vehicle monitoring (AVM)

For more complex networks, and those affected by more severe traffic congestion, automatic monitoring of vehicle location is desirable. Several systems have been attempted, such as BUSCO, introduced on London's 36 group of routes in 1984.

The following main options now apply:

(a) Use of a bus-mounted sensor which picks up signals from loops or roadside devices placed at frequent intervals, and converts the signal into coded form for transmission to a control centre. Similar coded messages may be sent and received by the driver (for example, an instruction to turn short). A major example is the system used to support the Countdown real-time passenger information system on route 18 in London, launched in Autumn 1992.

(b) Use of a standard commercial system, such as Securicor Datatrak, for which the operator pays a fee to receive frequently updated signals indicating the vehicle's position, identified through a system of triangulation (as used by Mainline in Sheffield). Communications with their driver or a real-time information system are then handled through the operator's own system. Another commercially available system is the GEC Bus Tracker (as used by Armchair Transport for tendered services in west London).

(c) Use of global positioning systems (GPS) using satellites – for example, by PMT, the main operator in Stoke on Trent.

All such systems are only of value if supported by a control strategy, such as drafting in extra vehicles and crews (if available) to fill gaps in service, re-allocating vehicles and crews between routes at termini, or turning trips short in one direction to cover a gap in the other (unpopular with passengers for obvious reasons). In many cases, scheduled running times do not reflect realistically traffic conditions often experienced. AVM systems or on-bus data recorders (such as the Optimiser) may be used to obtain a large sample of running times from existing operations, and hence set more reliable schedules (see also Ch. 5), reducing the need to introduce unplanned variations.

Passenger information systems

Quality of information provided on bus services remains poor. Even simple bus-stop displays of route number, destination and departure times are often lacking. Fares' information is very rarely provided. Simple displays, showing departure times from each stop for each destination may be more effective than use of full timetable sheets. Ready availability of maps, timetable leaflets and leaflets on fares provides the user with much of the information s/he requires. The most effective back-up would appear to be a telephone enquiry service with a well publicized number.

AVM systems can also be linked to passenger information displays to indicate when the next bus for a given destination is arriving. Following introduction of the Countdown system on route 18, London Transport is now extending this concept to the heavily used Uxbridge Road corridor, and plans wider use over its network. Experiments are also in progress (at 1994) in Southampton (Stop-watch) and Birmingham. Actual waiting times are not reduced, but the reassurance provided to the user and information on exceptional conditions, enables more effective planning of journeys. In several Canadian cities, the Teleride computer-based telephone answering system enables the potential user to call from home before setting out for the bus stop: this approach may be particularly appropriate in low-density suburbs. It may simply consist of a synthesized voice working from the fixed schedule, or, in more sophisticated versions, be linked with AVM.

Buses on road networks

In very broad terms, measures which benefit all road users also benefit buses. Traffic lights reduce accidents and delay at busy intersections, new roads improve traffic flow, and traffic-management measures enable existing networks to handle heavier flows and/or higher speeds. However, the opposite may also be true. One-way schemes increase route mileage, and may take buses away from passenger objectives. At traffic lights, a relatively long cycle time maximizes total flow but as shown below leads to significant and variable delays for buses. A case for bus priority can therefore be made, firstly, on grounds that buses should not suffer adverse effects from management schemes. As a wider policy, buses can be made more attractive, for example by permitting them to use a direct route via a contraflow lane when other traffic is re-routed around a one-way system. They can thus retain more passengers. In conditions of scarce road space, giving priority to the most efficient users of that space (buses) may reduce total travel time within the network.

Up to a third of bus journey time (especially in peak and/or congested conditions) may be spent stationary – roughly half at passenger stops, and half at traffic-light controlled intersections (together with other junctions, pedestrian crossings, etc.), which are in any case those with the heaviest flows. Reduction of time at stops may be attained through appropriate ticketing/boarding systems (see above). How can similar reductions be obtained at intersections?

For the majority of road users, average time taken to pass through an intersection is the only relevant criterion. The traffic engineer is also concerned with maximizing the flow of PCUs (passenger car units), in which a bus carrying 50 passengers receives little more weight than a single car. However, buses form a time-linked system, so that delays to one affect others.

Consider Figure 3.2. Buses are scheduled to depart from A at 3-minute intervals. Passengers accumulate at each stop at the rate of two per minute. Each takes 5 seconds to board, and hence average scheduled time at each stop is 30 seconds. Scheduled running times between stops and across intersections (20 seconds) are shown. Assume that the first bus just misses a green phase at the first traffic lights (or joins a queue of vehicles which does not discharge entirely during the first available green phase). It is delayed for 80, instead of the scheduled 20 seconds. When it reaches the next stop, more passengers have accumulated, and hence stop time is extended. This process is repeated at each stop, the bus running further and further behind schedule. The following bus has fewer passengers to pick up, and hence gains on schedule. If the first bus suffers a similar delay at the second traffic light, and the second bus only the scheduled delay at each junction, the two buses will be only 45 seconds instead of 3 minutes apart at B. Delay to passengers at stops is likely to be found particularly inconvenient and irritating, and is customarily given a value up to twice that of in-vehicle time.

This example also illustrates the effect of boarding times in aggravating irregularity, and the difficulty of running a regular, very high frequency service: the theoretical benefits of substituting small minibuses for full-size vehicles may be thus to some extent offset where small headways are already offered.

A simple solution would be to reduce traffic light cycle time and hence inter-

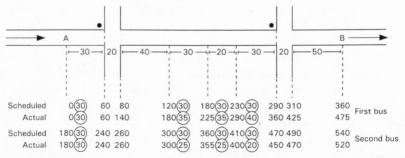

Total boarding time (in seconds) at each stop is shown thus ③⓪
Other timings are cumulative.
● Traffic lights

Figure 3.2 Effect of junction delays on bus service regularity.

vals between each green phase. However, this would reduce total junction capacity by increasing the proportion of inter-green time (i.e. that in which a green aspect is not displayed for any flow) and if the junction were already working near saturation, this could merely worsen congestion, in which buses would also be delayed. But if, as part of a comprehensive traffic-restraint scheme, traffic volumes over a wide area were reduced, this solution could apply.

At the least, one can ensure that each bus reaches the junction so that the next available green phase is used. By making the nearside lane bus-only, buses can overtake queues of other traffic. Many of these with-flow priority lanes were introduced during the 1970s, and they remain the most common form of bus priority measure. This success depends upon adequate enforcement (often lacking), and queues into which other traffic is placed not being so long as to obstruct other junctions which are also used by buses. Extra traffic wardens may be needed to deter kerbside parking in the bus lane. Variations in hours of operation of lanes (many are peak-only), and lack of physical separation of with-flow lanes from other parts of the road surface add to these problems. Colouring of the tarmac in the lane aids enforcement.

If the with-flow lane is taken right up to the stop line at the junction, this may reduce total junction capacity (in terms of PCU) and tempt motorists turning left to use the bus lane. It is standard policy to terminate the bus lane short of the stop line: buses can still get close enough to be able to use the first available green phase, but other traffic can also make use of the junction capacity.

In order to avoid extra running time and diversion from passenger objectives when one-way schemes are introduced, buses may be allowed to continue to use a road in both directions, those against the (new) one-way flow in a contraflow lane. Although a few may be separated from other traffic merely by a solid white line (as for with-flow lanes) most are physically separated by a series of traffic islands or raised curbs. Major examples may be found in London, such as Tottenham High Road or Piccadilly. In some cases the concept may be taken further by having a segregated section of road surface for two-way bus traffic, as near Gare du Nord in Paris.

A merit of contra-flow schemes is that they are largely self-enforcing, and substantial increases in bus speeds may be obtained. However, since the tarmac surface is used only by buses, rutting may develop, requiring more frequent resurfacing. One part of the Runcorn busway has been relaid in concrete slab form for this reason. There is also a problem of pedestrian safety, and it may be necessary to confine their movement to light-controlled crossings by use of barriers. In order to make them more conspicuous, buses now show their headlights throughout the day when in contra-flow lanes.

Another common means of giving buses priority is to exempt them from right turn bans, causing little delay to other traffic but giving significant time savings. Many examples can be found in London, notably at Parliament Square. Buses can also be given the benefits of selective detection approaching traffic lights, enabling either an extension of an existing green phase, or bringing forward the

59

start of the next green phase. Losses to other traffic may be compensated by extending green time on the next phase. Variation in delay to buses may be markedly reduced, especially when they are turning right. Transponders fitted to buses enable those vehicles entitled to such priority to be detected clearly. The MOVA demand-responsive software fitted at many isolated junctions has been adapted for this purpose.

Urban traffic control (UTC) schemes have been introduced in many cities, in which optimal use is made of an entire network – in terms of capacity, and/or minimizing delay – through central computer control. A common feature is the provision of a "green wave" in which a platoon of vehicles is able to experience a green phase on most signalled junctions it crosses, by the green phases at each successive junction being offset to allow for the average speed of vehicles in the platoon. However, running times of buses between junctions may be longer than for cars owing to the presence of intermediate stops and lower acceleration. Buses may thus fail to benefit, or even hit more red phases than before. A revised version of the traditional fixed-time linking system called Transyt was introduced in Glasgow, in which offsets between green phases were timed to suit buses, and duration of each green phase sufficient for buses to pass through after allowing for delay owing to intermediate stops. Bus speeds increased by about 9%, with no significant worsening for cars. More recent systems such as SCOOT (split-cycle offset optimization technique) have also been adapted to allow for buses. Other recent examples of bus priority include schemes in which the bus lanes continue up to the junction stop line, and an advance phase is provided for buses. Examples may be found in Swansea and in Shepherds Bush (west London). The latter is of particular value to the many buses turning right within the gyratory system.

It will be evident from the above that much of the benefit of bus priorities comes through reduced variability in journey time rather than any dramatic increase in average speeds. Their evaluation thus depends upon assessment of changes in passenger waiting time as much as that in-vehicle, as highlighted in the Buchanan consultancy study of London bus priorities in 1986.

Stations and interchanges

The great majority of bus passengers continue to board and alight at kerbside stops. For local services, this is in any case desirable in order to give good access to passengers' destinations, and permit cross-centre linking of services. The value of on-street stops can be enhanced by introduction and enforcement of parking restrictions, and provision of better shelters with timetable information. Their costs may be offset by advertising.

Bus stations are required for rural and long-distance services, and interchange – especially with rail in large cities. In some cases, however, they may have been

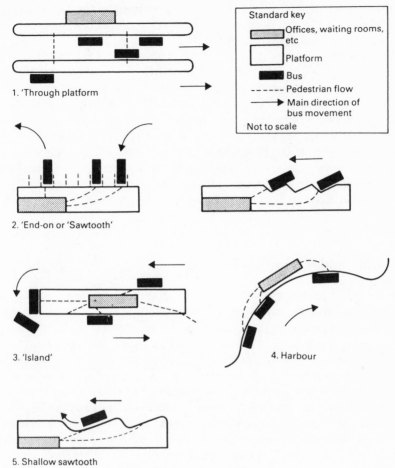

Figure 3.3 Bus station layouts.

built to "tidy up" town centres rather than aid bus passengers. Under pressure of competitive services following deregulation, some operations have shifted back to on-street stops in some towns where stations are poorly sited, and to reduce charges paid.

Figure 3.3 shows some common station layouts. For high-frequency services, a through-platform design is often best, buses moving parallel to it. Space between platforms should be sufficient for buses to overtake one another. However, a large area may be needed, and many points of conflict between bus and pedestrian movement occur. The end-on and "sawtooth" (or "echelon") layouts remedy this by providing only one platform area, on which all facilities such as waiting rooms and enquiry offices are concentrated, with the front doors of buses adjoining the platform. This layout is favoured for many rural/inter-urban or small town stations, but is limited by the need for buses to reverse on departing,

61

with associated accident risk: a modification introduced by Greater Manchester, the "shallow sawtooth", overcomes this. Other layouts offering minimal pedestrian/bus conflict, and concentration of activities, are the "island" and "harbour" types, as found at Newark and King's Lynn, respectively. The "island" type can be expanded by end-on loading of buses along each side, as at Preston. The main platform may also be entirely enclosed, and access to buses given through sliding doors. Many stations in medium-size towns combine both through-platform and end-on layouts for different types of service.

All of the above layouts may be used also for bus/rail interchanges, with a further aim of minimizing pedestrian conflict in access to the rail platforms. The "harbour" layout may be particularly suitable, or "island" where the railway is underground, access to rail platforms being given by stairs or escalator in the centre (as at the Broadway Centre, Hammersmith).

Busways and bus links

The concept of providing bus priorities on existing roads may be extended to that of allocating the whole road space to buses, and/or building separate busways, usually conventional road structures of about 7.0 m width, with one lane in each direction. They may provide new direct links, access to areas not open to general traffic, or routes parallel to existing congested roads.

The simplest form is where an entire street is restricted to bus and delivery vehicle use only, typically a town centre shopping street from which other traffic has been taken by an inner relief road. Buses thus continue to serve the heart of the town, and cross-linking of services is made easy. Major examples include Broad Street in Reading, Cornmarket in Oxford, and High Street in Exeter (the last for minibuses only). The traditional road surface may be retained, with separate pavements, or the whole area re-surfaced to permit mixed bus/pedestrian movement, as in Oxford. Average speeds may not rise substantially, but delays owing to congestion are largely avoided and excellent access provided.

Within residential areas, bus links may be provided, in which direct routeing is provided for buses, but other traffic is banned. Buses thus benefit from efficient network structures, but intrusion from other through-traffic is prevented (see also Ch. 5). Examples may be found in new towns such as Bracknell and Washington, and also in some older towns where previously indirect routeings have been replaced in this manner. Even for flows of only two or three buses per hour, operating cost savings can justify such investment, not to mention passenger time savings. However, buses in residential areas and others in which "traffic calming" is applied, have in some cases suffered from inappropriately designed speed humps. Recent work has established more suitable designs which may be negotiated safely by buses while meeting the objective of reducing car speeds (Hodge 1993).

In Halmstad (southern Sweden), an experiment involved the linking of short busways in housing areas with priorities on existing roads and in the town centre, together with the use of short raised platforms at bus stops, similar to those on light rail networks. Boarding and alighting was thus made much easier, by matching platform and bus floor heights. Stop time was reduced, and access for the disabled (including wheelchairs) made much easier. However, the very low floor design is more likely to be employed in future to achieve this aim (see above).

By these means, an incremental approach to investment can be adopted, in which many of the benefits associated with rail systems can be provided through gradual improvement of existing bus networks, also retaining the better accessibility of the bus. Unfortunately, current policies in Britain make even these modest schemes difficult to plan and finance (although, paradoxically, large-scale rail projects are more readily financed).

In terms of extensive new busway construction, the major example in Britain is in Runcorn New Town (discussed further in Ch. 5), where most of the network is provided by busways, enabling services to operate at an average of over 32 km/h, compared with about 19 km/h for buses entirely on conventional streets.

The busway concept has been developed recently into the guided busway – a narrower surface (although taking a standard-width bus of 2.5 m), on which the bus is guided laterally by use of small, horizontally mounted wheels set adjacent to the main running wheels, running against steel guide rails. The total width required for the busway is thus reduced by up to 25%, and the driver's task made easier. As with other busways, incremental development is possible, as buses fitted with the guidewheels can run quite normally on the rest of the road network.

The most extensive development of this idea has been the O-Bahn, pioneered by Mercedes-Benz in Germany. A 3.8 km section in Essen sharing space with a tramway opened in 1981/3. This has been followed by schemes elsewhere in Germany. Worldwide, the major example is the North East corridor in Adelaide, in which a guided busway serves a large residential area, both by park & ride facilities, and a network of through bus services into low-density housing areas. Rapid growth contrasts with decline in bus use elsewhere in that city: the scheme has been notably successful in attracting car users, and working-age male commuters.

In Britain an experimental section of guided busway, used by conventional double-deckers, operated in Birmingham (under the name Tracline) for a period in the mid-1980s. The first substantial application is on two corridors in Leeds, work on which began in 1994.

The most dramatic application of the busway concept is as an alternative to rail construction for heavy flows into the centres of large cities. Experience of such busways in several South American cities, and of reserved lanes in the Lincoln Tunnel in New York, indicates that passenger flows of up to 20,000 to 25,000 per hour per lane in one direction may be attainable, that is as great as any rail route in Britain. The critical factor is the capacity of intermediate stops, and hence passenger boarding rates. (Gardner et al. 1992).

In many respects, the choice between bus and rail technology (except where substantial underground operation is unavoidable) lies in passenger service quality, rather than peak capacity per se.

Conclusion

We can see that most immediate technical issues in bus and coach operation, are with the choice of vehicle itself, but also that there is great benefit to be derived from looking at urban bus operation in particular, as a system in which fixed investment in control and information systems and reserved track may produce many of the benefits normally associated with much more costly urban rail projects.

References and suggested further reading

Gardner, G., P. R. Cornwell, J. A. Cracknell 1992. *The performance of busway transit in developing countries*. Transport Research Laboratory Research Report 329.

Hodge, A. R. 1993. *Speed control humps – a trial at TRL*. Transport Research Laboratory report PR32.

White, P. R., N. P. Dennis, N. Tyler 1993. Analysis of recent trends in bus and coach safety in Britain. *Selected proceedings of the 1992 Sixth World Conference on Transport Research, Lyon*, vol. III, pp. 1785–96. Lyon: Laboratoire d'Economie des Transports.

A general guide to bus priority practice in Britain (including design and evaluation criteria) is given in *Keeping buses moving: a guide to traffic management in urban areas* (Local Transport Note 1/91). London: Department of Transport/HMSO, 1991.

CHAPTER 4

Urban railways and rapid transit systems

Early developments

During the nineteenth century, railways served almost all demands for mechanized transport, including those within urban areas. Specialized urban railways developed in the largest centres, notably the London Underground system from the opening of the Metropolitan Line in 1863. Main line railway companies also developed a strong interest in suburban traffic, especially where long-distance demand was limited. Thus, the railways to the south of London displayed markedly greater interest than those to the north and west. In smaller British cities, frequent steam-hauled services played an important rôle towards the end of the century, as in Stoke on Trent, Edinburgh and Birmingham.

The growth of electric tramways at the turn of the century, often under municipal ownership, caused a rapid transfer of short-distance trips to this new mode, which offered much better accessibility and frequency than railways, whose routes had been located primarily from the viewpoint of long-distance traffic. It was the tramcar, not the railway, which gave the first opportunity to the majority of the population to make frequent use of mechanized transport. The railways responded by closing some minor routes – leading eventually to the complete closure of local systems in cities such as Stoke or Edinburgh during the Beeching era of the 1960s – and concentrating on longer distance suburban flows, and movement within congested centres of very large cities, such as London. Suburban lines were electrified to improve speeds from the first decade of the twentieth century (for example, Liverpool to Southport, Ormskirk and Birkenhead; Manchester to Bury; and on Tyneside). In the London region this process greatly accelerated during the 1920s and 1930s to produce much of the present network south of the Thames. After World War Two this was followed by further extensions south of London, east London, and Glasgow. A renewed spate of investment led to further schemes north of London in the 1970s, notably extensions of the Glasgow and Merseyside networks. Main line electrification had also permitted local schemes as a by-product, notably in Manchester.

A more dramatic development was the growth of self-contained urban railway schemes, typically located underground in city centres, and often known as metros – after the Paris system, inaugurated in 1900. Other early examples included Hamburg, New York, Chicago, and Madrid. By 1940, seventeen such systems were in operation, including Moscow, Osaka and Tokyo. A boom in metro construction then followed from the 1950s. A further 49 systems were opened by 1984, and about another twenty have opened since. Within Europe, successively smaller cities, such as Oslo and Marseille, have opened metros, but some of the most heavily used systems are now found in the very large cities of Asia and South America, such as Hong Kong and Mexico City. Further growth in these regions is likely to produce much of the overall increase in metros.

In Britain, investment levels have been lower, but substantial improvements have been made to the London, Merseyside and Glasgow systems, and the Tyne and Wear Metro has been created largely from former BR routes. Light rail has been introduced in the form of the Docklands Light Railway (DLR) in London, Manchester Metrolink, and Sheffield Supertram.

In Britain also, the street tramcar largely disappeared during the 1950s, and only the Blackpool system remains. However, many medium-size cities elsewhere in Europe retained their systems, which have been developed into light rapid transit networks, acting either as the major framework in the public transport systems (as in Gothenburg or Hannover), or feeders to underground railways (as in Stockholm). New suburbs have been built around reserved track extensions, and older sections of the network placed on reserved track (sometimes in tunnel), so that most of the network is thus aligned.

Types of urban rail system

Four types of urban rail system may be distinguished, the first two using German terminology.

U-Bahn

This is an underground railway, usually running within the built-up limits of a city, giving good penetration of the city centre by tunnels (however, well over half the network may, in practice, be sited on the surface, or elevated track, outside the centre). Ownership is usually vested in the city transport authority, and the network largely self-contained. Close station spacing (about 1000m on average) permits a very high proportion of passengers to reach stations on foot, and all-stations operation of trains is normal. Simple fare systems, often flat rate or zonal, apply. Examples include the London Underground, Hamburg, Stockholm, Munich and New York. Although often adopted as a generic title for such systems, the Metro in Paris is in some respects untypical, with very close station spacing and short routes (apart from the RER regional express metro system).

S-Bahn

This term denotes those routes of main-line surface railways on which a frequent service geared to local traffic is offered. Station spacing within the inner city may approximate to that of the U-Bahn, but intervals of 2 or 3 km are more common. Average speeds are higher, despite lower acceleration rates. Peak service levels have often been limited by lack of track capacity, although there has been a general trend to segregate such services from long-distance operations through provision of separate tracks and stations. This may be taken further, to construction of new extensions purely for such systems, including city-centre routes in tunnel: this may offer a much cheaper alternative to building a new Metro, while giving many of the same benefits. Examples include Hamburg, Frankfurt, Merseyside and Glasgow. The Thameslink service, re-using an old tunnel between Farringdon and Blackfriars to create strategic cross-London links (such as Bedford–King's Cross–Gatwick) may also be placed in this category, albeit serving somewhat longer-distance traffic.

Light rapid transit (LRT) (also known as light rail transit)

This term is applied to electrically powered systems with characteristics similar to U-Bahn, but generally without block signalling (see below), full-height station platforms or ticket issue at all stations. Trains of up to three or four single cars, or one or two articulated cars, are usually operated. Many of the advantages of the "heavy" U- or S-Bahn systems are given, together with better accessibility, for a much lower investment, albeit at less capacity. Except in the largest cities, such systems are generally adequate for peak flows. Most have been developed from upgraded street tramways, but entirely new systems have been opened since the 1970s, including Calgary and Edmonton (both in Canada), San Diego and Buffalo (USA), Manila (Philippines) and Utrecht (Netherlands). The Tyne and Wear system uses some of the same techniques, but is closer to "heavy" transit. The Greater Manchester Metrolink, opened in 1992, represents the first British example of this new generation, using street-based technology to provide a cross-city link, while incorporating through running over former BR suburban lines.

In some cases, tramways have been upgraded to form an intermediate stage to "heavy" urban railways or metros. For example, the "pre-metro" in Brussels comprises city-centre tunnels and stations served initially by trams, and later by conventional metro trains. In other cases, a tramway may be upgraded by extensive construction of city-centre tunnels, and some stations at which all tickets are sold prior to boarding the vehicle ("semi-metro"), for example in Stuttgart. An advantage of such systems is that trams can be diverted into relatively short sections of tunnel as they are built, rather than waiting for a major portion of the system to be completed before operations can commence.

67

Automated systems

For some years, control technology has made fully automated operation (with no drivers or station staff) quite feasible. Several airport systems have been built, mainly in the USA, of which the Gatwick people-mover offers a British example, but the first such systems for general public use opened in Japan (Kobe and Osaka) in 1981. They have since been joined by several other Japanese systems, and the VAL in Lille (France), opened in 1983. The latter was the first to penetrate a traditional city centre, providing the same function as a traditional metro, and has operated very successfully. Further systems are now in use, including Vancouver's Skytrain. Flows handled are of similar size to those suited to LRT, hence the term ALRT (automated light rapid transit) being used in some cases. The DLR, the first part of which opened in 1987, also falls into this category, albeit retaining on-train "captains" for customer contact.

Basic system characteristics

Capacity

Capacity is a function of three variables:
1. *Passenger capacity of each car* Typically about 100 to 150, dependent upon the proportion of standing-to-seated passengers, level of comfort accepted, and size of car (LRT cars generally being smaller, and some "heavy" systems, such as Hong Kong, being built to a larger track and/or loading gauge than normal). A distinction may be drawn between "tolerable" loads, including some standing, and "maximum crush" (with greater standing densities) at the peak: in the case of London Underground tube stock, about 800 and 1,200 per train respectively. The proportion of seated passengers may be greatly increased by use of double-deck stock. This is found extensively on the Paris system for longer-distance commuting, and several other major cities, but is impractical in Britain due to the restricted loading gauge.
2. *Average length of train* Up to ten or twelve cars may be possible in the case of S-Bahn, but U-Bahn lines are generally limited by platform length to seven or eight (although newer systems may take more), as in the case of London. For LRT, up to three or four single cars, or two articulated cars, is typical.
3. *Headway between trains* Block signalling applies to all U-Bahn and S-Bahn lines, and some newer LRT routes (principles of which are described briefly in Ch. 9), implying a minimum headway of about 75 to 90 seconds. To allow some margin for minor operating delays, 90 to 120 seconds may be taken as a practical minimum (i.e. 30 to 40 trains per hour). LRT cars

may operate at intervals of down to about 45 seconds with control by drivers on sight distances.

Putting these factors together, the maximum passenger flow in one direction per hour (for a double-track route) can be estimated. For example, if each car takes 150 passengers, there are 8 cars to a train and 30 trains per hour, the flow will be $150 \times 8 \times 30$, or 36,000. In Europe, rarely is more than 25,000 required. S-Bahn routes may have lower capacity owing to sharing of track with other services and LRT routes a maximum of about 5000 to 15,000 per hour. In large cities of the developing world, higher capacities may be required: the Hong Kong Mass Transit Railway, for example, attains up to 80,000 per hour.

The DLR offers an interesting example, having been built to a modest capacity, partly as a means of stimulating land use development in London Docklands, rather than catering for existing passenger flows. However, development occurred more rapidly than initially envisaged, thus requiring the system to be rebuilt soon after coming into operation. Initially, single articulated cars with a capacity of 220 each offered 8 trips per hour on the section between the City and Westferry (1,760 passengers per hour). This was increased firstly by expanding frequency to 16 trains per hour and doubling train length (giving 7,040 per hour). By bringing the headway down to 2 minutes (i.e. 30 trains per hour) this can be further increased to 13,200 passengers per hour.

It is clear from the above that the time taken to clear a block section is a critical factor. This is determined firstly by the length of the section (in re-signalling schemes, introduction of shorter sections thus becomes one means of raising capacity), and secondly by the average speed through the section. This will be affected by presence of station stops, whose duration ("dwelltime") may be minimized by setting platform and train floor heights equal, and providing a large number of doors per car, of sliding or plug form. Lower platforms on some S-Bahn, and many LRT lines, may cause delay. Trams for operation on both street and in tunnel often have steps adjustable for loading at various heights. On some automated systems, a platform edge screen with sliding doors to match those on the train (as for a lift) are fitted, preventing passengers from falling on the track, and also minimizing delays: the Singapore Mass Rapid Transit also has this feature (in this case largely to permit efficient air-conditioning of stations). It is to be incorporated in new heavy metro lines in Paris, and the Jubilee Line Extension in London.

Delays in block sections owing to stops may also be reduced by adopting higher acceleration and retardation rates to/from running speed. New stock typically attains an acceleration of around 1.2 m per second per second, although older stock may be much slower. Higher energy consumption may be required as a result.

It will be evident from the above that one means of avoiding the need to build new tracks to raise peak capacity is to improve train performance. This may increase energy consumption and the capital cost of new rolling stock, but will generally be much cheaper than new construction.

69

The above statements assume implicitly that trains possess identical perform-ance. Where speeds and acceleration rates vary, peak flows may be much lower, especially where trains with urban performance characteristics and those for long-distance work are mixed on approach tracks to main-line stations.

Power supply and control

Direct current (dc) supply is typical, usually at 600–750 V, via a third rail. This form of current and voltage is suitable for use on trains without rectifiers or transformers but requires the provision of substations at very frequent intervals, about every 3–5 km. For dense urban traffic the cost of such substations is less than the extra on-train equipment, but for S-Bahn lines, especially those sharing intercity tracks, the 25 kV (25,000 V) ac system, favoured for long-distance movement (see Ch. 9) may be adopted as standard. BR standardized on this sys-tem for suburban routes in north and east London, Greater Manchester and Glas-gow, whereas the London and Glasgow undergrounds, Merseyrail and the network south of the Thames are based on third-rail dc. A third option is 1,500 dc by overhead supply, requiring about half as many substations as third-rail voltages, but using 750 V motors in parallel: this has been adopted for the Tyne and Wear metro (reducing substations from 13 to 7) and also on the Hong Kong Mass Transit Railway.

On trains, motors are usually mounted on the bogies, fed by current control-led through series resistor, chopper (dc), or thyristor (ac) switchgear. Immediate supply of full-traction current to motors in a train at standstill would cause com-ponents to burn out. The traditional series-resistor system consists of banks of resistances connected in series, through which current is passed to the motors. These are successively switched out as acceleration occurs. About fifteen such steps occur in reaching full speed. A further sequence may be inserted by con-necting the motors in series during the first stage of acceleration, and then in par-allel.

The series-resistor system is very well established and reliable, but involves a waste of energy as the resistances are heated (warming the passenger saloon is one use for this by-product in cool climates). The alternative chopper/thyristor system is now in general use on new stock. It is a solid-state switching device, originally applied to ac equipment, in which a "gating" pulse of a few millisec-onds breaks the main current flow at intervals which are varied to change its volt-age. In the acceleration phase, waste of energy is avoided, and smoother performance given, of particular value where high acceleration rates are required. Provided that problems caused by high-frequency interference from the gating pulses to telecommunications equipment can be overcome, this system offers clear advantages. It also makes the use of regenerative braking (see below) much easier.

In Britain, a more conservative approach has been adopted by manufacturers and operators, and only with the introduction of the BR Networker class 465 in 1992, and the new Central Line stock for London Underground in 1993 has it become standard. The Hong Kong stock built in the late 1970s/early 1980s was initially of conventional series-resistor form, but has been rebuilt with chopper controls, in view of the energy savings obtained. A further development in modern European stock is the use of three-phase motors fed by inverters on the train, giving further savings in energy consumption and maintenance costs.

Electric urban trains are almost entirely of the multiple-unit form, in which the switchgear is carried on each power car, which picks up current direct from the third-rail or overhead, being operated by controls from the driving car. A high proportion of axles in the train can be motored where high acceleration is required, without reducing passenger capacity, as all motors and control gear are mounted under the floor. Some push-pull working using separate locomotives linked to a control cab in the car at the opposite end of the train is also found, notably on SNCF lines in Paris and – using diesel locomotives – the GO Transit suburban lines in Toronto.

Energy consumption

Energy consumption is determined by two main factors:
1. *Acceleration* Energy used is proportional to the mass of the train (including payload) multiplied by the square of the maximum speed attained.
2. *Overcoming rolling resistance* Energy is used while accelerating and maintaining a steady speed, and is proportional to mass.

Aerodynamic resistance is of little importance at the fairly low speeds attained by urban railways, although critical for intercity modes. However, it is a factor in tunnels, where little clearance is provided between train and tunnel, creating a piston effect. The need for frequent bursts of high acceleration, owing to close station spacing, creates a much higher energy consumption per gross tonne-km for urban stock than intercity: high acceleration may itself impose a weight penalty, owing to the higher proportion of motored axles (up to 100% for rates of 1.0m per second per second and above) thus required.

The energy required for the acceleration phase is often the greater part of total consumption, especially where stations are less than 1000m apart. Since it is proportional to mass, and urban rail stock is heavy relative to road vehicles, much of the expected energy advantage that one would expect *vis-a-vis* buses owing to lower rolling resistance disappears. Except where very high load factors are attained, energy consumption per passenger-km may be higher for urban rail than bus, as appears to be the case in Britain. A typical unladen weight per passenger space for a bus is about 125kg, that for "heavy" urban rail stock about 250kg.

Many techniques for reducing rail energy consumption are available:

- *A downward gradient* On leaving a station at about 1 in 20 (5%) this aids acceleration, and retardation is likewise aided by an upward gradient on entering. This is used on some London tube lines, but for subway or surface routes such frequent variation in vertical alignment is less easy to incorporate.
- *Reduced unladen weight of train* Older motor cars may weigh as much as 45 tonnes, but new stock is much lighter. Use of stainless steel instead of conventional construction can bring the weight of a trailer car to about 25 tonnes. Further reductions may be obtained through aluminium or light alloy construction. BR EMU (electric multiple unit) stock built in the 1970s featured aluminium cladding on steel framework, but then reverted to all-steel construction, using the Mark 3 intercity coach shell (classes 317–322, and 455). Nonetheless, substantial weight savings were obtained, a four-car 455 set weighing 129 tonnes. More dramatic savings have been obtained in London Underground's D78 District Line stock, in which use of longer cars, and a lower weight per car, enables a saving of 40%, through a six-car train of 146 tonnes replacing a seven-car train of 242 tonnes. Using longer cars (within limits imposed by the loading gauge) enables the number of bogies to be reduced, in addition to savings from lower body weight. Where longer cars are not feasible, articulation of adjoining cars over common bogies achieves a similar gain, as in the Tyne and Wear metro stock (a two-car set weighing 38 tonnes), or three-car sets as on the Hamburg U-Bahn.

  The stock placed in service on London Underground's Central Line from 1993 uses large welded aluminium extrusions to give a weight of only 24 tonnes per car, all of which are motored. Identical cars operate the Waterloo and City line in London, and BR also has adopted aluminium construction again with the class 465 Networker. However, when the high-energy requirements for aluminium production are borne in mind, it is only for vehicles operating high distances each year that a net overall energy saving is obtained.
- *Reduced length of train* Some systems run shorter trains at off-peak periods. However, since the cost of electricity is determined largely by the peak (see below), this is probably more useful in reducing maintenance costs.
- *Coasting* By cutting off power after the initial acceleration phase, energy consumption can be reduced substantially as rolling resistance has to be overcome only during the acceleration phase, i.e. that shown as phase t_1 in Figure 4.1. Where constant speed is maintained during phase t_2 a trapezoidal speed–time curve results, but an irregular curve is produced when coasting is used, as shown in Figure 4.1b. The area under the curve represents distance (i.e. speed × time). By using a higher initial acceleration rate the station-to-station trip may be completed in the same time, even with coasting.

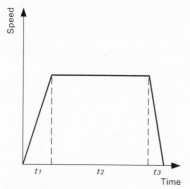

(a) Simplified trapezoidal form, train running at steady speed after acceleration period

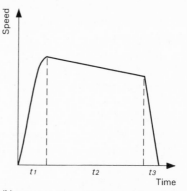

(b) Form in which a higher rate of acceleration is followed by a "coasting" period

t_1 - time during which train accelerates

t_2 - time during which train runs at steady speed or "coasts"

t_3 - time during which train decelerates

Figure 4.1   Energy consumption curves for urban rail services.

Owing to the low rolling resistance on steel rail, loss of speed through coasting is marginal. For example, if two stations are 750 m apart, and a train accelerates at 0.49 m per second per second (m/s/s) and decelerates (phase t_3) at –0.75 m/s/s, then at a steady speed of 9.89 m/s during phase t_2 the trip takes 92.5 seconds. If the train is allowed to "coast" during phase t_2, losing speed at –0.025 m/s/s, the same distance is covered in 98 seconds, an increase of only 5.5 seconds, or about 6% – yet an energy saving of about 25% would be obtained. The additional journey time between stations might be offset by reducing station dwell time.

- *Use of regenerative braking*   With friction braking, kinetic energy is converted wastefully into heat and noise. However, the electric motor of the train may be used as a form of retarder, generating current in this process. The simpler form is known as rheostatic braking, in which the current is fed into resistors to produce heat. This reduces wear and tear on the friction braking system, and the heat may be used inside the car where climate requires. Better use of the current may be made by feeding it back into the power supply for use by other trains, known as regenerative braking. In theory, savings of up to 30% or more in net energy requirements may be obtained, although in practice this may be limited by factors such as the acceptability of regenerated current at substations, and number of other trains on the system at any one time which can use the regenerated supply. This has limited the net gain in most cases to around 15% to 20%, but with more comprehensive system design to make better use of regenerative motor characteristics from the outset, gains closer to the theoretical maxi-

73

mum may be expected. Regeneration has been made much easier through the use of chopper/thyristor technology, and is now general on new systems, such as São Paulo and Dublin. It has now been adopted in Britain through the Networker and Central Line stock. Substations on the Sheffield Supertram are designed to accept regenerated current.

- *Other forms of energy storage*   As in the case of buses, energy may also be stored on the vehicle itself through high-speed flywheels or batteries, thus overcoming the problem of finding other trains to use regenerated current. Rail vehicles can incorporate the weight and bulk of such equipment more readily than buses, but conventional regeneration is probably more practical. Flywheels have also been used to store regenerated current at a substation on the Tokyo network, thus overcoming the problem of feeding it back into the main supply system.

Putting all these factors together, one can see scope for reducing energy consumption on some older systems by about 50%, mainly through a combination of reduced stock weight and use of regenerative braking. The main constraint in many cases is the rate of renewal of rolling stock. Longevity of rail stock makes it possible to aim for lives as high as 35–40 years (with interior refurbishment), but in consequence the rate at which energy-saving technology can be introduced is very slow. If energy costs rise, a more rapid rate of renewal may be justified.

Internal layout of rolling stock

For many years, a pattern of three or four sliding doors on each side of the car, with a high proportion of standing space, has characterized U-Bahn stock. Seating is often arranged longitudinally to assist this. In some recent London Underground stock a single-section sliding door has replaced the traditional double-leaf door (for example, 1983 tube stock on the Jubilee Line), giving reduced maintenance costs without significant extra dwell time. High rates of acceleration necessitate many grab rails.

For S-Bahn services, a higher proportion of seats, and fewer doors, are usually provided. This difference can be observed in London by comparing the C69 Circle Line stock (with four sets of double doors per car to permit rapid loading), with the A60 stock on the Metropolitan Line to Amersham (with three sets of doors and five-across seating). On British Rail, the antiquated layout of slam doors was retained in new stock until the late 1970s, but here also sliding doors are now general.

The sliding-door layout permits driver control, and with certain other modifications (notably mirror or closed-circuit television display at platform ends) enables driver-only operation (DOO) to be introduced. In Britain, it has applied from the start on the rebuilt Glasgow Underground, Tyne and Wear Metro, and Manchester Metrolink. It applies to several BR suburban and London Underground lines, and is being steadily extended. On heavy rail systems, the driver

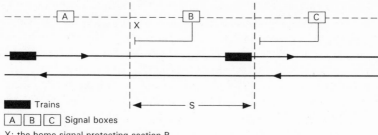

Trains

A B C Signal boxes

X: the home signal protecting section B

S: safe braking distance

Figure 4.2   Block section signalling.

remains responsible only for driving as such, but on light rail he/she may also collect fares from some passengers, as on bus services. A passenger entrance adjacent to the cab may thus be required.

The closing of sliding doors is controlled automatically by the guard or driver, but their opening may be actuated selectively by passengers, as on London's D78 stock. This avoids the needless entry of rain and cold air, especially on surface stations.

Where double-deck stock is used, as in Paris, this takes the form of an entry vestibule over each bogie, with steps into upper and lower saloons, the latter within a well section of the chassis.

Signalling and control

A system simpler than that found on main-line railways can be used, owing to regular timetable patterns, and lesser variation in speeds, braking distances, etc. The network of most U-Bahn systems is fairly simple, with few junctions and crossing points only at terminals or certain intermediate stations. S-Bahn may be somewhat more complex, owing to mixing with other rail traffic, but even in this case, tracks are often largely segregated from parallel main lines (between Euston and Watford, for example).

A semi-automatic sequence of trains can be programmed, with manual control as an override to handle exceptions and emergencies. An entire network can thus be controlled from a single centre, such as that on the Tyne and Wear Metro.

As on main-line railways, the basic signalling system is that of block working. A train may not enter a block section until the previous train has cleared it. Figure 4.2 shows this in simplified form. The train in section A cannot enter section B until the train in that section has entered section C. The minimum length of block section is normally at least equal to the minimum safe braking distance from the maximum speed permitted, where signals are of the simple two-aspect (red/green) type.

On surface railways; the presence of the train in section was observed from

75

signal-boxes manually, as shown in Figure 4.2. On the tube lines in London such a method was clearly impracticable and at an early stage a system of semi-automatic block working was devised. Quite apart from the traction current (from third rail, or overhead), a low-voltage track circuit current may be fed through the running rails (ac where traction is dc, and vice versa). When a train enters a section it shorts the circuit set up by this current, thus indicating on a control panel that the section is occupied. The circuit can also be interlocked with signals to ensure that the section is protected. Together with a trip-arm which ensures that a train passing the red signal will brake automatically, the system makes collisions between following trains on the same track almost impossible. The track circuit principle has also been adopted in main-line railways (see Ch. 9).

Complete automation of "heavy" urban railways is possible. To date, this has mainly taken the form of automatic control of the train running between stations, with the driver remaining responsible for starting the trains, as on the Victoria Line in London, and the Paris Metro. High-frequency pulses through the traction supply determine rates of acceleration, maximum speed and retardation. A more efficient cycle can thus be followed – for example, to make the best use of opportunities for coasting described above. However, there is a danger of monotony for drivers as a result, and on the Paris Metro the automatic control is not applied running at off-peak periods. French systems are now pioneering full automation of heavy metros, beginning with the MAGGALY system on Lyon's Line D in 1992. This also incorporates moving-block signalling (as distinct from the fixed block described above), enabling spacing of trains related to braking distance for the speed currently performed. Proposed for Paris is the Meteor line which will offer capacities in the order of 30,000 passengers per hour with fully automated working. The SELTRAC central system, introduced on the Beckton extension of the DLR, also incorporates the "moving block" concept.

Information from track circuits and control centres can also be used to activate platform indicators. In the traditional form in London, these simply display the sequence in which trains are due to arrive. These are being replaced by dot-matrix indicators, which display a real-time estimate of the number of minutes in which the train is due. This information has been found to be acceptably accurate, and of considerable help to passengers.

Stations and interchanges

Much of the high labour productivity resulting from one person driving a train with over 1,000 passengers on a heavy transit system may be offset by the need to staff stations throughout the day. Ticket issue may be automated to a large extent by use of machines designed to cover all destinations and ticket types. Cash sales may be further reduced by pre-sale of travelcards (see Ch. 7) and stored value tickets, which are decremented on use. On some older systems, station staff are retained to handle some types of ticket issue, as in London, but complete destaffing is technically feasible, as the Tyne and Wear Metro has demonstrated since opening in 1980. Ticket inspection may be automated by use of barriers which read magnetically encoded tickets, checking their validity, and if necessary re-encoding. Such stored-value tickets are used on the Hong Kong and Washington systems. If a complete closed-entry system is used, they may be re-encoded at the end of each journey to allow for distance covered and rate applied (peak or off-peak).

On some systems, a simpler approach is adopted, as on the DLR, where the passenger is required to hold a valid ticket on entering the platform, but not to pass through a barrier as such. Strict enforcement through random inspections is a necessary feature on such systems, backed up by penalty fares and fines. Reliable ticket-issuing machines, to ensure that all passengers have had the opportunity of buying a ticket before commencing their journey, are also essential.

In designing stations it is desirable to minimize the number of changes of level, and make such changes as are necessary easier by use of escalators and lifts. The latter may also improve access for the disabled. Conflicting pedestrian flows should be prevented by use of separate passageways where possible. Well lit passages and platforms, with no blind spots, are desirable.

Escalator width required for one person is about 60 cm, 80 cm with luggage, or about 1 m to allow overtaking. In order to reduce energy consumption created by continuous operation, escalators may be activated by passengers breaking a photo-electric beam. Increased emphasis is now being placed on accessibility for elderly and disabled users, which may justify use of lifts in addition to escalators.

Passages and other entrances to the platform should be located at different points on successive stations so as to distribute passenger loadings throughout the train. If only one entry can be provided, the mid-point is best, if two (or separate entry and exit), then at quarter length from each end. The situation to be avoided if possible is the repetition of the same entry/exit positions at successive stations, which result in some parts of the train being overcrowded, others almost empty. The terminal layout is particularly unsuited to suburban operation, as boarding passengers may concentrate at only one end of the train, while seats at the other remain empty. Further arguments for through-running in place of terminal working may be found in Chapter 5.

Where different routes can be arranged to run parallel at an interchange, cross-platform passenger movement may be possible, as at Oxford Circus (Victoria/Bakerloo Lines) or Hammersmith (District/Piccadilly Lines) in London.

Track and structures

The cross-sectional area of rolling stock is determined primarily by the height of standing passengers, use of standard track gauge, and the clearance required for motors and equipment below the train floor. A square cross-section of about

3.5 m is typical. Where power is supplied from overhead wires, a vertical clearance of about 4.5 m may be required. More limited clearances may apply to light-rail systems, and on automated systems such as VAL (Lille) a narrower vehicle width can be adopted to reduce tunnelling costs: the high frequency possible with unmanned trains provides capacity to compensate for the reduced size of each car. On curves, swept area is a function of radius, body width and length. Shorter vehicles, or tapered ends, may be adopted (as on street tramways) to reduce lateral clearances.

Surface tracks may be relatively simple, although use of continuously welded rail is now common as a means of ensuring a smoother ride (although not, as yet, on the London Underground). Conventional rail track, with sleepers and ballast (see Ch. 9) is generally used, although grooved rail is still used on street tramway sections of light railways, and concrete slab-base track is now used on new tunnel sections, to reduce subsequent maintenance costs and access delays. Tramways continue to operate through pedestrianized areas, and even new light-rail alignments of this sort are now accepted, as in Manchester. Bremen in north Germany was the first major city to pedestrianize its centre in the early 1960s, and the trams remain the only vehicles in major shopping streets. The swept area of cars is indicated by distinctively coloured paving.

Where land is not available, the cheapest alternative alignment is an elevated structure. This may also be a means of avoiding conflict on the same level with other modes. This solution was common on early systems – the DLR partly follows such an alignment first built in 1840 – and substantial sections remain in New York and Paris. However, the environmental effects of such structures are often criticized. Newer elevated structures, using concrete, are much less intrusive, and noise levels may be reduced by adoption of rubber-tyred stock, as on the Marseille and Lille systems.

An underground alignment became necessary in the largest cities because of the high land costs and environmental effects of elevated structures. Most systems are subways, i.e. usually aligned not more than 10 m below the surface and built on the "cut and cover" principle, often along existing major roads. The first London lines, such as the Metropolitan, were of this pattern, but at an early stage opportunities at this level were restricted by existing railways, sewers and the Thames. The deep-level tubes such as the Bakerloo were therefore built by shield tunnelling, of about 3.5 m diameter. Reduced cross-sectional area limits train capacity and room for motors, etc.

The depth required for access by escalator or lift, instead of a short flight of stairs, increases passenger access time, which will itself deter use especially for short trips. Hence, this alignment should only be adopted if unavoidable. A subway alignment, even if incurring more disruption during the construction phase, is generally preferable. Whereas the sub-surface metro in Paris is appropriate for short trips, the deep-level tubes in London require bus duplication for such travel. Londoners' habit of referring to all underground railways as tubes is inaccurate in their own city, and even more so in respect of others, Moscow being the only other major example.

Construction costs vary greatly according to local circumstances, including geology: as a very rough guide, they are in the order of £50 million upward per double-track route-km for subway or tube routes, with a similar additional cost per deep-level station. Elevated track may be much less than half this figure, with surface (especially if following existing alignments) cheaper still. The last point is well illustrated by the Manchester Metrolink, which uses light rail technology to provide the cross-city centre surface link, at very much lower cost than the previously proposed conventional rail with cross-centre tunnels.

Current prospects

The urban rail revival of the 1960s and 1970s is largely over so far as new "heavy" rail systems in North America and Western Europe are concerned. Falling population densities make substantial new construction difficult to justify. However, those systems which have been built are generally well used, and have retained their ridership with much greater success than buses mixed with other traffic. Further expansion is likely to take the form of modest extensions to existing networks, rather than entirely new ones or additional routes involving substantial extra tunnelling. However, major renewal investment will be needed, creating the opportunity for energy saving, improved labour productivity and better conditions for passengers.

In Britain, urban rail use is dominated by London. Following the rapid growth in ridership during the 1980s (see Ch.2), extensive proposals for improvement have been put forward. These include the Jubilee Line Extension (JLE) to serve growing development in Docklands, for which the DLR may not be sufficient; the CrossRail scheme, linking Liverpool St and Paddington BR services in similar fashion to the RER of Paris; expansion of the Thameslink service to provide a high-density north-south link across the central area, and a light rail system in Croydon, linking existing local BR lines with surface running through the city centre, akin to Manchester.

The Central London Rail Study of 1989 evaluated options in central London (but not the JLE, subject of a separate study), indicating a positive cost–benefit analysis for CrossRail, and, more markedly, for expansion of Thameslink to increase capacity. Government approval for construction of JLE was finally given in October 1993, following confirmation of previously negotiated private sector contributions. The future of the CrossRail proposal remains uncertain.

Improved access to airports plays a major rôle. Following the Piccadilly Line extension to Heathrow in 1976 (and the loop to serve Terminal 4 in 1984), the Heathow Express (largely funded through private sources) is now being built, to provide a high-speed link from the Paddington route. The Tyne and Wear Metro was extended to serve Newcastle airport in 1991. A new spur to Manchester airport was opened in 1993, served by local and regional services. Proposals for rail access to Glasgow and Edinburgh airports are being evaluated.

In the West Midlands, the main cross-city route on the largely diesel-operated network has been electrified at 25kV. Further plans for development in Glasgow, Edinburgh and Merseyside are active.

As in the case of bus operation, increased interest is being shown in improving access for elderly and disabled users on urban rail systems. London Underground lifted its previous ban on wheelchair users form October 1993, and the JLE will be fully accessible, together with limited number of central area stations on other lines. The Manchester Metrolink offers improved access through raised platform sections within central Manchester (elsewhere, former BR stations provide high-level platforms in any case), to permit access for wheelchairs. In parallel with bus design, very low-floor models are being developed, as in the trams being built by ABB Transportation in Britain for the new Strasbourg system.

Taking a broader view of developed countries, a higher level of rail investment may be seen. The construction of fully automated systems is evidence of this: the initial VAL line in Lille has been followed by a second route in that city, and other systems, such as Toulouse. Some standardization of future automated systems is being attained in Japan. Capital costs are very high, but there is greater scope for covering operating costs than on traditional labour-intensive systems. A much higher quality of service, especially in terms of frequency, can be offered.

A common feature of automated systems is the nationalistic basis on which they have been developed to date, with each country designing its own system. Not only does this lead to high initial costs, but also the risk that a successful system will not be adopted for use elsewhere, nor economies of scale from mass production attained.

A feature of rail development in Britain until recently has been the need for each project requiring compulsory purchase or significant extension to existing schemes, to obtain a Private Act of Parliament: this process has been used for initial stages of DLR, Manchester Metrolink, and extension of the BR and LT networks. The rapid growth in rail schemes during the 1980s resulted in many such Bills being put forward, and the need for a simplified system was recognized. Under the Transport and Works Act 1992 rail and busway projects may be approved through an enquiry and ministerial order of similar form to that applied to road schemes: the first use of this mechanism is for the planned extension of the East London Line (New Cross–Shoreditch) to Dalston. However, separate Bills may still be required for controversial major rail projects, such as the Channel Tunnel Rail Link.

References and suggested further reading

A comprehensive review of recent research on the impact of major urban rail projects in Western Europe and North America, with their implications for Britain, is given in *The effects of rapid transit on public transport and urban development* by David Walmsley & Ken Perrett, published as *State of the Art Review 6* by the Transport Research Laboratory (London: HMSO, 1992).

Frequent coverage of urban rail development is given in *Modern Railways*, and *Railway Gazette International*, with further coverage of light rail system developments in *Light Rail and Modern Tramway* – all monthly.

Major proposals for London were set out in the *Central London rail study* (London: Department of Transport, 1989).

A description of the Transport and Works Act 1992 is given in *Blackstone's Guide to the Act* (London: Blackstone, 1993).

Issues concerning station design, especially with reference to pedestrian movement, are reviewed in "New modelling techniques for assessing alternative railway station designs", by N. Ash, a paper at the PTRC Summer Annual Meeting (published in Proceedings of Seminar D, by PTRC, Hammersmith, 1993). The public transport stream at the PTRC Summer Annual Meeting (known from September 1994 as the European Transport Forum) frequently contains papers on modern urban rail developments.

CHAPTER 5
Network planning

Typical structures

The task of a traffic manager or transport planner is to effect the optimal balance between the desired door-to-door trips of individual users and characteristics – especially speed, capacity and cost – of the mode(s) available.

A consequence is that different modes of transport serve different traffic densities, which in turn affects network structure. The minimum average load for a conventional bus service to be viable – averaged over the whole day in both directions – is about twelve passengers (if all costs, including replacement depreciation, are to be covered). Lower traffic densities may be handled either by a smaller vehicle, such as minibus or shared taxi, and/or by a service financially supported by a local authority. For rail very much higher densities are required: for a new route several thousand passengers per hour would normally be needed, although many routes at very much lower densities continue to be justified by the fact that investment in infrastructure has already taken place (or existing alignments may be re-used at low cost).

A distinction may be drawn between public, scheduled services operating for most of the day, to which the above comments would apply, and those timed for specific traffic flows, such as from a housing estate to a school, on which only a few journeys may be operated. However, although total daily flows on such routes may be low, the break-even load per trip may be considerably higher when peak-only operation is involved, as discussed in Chapter 6.

Within this chapter, networks in urban areas and the adjoining rural zones are examined. Aspects of rural networks as such are considered in Chapter 8, and long-distance networks in Chapter 9.

Given the typical loadings mentioned above, many public transport services are confined to radial routes into town centres. In towns of up to 100,000 little else may be provided, save for school or works specials. As town size increases, inter-suburban traffic may justify regular all-day services. Such services become more firmly established in larger cities, linking inner suburbs at high frequency as in London and Birmingham. Larger cities are also parts of conurbations, such as Greater London, or the West Midlands, which have been formed from a group of formerly separate towns. Local bus networks focus upon each of these, over-

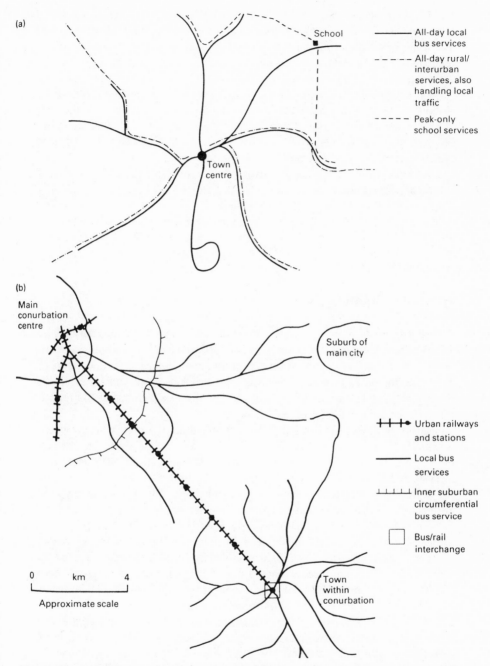

(a)

School

——— All-day local
bus services

– – – All-day rural/
interurban
services, also
handling local
traffic

- - - - Peak-only
school services

Town
centre

(b)

Main
conurbation
centre

Suburb of
main city

+++• Urban railways
and stations

——— Local bus
services

⊥⊥⊥⊥ Inner suburban
circumferential
bus service

☐ Bus/rail
interchange

0   km   4

Approximate scale

Town
within
conurbation

Figure 5.1 Typical network patterns. (a) In a small town (about 50,000 population). (b) In a sector of a conurbation (1 million population, or more). For simplicity, the latter excludes school and inter-urban bus services.

laid by other bus and rail links to the main conurbation centre. Thus, local networks may be found in Stockport, Bury, Oldham, etc. together with rail services and trunk bus routes from each to the centre of Manchester. Such a situation lends itself to the creation of integrated bus/rail networks, especially where the local centre has a convenient interchange, as at Bury and Altrincham.

Within large city centres, additional distributor services may be needed where walking distances from terminals become excessive. Within London, the Red Arrow buses from Waterloo, Victoria etc. are one example, although the radial bus and underground lines provide most of this function. City-centre bus services are also offered in smaller cities, such as Nottingham.

Rail rapid transit's high capital cost confines it to major radial corridors and central area distribution, although the North London Link does provide a somewhat exceptional service linking inner suburbs.

Figure 5.1 illustrates in simplified form the typical network forms mentioned above.

Urban form and land use

The starting point of any public transport network must be the pattern of land use, which strongly influences the potential traffic. The public transport network itself may also influence the land-use pattern: although the car is now the main influence, the past structure of rail, tram and bus routes had a major effect on urban form, and improved rail services for long-distance commuting continue to affect the housing market around London.

Density of population has a major effect on public transport demand: where it is higher, a better level of service may be justified, and/or lower fares be viable. A longer operating day and week, perhaps including all-night services, may be sustained. Housing density is perhaps the most important factor, followed by the degree of concentration of workplaces and shops. The two are in any case correlated to a large extent, often also with the age of the city.

Two measures of residential density must be distinguished: "gross" is that estimated from the population divided by total land area, including roads, schools, open space, etc. "Net" density is that of the area actually occupied by houses, private gardens, access roads, etc. and thus higher than the "gross" density for the same area. Table 5.1 relates housing type with residential density.

In Table 5.1, a household size of about 2.5 persons is assumed, based on the national 1991 Census average. The average has declined, as more old people live in households of one or two persons and size of completed family falls. Typical densities are also falling as more space per house is required – for example, to provide garage space – although it may be the case that fewer rooms per house may be needed as the number of occupants declines.

Although there is a general personal wish to enjoy more space per household,

Table 5.1   Typical net residential densities.

Housing type	Persons per hectare (ppha)
High-density Victorian, with multi-occupation (e.g. inner London)	350–400
Inner-city redevelopment, slab or tower blocks	175–250
Local authority estates and higher-density private estates	90–150
Private housing, low density	40–80

evident in some very low densities – or scattered rural development – in recent new construction, public costs are also incurred which may not be reflected in those perceived by the householder. There may be a case for higher densities, and a greater variety, than currently found. At the highest extremes, as in some Victorian cities and developing countries today, health may suffer from over-crowding and lack of open space. Construction costs may also be high where multi-storey dwellings require greater structural strength, provision for lift shafts, etc. Estimates some years ago by Stone suggested that construction costs (excluding land costs) are minimized at about 150 persons per hectare (ppha), with two or three-storey dwellings.

Much new housing is at densities well below this, incurring the following resource costs:

- Basic utilities such as gas, telephone, electricity and water require a greater length of pipe or cable to serve each residence, increasing capital and maintenance costs.
- Other services such as postal deliveries and public transport provision require regular servicing of the household. A lower density increases the cost of maintaining a given level of service, which rises further with growing real labour costs, unless offset by productivity growth.
- As urban areas expand, a loss of open space and natural habitats occurs.

Little incentive to higher densities is given by the present council tax system, and costs such as those of postal delivery are (unavoidably) averaged out, resulting in a cross-subsidy to low-density areas. From the public transport viewpoint, the situation is worsened by the stimulus given to car use and ownership in low density areas, as it becomes necessary to make trips that previously were within walking distance (for example, to the local shop) by this mode.

A stimulus to higher densities might be given by reform of the local taxation system, if council tax were aligned more closely to a charge for services rather than an arbitrary assessment based on a notional value per house. Further arguments in favour of higher densities and illustrations of attractive designs that can be provided (retaining ground floor access for all dwellings) are given by Sherlock (1991).

The densities of shops and workplaces have also tended to fall over time, although less so for some types of office work. From the public transport operator's viewpoint, it is not so much the density as location of such development which is important. New out-of-town superstores are obviously far more attractive to car users, although some bus services are generally provided. If new office development outside traditional city centres can be encouraged to locate at public transport interchanges rather than greenfield sites, then there is a higher chance of retaining traffic. This pattern can be seen in the London area, where much new development has been outside the traditional centre, but near suburban rail stations such as Croydon, Wimbledon and Hammersmith.

Town planning in Britain

Until the late nineteenth century, urban growth was virtually uncontrolled. Housing conditions were insanitary, often with very little open space. Industry and housing were intermixed. Certain aspects of the subsequent shift to a planned approach may be seen as a reaction against such conditions, notably the New Town or Garden Suburb movement. Writers such as Ebenezer Howard in 1898 proclaimed the advantages of life surrounded by green open space, where housing and industry were separated. Rapid transit links between the areas of housing and industry thus separated were shown in the original concept, but often forgotten in later versions.

Although construction of Garden Cities (notably Welwyn) began, the major impact was on suburban development from 1919 onward, in both the first large-scale local authority schemes and the semi-detached boom of the 1930s. The low-density concept remained, but without the related planning for public transport or local facilities. This development – in-filling areas between tramway routes and beyond them – was made possible by the growth of bus services and private car ownership.

The growth of motor traffic also demanded better roads. Principal radial roads were widened and extended beyond the previous built-up areas, such as the Great West Road in London. Bypasses (often now within the built-up area) and ring roads were also constructed. In broad terms, the same "ring and radial" principle may also be seen in later urban motorway plans.

Parallel with the Garden Suburb of the inter-war period was the "neighbourhood unit" concept, based on the vision of a relatively small-scale community permitting face-to-face contact, yet of sufficient size to justify facilities such as primary schools and shops. Within the neighbourhood unit, most facilities would be within walking distance, and through-traffic routed around the area – hence major roads were not well sited for bus services penetrating such areas. Similar developments occurred in other European cities, but at higher densities, and with the fundamental difference that municipal tramways were normally projected through the area, enabling public transport to offer good accessibility with little environmental disturbance – for example, in Stockholm. Some British cities also incorporated such tramway links, as in Leeds at Middleton Estate (to be revived in current light rail plans), but in London, large estates were poorly sited with respect to railways. This trend continued after the Second World War, with little allowance made for public transport in land-use planning. The supposed flexibility of the bus may have proved a handicap, in encouraging planners to assume that public transport routes could be fitted in at a later stage, rather than incorporating them from the design stage.

The concept of segregating through traffic from local movement was taken further in Alker Tripp's book *Town planning and road traffic* in 1942. He suggested that effective reduction in accidents could be obtained only by such means, through motor traffic being confined to a network of purpose-built roads without direct access. The areas thus bounded by through, or arterial, roads were named "precincts". The same concept can be seen in the "environmental areas" of the Buchanan Report of 1963. From the traffic safety and environmental viewpoint such an approach is clearly desirable (although incorporating the new roads for through traffic in existing urban areas can prove very costly and disruptive), but the need for good access within the areas thus defined for public transport and other services was often overlooked.

The immediate post-war period in Britain was characterized by an expansion of the New Town concept, often stressing the neighbourhood unit principle, and with little explicit consideration for public transport provision. The first generation was built mainly around London (such as Stevenage and Bracknell). This was followed by second generation, often in older industrial areas, accommodating rehoused populations from older industrial cities (such as Skelmersdale, near Liverpool). Public transport provision in such cases was often even worse, as road layouts were adopted which made through operation into housing areas very difficult. Ironically, most of the second generation towns were built in regions of exceptionally low car ownership and use. Access to railways for inter-urban travel was also poor.

The 1960s also saw re-development of poor condition, high-density older urban areas. Partly to provide replacement stock at high densities, the building of blocks of flats of up to twenty stories became popular, with results that are well known. The communal open space was not perceived in the same manner as gardens attached to individual houses, facilities for children were poor, and lifts unreliable. Growth of vandalism and crime – not entirely attributable to the physical design as such – made them even less acceptable. The end of the 1960s saw a reaction against "high-rise", with a shift toward low-rise building, and rehabilitation of older housing stock. At the same time, many private schemes on the fringes of urban areas, or "adventitious" settlements in rural areas, were built at successively lower average densities, making provision of public transport services exceptionally difficult.

The third generation of new towns, designed during the 1960s and now reaching maturity, has been strongly influenced by transport requirements, but in very different ways. Runcorn, with a population of about 80,000, is laid out on a figure-of-eight pattern, which is followed by a high-capacity expressway for general traffic, and also, parallel with it (but passing through the centres of neighbourhood units), a busway (as described in Ch. 3). By placing public transport on a segregated track, good penetration of the housing areas can be obtained, and a high average speed. Busways and bus links are also incorporated in Redditch and Washington.

Milton Keynes and Telford are, in contrast, designed almost exclusively around the private car. A grid road structure permits a spread of traffic over the network so that little congestion occurs, and penetration of the housing areas by public transport becomes very difficult, although alleviated to some degree by growth of minibus operation in the late 1980s.

Design of public transport networks

Stop and route spacing

The total time for a one-way door-to-door trip comprises:
- walk to public transport stop or station
- wait for vehicle
- board vehicle
- vehicle accelerates to steady speed
- vehicle runs at steady speed for each vehicle
- vehicle decelerates to stop

} cycle repeated for each intermediate stop

- intermediate stop
- alight from vehicle
- walk to destination, or to an interchange point for further transport ride as part of a trip.

For urban bus services, a simple average speed may be taken (typically around 18km/h) for the in-vehicle ride, varied according to traffic congestion and boarding time (see Ch. 3). For rail systems, where acceleration/deceleration rates, and maximum running speed can be specified more precisely, they may be considered explicitly.

As shown in the appendix to this chapter, an expression can be derived for the components of total time listed above, incorporating speed and average length of line-haul trip, and vehicular characteristics. The line-haul part of the trip is that which takes place on the major public transport mode used. In conditions of fairly uniform population density along the whole route, with some concentration around stops or stations, the feeder trip length is equal to about one-quarter of the average spacing between stops.

For a given set of speeds, acceleration rates and trip lengths, the expression thus derived can be simplified to contain only one unknown quantity – the average stop spacing. If this were very small, total trip time would be high, since each passenger's journey on the major mode would be interrupted by many intermediate stops. On the other hand, if stop spacing were very wide, feeder trip

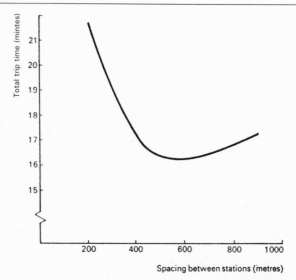

Figure 5.2   Optimal stop spacing to minimize total travel time.

times would lengthen, outweighing the benefits of a faster "line haul" section. By differentiating the expression, as shown in the appendix, the spacing which minimizes total time can be calculated.

Figure 5.2 shows such a case, for an average line-haul trip length of 5 km, walking as the feeder mode (at 1 m per second), and a vehicle with an acceleration rate of 1.0 m per second per second and steady speed of 12 m per second. Trip time is minimized at a stop spacing of about 550 m. By substituting different values for each variable, trade-offs between them can be illustrated:

1. If acceleration and/or retardation rates are increased, optimal stop spacing will narrow (i.e. an intermediate stop imposes a smaller time penalty).
2. If steady running speed attained after acceleration increases, optimal spacing will widen (i.e. an intermediate stop will impose a greater time penalty).
3. If the speed of the feeder mode is increased, optimal spacing will widen.
4. If stop time is reduced, optimal spacing will narrow (as for 1).

Many examples of these effects can be quoted. As Newell & Vuchic (1968) have argued, replacement of walking or bus as feeder mode to an urban rail system by park-and-ride substantially increases feeder trip speed, and hence optimal spacing becomes wider. US urban rail systems of the 1970s, such as the Lindenwold Line in Philadelphia, and BART in California, illustrate this trend.

Where a more comprehensive local service is being provided, with most users gaining access on foot, then additional stations may be created, and the resultant delay to through-passengers offset by using higher acceleration stock, as on the Docklands Light Railway in London. Where additional local stations have been adopted in areas served by diesel multiple units, as in West Yorkshire, there is

89

some risk of journey times being increased as a result of the lower acceleration of such stock.

Most urban flows are concentrated on the central area and hence loadings on buses or trains will be heaviest on the inner sections of radial routes. The penalty imposed by an additional intermediate stop to existing occupants will thus be greater the closer to the centre it is located. On the other hand, density of population in the catchment area may be much greater. When additions of this sort on existing networks are being evaluated, each must be considered on its own merits, to establish the overall trade-off in passenger time.

Given the higher traffic densities on the inner sections of radial routes, limited-stop operation may be justified, with outer suburban services running nonstop through the inner suburbs – apart from selected interchanges – and a parallel local stopping service offered. This can be seen on most rail corridors into London, for example. In the case of bus services, limited-stop operation may be introduced to give an equivalent effect, as in the Timesaver services in the West Midlands. Limited-stop operation may also be sometimes justified on high-density inter-suburban corridors, as on the Uxbridge Road in west London.

For the vast majority of local public transport services, walking is the access mode. The maximum convenient walk thus determines spacing between stops and between routes. For urban bus services, a typical upper limit of about 500 m may be taken. Normally about 95% of the urban population is within this distance of the nearest stop. The 1989/91 National Travel Survey shows that 88% of respondents were within 6 minutes' walking time of a bus stop, and a further 8% within 7–13 minutes' walk – furthermore, this includes rural residents. However, only 20% were within 13 minutes' walk of a rail station (NTS 1989/91, p. 101).

A similar walking distance emerged from theoretical studies as part of the Runcorn New Town Master Plan. It corresponds to about 5 minutes' walk for the average adult, but can take up to twice as long for someone with a pushchair or an elderly person. Passengers will also tend to walk to a stop in the "right" direction of travel, and not necessarily the closest one.

From this, one can suggest that different network densities may be appropriate for different types of passenger. Peak school and work journeys can be handled on fairly widely spaced routes largely on main roads, offering high frequency and/or using large vehicles. At off-peak times, users may be much more sensitive to walking distances. The development of "hail & ride" operation – picking up and setting down at any safe point, usually off main roads, and generally associated with minibus operation – has provided such a facility, of particular benefit to those with heavy shopping or the elderly. It tends to be used more on the homeward journey than the outward trip, for which fixed stops still provide an easily understood point, at which information can also be displayed.

In the case of railways, a wider stop spacing is adopted. Although acceleration/retardation rates may be higher than for buses, intermediate stops incur a greater penalty, owing to higher running speeds, and higher energy consumption

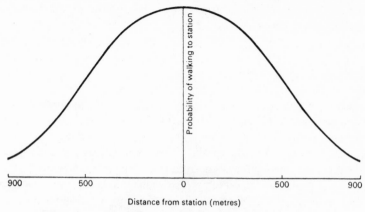

Figure 5.3   Probability of passengers walking to a station.

(see Ch. 4). The capital and operating costs of stations are high, especially if requiring underground construction and/or staff on duty. A spacing of about 1,000 m is typical of U-Bahn networks, falling toward 500 m in city centres, and somewhat lower on light rail. Rail station spacing is also affected by the extent to which that mode is expected to provide a general local service, largely accessible on foot (older parts of the Paris Metro, for example), or be supplemented by parallel buses for local movement (as is generally the case in London).

To a large extent, a wider rail station spacing is accepted by passengers (partly reflecting the emphasis on work journeys). The average line-haul trip by rail tends to be greater than that by bus, and hence a longer feeder trip will be acceptable within the minimization of total trip time described above. A walking catchment radius up to about one kilometre may be assumed, although the probability of being willing to do so falls off roughly in line with a normal distribution (Fig. 5.3). Such estimates have formed the basis for planning housing densities in Stockholm, in which the innermost zone around a station is reserved for the highest densities, the outermost for single-family dwellings. In London, however, a survey in 1969 was unable to detect significant differences in willingness to walk within an 800-metre radius.

The other main element in total journey time is waiting. This is affected mainly by service frequency and reliability. Its impact on demand may be incorporated through use of a "service elasticity" as described in Chapter 2. Use of smaller vehicles clearly enables higher frequencies to be offered, but at a higher cost per passenger. Waiting time may also be reduced by bus priority measures, as described in Chapter 3, and its perceived effect by better information systems, as shown in chapters three and four.

There are, however, two trade-offs between waiting time and network density outlined above. First, a wider spacing between routes and/or stops will give a greater density of traffic at each, and hence a higher frequency, for a given vehicle size, may be justified. Secondly, development of limited-stop services may help to reduce in-vehicle time, but increase waiting time through the lower frequency offered at intermediate points.

Route length and headway

For purposes of illustration, this section is written largely in terms of bus operation, but similar considerations apply to railways.

After selection of route and frequency for a proposed service – the latter usually a function of peak demand (peak:interpeak service ratios are discussed further in Ch. 7) – a running time is derived from previous experience (many new routes are in fact a restructuring of old ones rather than totally new road mileage) or a sample of test runs. Where an existing section is incorporated, past data from automatic vehicle monitoring (AVM) systems, as described in Chapter 3, may provide a much larger sample. The running time set should reflect conditions which vary by time of day and a desired level of reliability. Setting the mode or mean average time may result in many journeys not being able to cover the route within the scheduled time. Hence the return trip may also be late, and passenger waiting time greatly increased. It is far more realistic to assume a distribution of running times than a simple average, and set a proportion, such as 95%, which the schedule should cover. This may result in apparent inefficiency, as many buses and crews will spend longer at the terminal than necessary, but will provide a better passenger service.

This approach was adopted on London route 220 (Tooting–Willesden Junction), serving congested inner suburbs, where the same number of buses and crews was re-scheduled to allow more realistically for variations in running time, mainly by increasing lay-over time at terminals. Although the average scheduled frequency fell, actual average passenger waiting time was reduced by about 4% (Weston 1982).

It should be noted that variability in running time is much less of a problem for railways, being unaffected by general congestion, and in any case needing to plan train paths with much greater precision. However slightly greater running time should be allowed at peak periods, owing to increased station dwell time, and delays at junctions. Rail timetables also allow a small recovery time in addition to the scheduled running time, to allow for minor delays.

The number of vehicles and crews needed to work a service is equal to the round trip running time (single-trip running time in each direction, plus lay-over at each end), divided by the proposed headway.

The following examples illustrate this:
- The single trip is 30 minutes each way, and if 5 minutes lay-over is allowed at each end, round-trip running time will be 70 minutes. If a 10-minute headway is operated, 70/10, or 7, buses will be needed. If a 15-minute headway were intended, then the number of buses estimated would be 4.66; in practice, 5.

This wastage becomes more serious the wider the headway, and the shorter the round trip time.

It may be possible to interwork two routes at a common terminus so that the combined round-trip time is an integer multiple of headway:

- If the 15-minute headway were desired on the above route, it could be linked with one having a round-trip time of 35 minutes (itself using 3 buses inefficiently, if also on a 15-minute headway). The combined round-trip time of 105 minutes divides by 15 to give exactly 7 buses. Alternatively, the original route could still be worked separately with a round-trip time increased to 75 minutes (i.e. fully using 5 buses), the extra time being used to increase layover (with reliability benefits mentioned above), or to extend a short distance without extra buses being required.

Another approach is to set the round trip time and number of vehicles, and then derive the headway:

- If 5 buses work a route with 70 minutes round-trip time, a headway of 14 minutes could be offered. However, the "clockface" headway (one giving the same departures past each hour) would be lost, making the service more difficult to follow for users and crews. Such an approach is only sensible where the headway is low enough for passengers to arrive at stops at random, rather than aiming for a specific departure (typically about 12 minutes or less).

The operator should aim to make best use of crew paid time. If drivers do no other work, then driving time per shift is to be maximized. This will be subject to legal constraints, under current UK domestic regulations for local services these being:

- maximum driving time before a break: 5 hours 30 minutes
- maximum driving time per day: 10 hours 00 minutes
- minimum rest between shifts: 10 hours 00 minutes.

The last limit effectively imposes a maximum range between the start and end of driving (irrespective of the number of hours actually driven), if the same day's duty is to be repeated the following day, of 14 hours. Within the paid work shift, time must also be allowed for signing on and signing off, as well as driving per se. In addition to "straight" shifts of continuous work apart from the break(s), crews may also work "split" or "spreadover" shifts, i.e. in which two separate spells of driving are worked during the day, typically to cover the peak periods. Implications for costing of peak services are considered in Chapter 6.

In rail operations, trade-union agreements, rather than legal limits, generally set the crew scheduling constraints. Split-shift working is not generally practised, for example, although adoption of flexible rostering in recent years has enabled length of shift to be better matched to round trip running times, hence increasing driving time per shift.

Bus network planning methods

So far as rail operations are concerned, a fairly systematic planning approach is clearly required, owing to the high cost of infrastructure and rolling stock. Even a change in the pattern of service on an existing network involves planning a year ahead to fit in train paths, connections, etc.

In bus networks, much less formal planning may appear to be necessary, as little infrastructure is involved. In deregulated areas, only six weeks notice of service withdrawal or change is required. For certain types of change, an *ad hoc* approach may well be appropriate. Apart from determination of the schedule for crewing purposes as described above, passenger reaction may be gauged largely by monitoring use of the service once introduced, by use of ticket sales data and simple on-vehicle surveys. For example, varying the number of journeys on an existing route may be handled in this way, although a simple vehicle-km elasticity can be used to make an initial estimate of likely patronage effects. This simple approach may also be applicable to new services directed at very specific markets, such as direct shoppers' services to a new superstore, or the commuter coach services into London which have developed since the 1980 Transport Act.

However, within a complex urban network, and/or where a radical restructuring of routes is taking place, such methods are not sufficient. Even on a simple, small-town network such as that shown in Figure 5.1, many possible combinations of cross-centre linking, and combined headways on common sections of route, may be feasible. A series of *ad hoc* changes may identify some of these, but is unlikely to produce an optimal pattern. The operator may wish to assess the likely demand for new routes which do not serve a single well defined market, such as an all-day inter-suburb service. He/she may also wish to reassess running times over the network, and investigate the case for traffic management measures to assist buses.

Comprehensive land-use transportation studies of the type described in Chapter 2 are not generally appropriate for this purpose. True, they give a picture of the main corridors of demand and market share bv mode at one period, but they soon become out of date. Zone sizes are usually too large to assign passengers clearly to specific routes, and household surveys based on too small a sample to give confidence in data for particular routes by time of day, etc. The LUTS approach is useful for major infrastructure planning, especially rail, but other methods are needed for detailed short-to-medium term planning.

Two main techniques have been developed:
- *Manual* The first major example was the Market Analysis Project (MAP), developed by the National Bus Company in conjunction with Buchanan and Partners in the mid-1970s, and applied on an area-by-area basis to most of its local bus network by the early 1980s, covering both town networks and adjoining rural areas (see Ch. 8). It was also applied to the National Express coach network (Ch. 9) in 1978–80 as "Coachmap", and to the Scottish Bus Group network as "Scotmap" in the early 1980s. The manual

element related to the network design process as such: computers were used from the start to collate and classify data for the network designer. Following developments in computer technology, QV Associates produced the BusDriver model (able to work from microcomputers rather than main-frames) in the mid-1980s (MacBriar 1986).

- *Computer-based systems* The major example is the Volvo Interactive Planning System (VIPS), initially developed by Volvo Transportation Systems in Sweden, and applied in many other countries. Studies in Britain and South-East Asia have been undertaken by the MVA Consultancy. London Transport and West Midlands PTE used the system directly, under licence, LT subsequently developing its own system based on similar concepts. A refinement of the original system, known as VIPSII is now available.

Both methods involve similar initial stages:

1. The identification of network to be studied, not necessarily the whole network of one operator, but typically one focusing upon a market town or city centre, e.g. the Guildford area (subject of an MAP scheme in 1980 which included rural services and several different operators), Coventry (first application of VIPS in Britain), or part of a complex network within a large conurbation (such as that based on Wandsworth within London, recast in 1991).

2. Assessment of existing services in the area, including running times, frequency, peak vehicle requirement, etc.

3. Extensive on-vehicle surveys to obtain a detailed picture of existing bus users, with exact origin and destination, extent of linked trips, journey purpose, etc. Patterns for different periods of the day are observed, as those in the peak may differ radically from shopping periods, or late evening. A sample covering all scheduled bus journeys within a short period (such as one week) is usually taken, and a high response rate obtained with simple self-completion forms, collected on-vehicle. The current survey adopted for this purpose in London is known as BODS (bus origin and destination survey).

4. This may be supplemented by additional background data, on market composition by age, sex, car availability, etc. This may be derived through the on-vehicle surveys, but generally a much smaller sample suffices. Household surveys may be used to collect attitude data, and trips by other modes.

5. The data thus obtained is coded, edited and grossed-up to reflect total movements, making use of simple counts, etc. This process is far more reliable if carried out locally by the survey team who are familiar with the area and any problems encountered. For example, in the Scotmap work, on-line terminals were installed in each company's planning office into which data were entered directly, giving much better quality than in earlier MAP work in NBC, in which editing and coding was carried out centrally. The need for some supplementary surveys may be identified.

95

From this stage two methods differ. In MAP and its descendants, the computer was used to present data for zone-to-zone flows by time of day, and network planning was undertaken manually. In VIPS, and LT's planning, the existing and proposed networks are represented in computer form. A route network analysis (RNA) is then undertaken, in which zone-to-zone links are assessed in terms of journey time, frequency, and extent of interchange. In VIPS, a direct demand model is calibrated for zone-to-zone flows, based on zonal data (such as population and workplaces, as one would find in LUTS), and public transport service characteristics. The manual and computer-generated networks are developed, and evaluated using the RNA. Alternative cross-centre linkages and frequencies may then be evaluated. In the subsequent development of network planning by LT, a simplified approach has been adopted, in which existing demand is taken as the base, and variations which would result from changes in frequency and interchange (applying established elasticities and interchange penalties) are calculated, rather than modelling total demand as such.

In both methods the planned network is then assessed by local management and may be subject to public consultation with local authorities and user groups (this last aspect has virtually disappeared following deregulation in Britain, except in London where a different approach is adopted in any case, and some consultation is required by statute). A preferred network is then chosen, and detailed scheduling work completed. Introduction of the new network is usually marked by extensive publicity, and sometimes adoption of a new fleet name or local marketing title, the latter being common in many NBC schemes of the late 1970s.

Both systems enable a better matching of supply with demand, and hence either a better level of service without extra resources being required, or savings without substantial losses of traffic and revenue. Better crew and vehicle utilization (especially in terms of passengers carried) is obtained. The emphasis in most MAP schemes was on cost reduction while minimizing traffic losses, given the limited amount of financial support provided by non-metropolitan counties. Typically, peak vehicles were reduced by 25%, and mileage by 15–20% while revenue fell by only about 7%. The peak:interpeak ratio was lowered, and larger vehicles were used to handle school traffic. In Scotmap, traffic losses were less, and daytime off-peak services generally maintained or even improved.

Following deregulation, comprehensive network planning has been largely abandoned. Operators make individual service changes, exploiting opportunities such as the higher frequencies permitted by minibus conversion. However, while this has produced specific local innovations of value, the acute instability in the network is a major factor in loss of ridership. Competing behaviour by different operators in the same area does not necessarily produce an optimal overall network. Resources are likely to be concentrated on busier routes at busier times, often increasing frequency where it is already good, and giving little ridership growth in consequence. The separate provision of commercial and tendered services also has the consequence of fragmenting network planning. There is strong evidence that many service changes are made, not in consequence of changes in passenger behaviour, or perceived opportunities to influence it, but in reaction to competing changes made by other operators.

As indicated in Chapter 10, the overall impact of the approach taken in London has been much more positive than the post-deregulation experience elsewhere, especially in the metropolitan areas. However, some scope still remains for making the centralized system more sensitive to local service improvement opportunities. Some of the London Buses' subsidiaries, mainly in west London, have been particularly active in pushing the midibus concept, for example. There may be scope for making the planning models more user-sensitive by segmenting the market by user type (some users are far more sensitive to interchange penalties than others, for example).

VIPSII offers refinements over the earlier techniques, notably in more realistic simulation of user behaviour in terms of choices made between routes of different service frequency and other characteristics serving the same catchment area (Jansson 1992).

Applications of computers in scheduling

As well as being used in network planning, computers are also used to assist in scheduling, traditionally a manual process. Two major packages are currently available, the Busman suite of Leeds University/Hoskyns, and Hastus suite developed at the University of Montreal, used largely in North America but now also in Britain.

Commonly used elements in the Busman suite include TASC (timetable and schedule compilation), which sets out the basic sequence of vehicle movements on an all-day service, and CREWPLAN which sets out the crew duties. The latter task is considerably more complex, whether undertaken manually or with computer assistance. In practice, the set of runs to be covered is not totally rigid. If, for example, the last run in the evening required an extra crew to be brought in, a manual scheduler would probably delete that journey from the timetable (perhaps re-timing some others). This facility is incorporated in the CRUSCHED programme of Darby–Dowman and Mitra, which takes a given number of crews and bus journeys to be covered, then indicates which (if any) may not be feasible.

The use of computer scheduling packages is unlikely to bring enormous savings (although even small reductions in vehicles and crews needed will easily justify the cost of using them), but assists the manual scheduler by enabling many more options to be tested, and compensating for loss of skills as older schedulers retire.

Interchange

Within an all-bus network some interchange will occur owing to the problem of dispersed demand for which through services cannot be offered. Although a high proportion of passenger trips is undertaken without interchange, and may be increased through techniques such as VIPS, there will always be some trips involving interchange, commonly including hospital visits, those to friends and relatives, and home-to-work journeys where the workplace is outside the central area or not large enough to be served by a special route. As populations become more dispersed, these trips will become relatively more important, even though public transport has a small share in these markets.

Within larger cities, the proportion of bus trips involving bus-to-bus interchange grows, especially where separate services are required in the central area. Where rail networks are provided, some bus-to-rail interchange may occur spontaneously to save time, and may be encouraged by through-ticketing, clear information, etc. Interchange between urban and long-distance modes is also important.

In modelling of flows using generalized cost as a measure of deterrence (see Ch. 2), interchange may be represented by a time penalty (i.e. over and above observed interchange time) of about 5 minutes (a range from about 2 to 10 minutes). However, this is highly dependent upon ease of interchange, type of passenger, etc. Systems such as Stockholm and Hamburg have succeeded in stimulating high levels of public transport use, despite the high proportion of interchange (generally bus/rail) involved. The high proportion of passengers using travelcards clearly assists in this, and the very rapid take-up of London's Travelcard from May 1983 (in a network with a high proportion of interchange) also illustrates its attractiveness to users in such circumstances. Some 70% of London bus travellers now use travelcards, bus passes, or concessionary passes. This makes it easier to plan networks with a higher element of interchange (for example, shortening very long routes to offer improved reliability on each section) than in cases where the majority of passengers would incur a financial penalty under a cash-paid fare system.

Interchanges themselves form another criterion for station location, especially where a new rail route is added to an existing network: on London's Victoria Line all stations but one are interchanges with other rail routes.

If interchange penalties can be minimized, then systematic substitution of line-haul rapid transit for existing through bus services can be envisaged. Slow, unreliable and costly bus operation on inner sections of congested radial roads can be replaced by reserved-track rapid transit, being less labour-intensive and of higher quality. The outer sections of bus routes are then converted to rail feeders. The cost aspects of such a process are illustrated as a break-even chart in Figure 5.4. So far as the operator is concerned, the fixed-cost element may have been met largely by central or local government grants (whose justification would also have rested on estimated time savings to users, increased traffic, etc.).

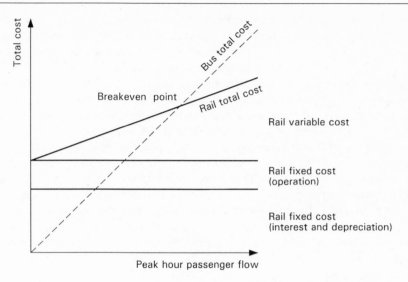

Figure 5.4   Break-even chart for bus and rail services in an urban corridor.

The main example of such an integrated network in Britain prior to local bus deregulation was that in Tyne and Wear, where the Metro was opened in stages from 1980 to 1984. Buses were converted to feeder services through purpose-built interchanges such as those at Regent Centre and Heworth. Overall, the system proved successful in retaining a high level of public transport use despite other adverse trends. However, there were problems when all bus passengers were required to transfer to rail, if the rail journey leg was short. This is the case at Gateshead, where bus/rail interchange occurs within 1.5 km of the centre of Newcastle, and through bus services were offered once again after deregulation. However, many of the other bus feeder services to Metro interchanges have been retained since deregulation, and even some of those at Gateshead reintroduced.

Elsewhere in Britain, parts of conurbations have bus/rail integration of this sort, where convenient interchanges can be made onto railways with good central-area penetration (e.g. the Birmingham–Longbridge corridor, or the rôle of purpose-built interchanges at Bury and Altrincham, which now serve the Manchester Metrolink). In other major European cities, integrated bus/tram/rail networks are the norm. Typically, through bus services are provided within a radius of about 5 km of the centre, with an outer bus network feeding rail interchanges: this is the pattern in Paris, for example.

Non-central area trips

Some trips of this type are handled along existing radial corridors into the central area, their origins and destinations both being within the same corridor – for example, to a suburban shopping centre on a main road, or a school similarly sited. A tendency for households to relocate outwards along the same corridor assists this. Linking of radial routes across a city centre can also assist, as can easy interchange within the central area between radial routes. However, congestion within the centre can deter the former, since unreliability would thus spread more extensively through the network.

In many cases, however, use of radial routes for suburb-to-suburb trips would be highly inconvenient, and specialized services will be needed. Since these will generally be of low frequency (typically half-hourly or worse), adherence to schedule is essential, and timetabled connections between such services (and radials) essential. The Canadian concept of the timed transfer focal point, at which several services converge on a centre at fixed intervals, takes this one step further. In a small town, this approach can be applied to the whole network.

Within suburban areas, it is helpful if land uses such as office employment, shops, health centres etc. can be concentrated at nodes which also have public transport interchanges, such as the Broadway development at Hammersmith.

Park & ride (P&R)

The private car can also be used as a feeder mode to public transport, generally rail in large cities. It is particularly important in low-density suburbs of large cities, where local bus services are thin, and much housing beyond walking distance to the station, yet the railway is an attractive mode for the radial trip to the city centre. Some spontaneous development has occurred, but to an increasing extent P&R is being encouraged through provision by transport operators or local authorities of car parks at stations. Many of these are former railway goods yards, especially around London, not ideally shaped or sited. However, new sites have also been developed, and for long-distance travel specialized Parkway stations such as Bristol, have been built almost exclusively for this mode.

Motorists tend to "railhead", i.e. drive fairly close in to the city centre, before transferring to rail, rather than driving to the nearest station. This tends to reduce public transport revenue without corresponding changes in cost. If the point of transfer can be placed as far as possible from the central area along a rail route, the financial position of the operator will generally improve, and fewer problems of on-street parking and traffic congestion caused by cars in inner areas.

A certain amount of time (or cost) saving is usually required to offset the perceived interchange penalty (see above). Unless there are severe physical or price restraints, voluntary diversion is unlikely for trips of less than about 6km. Generally speaking, one would not expect significant P&R demand within cities of less than about 500,000 people, as most trips would be under this length, and rail or rapid transit systems are not provided. Within Britain, most P&R use is found in London and the metropolitan areas. In some cases, such as the West Midlands, free parking is provided: this can be justified by the reduction in traffic congestion thus obtained.

There are, however, some exceptions. Where parking is very limited, as in some older cities, or at certain periods, such as the Saturdays leading up to Christmas, bus park & ride may be attractive. Many towns run pre-Christmas P&R bus services to supplementary car parks. In others all-year-round Saturday shopping services are operated. In Oxford, where the historic city centre imposes limits on road space and parking, and buses enjoy very good access through priority measures (see Ch. 3) all-day P&R services were established in 1974: 3,000 parking spaces are now provided at three sites, with plans to expand to 5,000. Bus park & ride has also expanded in similar historic cities, such as Chester and York. Some schemes are now financed through TSG, and government support has also been evident in allocation of credit approvals for P&R schemes.

The future of park-and-ride has four aspects:

- A means of enabling existing car trips originating in low-density, or poorly served areas, to transfer to public transport (normally rail) without the need to provide additional feeder services.
- Catering for further dispersal of the population by creating railheads through which trips can be channelled. For example, the intercity station at Stevenage serves the north Hertfordshire area.
- A means of enabling restrictions on car use in town centres, for traffic congestion or environmental reasons, to be implemented. Demand from dispersed origins may be concentrated at one or a few points. In addition to examples already quoted, St Ives in Cornwall restrains summer visitors' cars for environmental reasons. A P&R scheme was set up in 1978 on the branch line from St Erth, used by several hundred cars per day.
- On new suburban rail routes, the optimal spacing between stations could increase if a high proportion of feeder trips were by car (see the argument given earlier in this chapter).

A variant on P&R is "kiss & ride" in which the commuter is driven to the station by their partner, so that all-day parking is not required. In new interchanges, parking areas specifically for this purpose may be designated. Its pattern of use is often asymmetric – for example, a lift to the station in the morning, but not the evening, when a feeder bus may be used instead.

Public transport in low-density situations

Variations in traffic level are handled mainly by changing service frequency. Network density may also be varied by not running some routes at certain periods, and/or a simplified network at certain periods such as evenings and Sundays. This reaches its extreme (in urban areas) in skeletal all-night bus networks operated in cities such as London. Limited-stop services may be confined to busier periods only, their vehicles augmenting intermediate stopping services at other times. These problems are, of course, particularly acute in rural areas, considered separately in Chapter 8.

Where a mixture of minibus and full-size operation is found in the same network, minibuses and single-deckers may be deployed to cover almost all evening and Sunday work, thus enabling a similar route structure to be offered throughout the week, but at lower cost. The smaller vehicles may also be particularly appreciated in terms of passenger security when small loads are carried.

The alternative of less direct routeings offered at low-density periods (to combine traffic), or the absence of limited-stop workings, will of course result in longer journey times for some passengers, but these will be offset by a higher frequency than might otherwise be the case. Loadings are likely to be low, and higher scheduled speeds may be set when there is little traffic congestion.

The "dial a ride" concept was introduced during the 1970s, offering variable routeing in defined area, responding to requests by phone, in writing (normally a standing order for a regular trip), or on boarding the vehicle. Minibuses of about 16 seats were generally used. Telephone requests were handled by a radio control centre, sometimes making real-time use of computers to plan minimum-time routes. The very high unit cost per passenger which resulted made these services difficult to justify as general public services, and have all now been withdrawn, although a few similar services continue to operate elsewhere in Europe, where higher levels of support are generally given.

In Britain, the dial-a-ride concept has been adopted for specialized demands, notably many services for the disabled, using minibuses adapted to carry wheelchairs. Examples include the local dial-a-ride networks within London, "Ring & Ride" in Manchester, and Readibus in Reading. Despite the failure of dial-a-ride as a general purpose mode, there has been considerable expansion of radio-controlled single-hirer taxis. In some other countries taxis are used as planned substitutes for conventional buses at times of low demand, notably some evening/all-night services in West German cities. The legalization of shared-taxi operation in Britain since 1986 should have made this sort of mixed-mode operation much easier, but there has been little impact to date.

Conclusion

The process of matching supply to demand through design of the appropriate network structure has become much more systematic in recent years through the adoption of extensive passenger surveys with computer-assisted planning techniques. However, the pattern of land use has major effects on the ability of public transport to provide a good level of service, and public transport planners and operators should seek to influence it where change creates such opportunities.

Appendix: A technique for determining optimal interstation spacing

The components of total travel time are defined as on (page 88), the notation as:

L average line-haul trip per passenger (metres)

D average interstation spacing (metres)

S station stop time (seconds)

A distance covered by train in accelerating to normal running speed, and in retardation from normal running speed (symmetrical speed/time curve assumed) (metres)

B time occupied in same process as (A) (seconds)

V steady running speed of vehicle or train (metres/second)

F average speed of feeder mode to station (metres/second)

T average feeder trip length from origin (metres) to station
(as a working approximation, take T as equal to $0.25D$)

Some behavioural studies have suggested that passengers experience losses while walking and waiting equal to about twice the average valuation of travelling time. The component for feeder trip time could on this argument be multiplied by two if walking were the feeder mode. Waiting time is a function of service frequency and thus is not affected directly by spacing. It is therefore not considered in this calculation, but walking has been assumed as the feeder mode.

Total travel time = feeder trip time ($\times 2$) + (number of intermediate station stops $\times$ station stop time) + (number of interstation runs $\times$ acceleration and deceleration time) + (number of interstation runs $\times$ time on each run at steady speed)

$$\frac{T}{F} \times 2 + \frac{L}{D} \times S + \frac{L}{D} \times B + \frac{L}{D} \times \frac{(D-A)}{V}$$

In the expression as shown, stop time at the station where the passenger boards the train or vehicle is included, since normally s/he would arrive before the train or vehicle stopped. The values of A and B are calculated for given rates of acceleration and maximum running speed.

In this example the following values are assumed:

$L = 5000\,\text{m}$

$A = 144\,\text{m}^*$

$B = 24$ seconds*

$V = 12\,\text{m}$ per second

$S = 20$ seconds

$T = 0.25D\,\text{m}$

$F = 1\,\text{m}$ per second

* Based on a constant acceleration/deceleration rate of $1.0\,\text{m}$ per second per second

Inserting the values into the equation above we obtain

103

$$\text{Total time} = 0.25D \times 2/1 + (5{,}000 \times D) \times 20 + (5{,}000/D) \times 24 +$$
$$5{,}000(D{-}144)/(D \times 12)$$
$$= 160{,}000D^{-1} + 0.50D + 417$$

Differentiating with respect to D we obtain:

$\mathrm{d}TT/\mathrm{d}D = -160{,}000^{-2} + 0.50$

By setting the value of this expression equal to zero we can obtain the value of D for which time is minimized:

$O = -160{,}000D^{-2} + 0.50$

$D = 565.5\,\mathrm{m}$

The values inserted are typical of an urban light railway fed entirely by walking trips, and station stop time is an average for stock with sliding doors. In practice, a calculation of this type need not be made to within limits of less than $\pm 100\,\mathrm{m}$, since curvature, location of entrances, etc., will affect site availability, and stations themselves may be up to 100 m long.

In the case of bus operation, stop time can be represented as a constant, which for a one-man bus is about four seconds, plus a time per boarding passenger. The latter ranges from about two seconds on systems with simple fare scales and no change-giving up to about six seconds. The boarding time related to the number of passengers could be regarded as a constant total and only the four-second period be included in the optimal spacing calculation. In the long run, however, stop spacing will itself affect demand, and hence total delay caused by boarding passengers. (Widening the stop spacing would cut out some short trips, but encourage more long-distance ones, and vice versa.)

References and suggested further reading

Jansson, K. & B. Ridderstolpe 1992 (August). A method for the route-choice problem in public transport systems. *Transportation Science* **26**, 246–51.

MacBriar, I. 1986 (July). NBC's BusDriver Project. PTRC Summer Annual Meeting, July 1986, Seminar L.

Newell, G. F. & V. R. Vuchic 1968. Rapid transit interstation spacings for minimum travel time. *Transportation Science* **2**, 303–309.

Sherlock, H. 1991. *Cities are good for us*. London: Paladin.

Weston, J. G. 1982. Testing bus scheduling and control options. Paper presented at 14th Annual Seminar on Public Transport Operations Research, University of Leeds.

CHAPTER 6
Costing and
cost allocation methods

Introduction

The themes of costing and pricing are the subject of many entire textbooks, and in this book only a fairly brief outline can be given. Developments specific to public transport are described, with reference to other texts for general theory. The basic structure of costs is examined, followed by methods of allocating costs to specific activities, highlighting the contrast between fully allocated approaches and those based on determining avoidable, or escapable, costs. Some simple relationships between costs and prices are discussed in Chapter 7, followed by pricing techniques based on user perception. Particular emphasis is given to recent changes in pricing structures, of which traditional economic theory takes little account. The question of cross-subsidy is examined, in relation to allocation of revenues as well as the more traditional emphasis on costs.

The structure of costs

Classification

The costs involved in a transport operation may be classified in three ways:

1. According to inputs.
   Groupings such as wages and salaries, other staff-related costs (National Insurance, pensions, etc.), energy, spares and materials, insurance, depreciation, rent and interest charges indicate the main inputs and their relative importance. For example, in countries such as Britain the staff-related costs comprise about 70% of the total, but energy only about 5% to 10%. This type of classification is useful in highlighting the importance of different inputs and hence likely future trends: thus change in real labour costs is likely to be the predominant factor in determining overall rates of

change (in the absence of productivity change), rather than that in energy costs.

2. According to the activity within the transport operation.

For example, in analyzing bus operators' costs, the following classification based on that by CIPFA (the Chartered Institute of Public Finance and Accountancy) has been found helpful:

- traffic operating costs
- drivers, conductors and supervisory staff, ticket equipment, uniforms, miscellaneous supplies
- fuel and power
- servicing, repairs and maintenance
- staff costs, materials and spares, maintenance of buildings, machinery, etc.
- management, welfare and general
- administration, insurance, welfare and medical facilities, etc.
- (interest, taxation and depreciation are treated separately).

The advantage of this type of classification is that it highlights the relative importance of certain types of activity within the organization. Although similar in some respects to the input classification above, it gives a more useful guide to where costs arise. For example, it can be shown that the cost structure for urban bus operators in Britain changed during the late 1970s as one-person-operation became widespread. Traffic operating costs were thus held down as conductors were lost, falling from 62% of total operating costs in 1975–6 to 57% in 1979–80, while servicing, repairs and maintenance rose from 23% to 26% of the total over the same period, as more complex rear-engine double-deckers replaced simpler front-engine types, and operators failed to reduce the scale of their workshops in line with falling fleet size (Higginson & White 1982). From deregulation in 1986, sharp reductions in labour costs have been made, especially in maintenance and administrative staff (see further comment in Ch. 10), with smaller cuts in driving staff costs. This is consistent with the evidence for scope in cost reduction prior to 1986.

3. According to their basis of variation, and escapability over time.

Table 6.1 shows the main elements identified in the CIPFA/NBC classification developed in the early 1970s. Note that variation by time is much more important than variation by distance, reflecting the major rôle of time-based labour costs in the total. Peak vehicle based costs are those associated with all vehicles required to cover service at peak periods, not merely those used only at such times.

The examples above have been drawn in terms of the bus industry. Compa-

106

rable examples for railways in (2) would include train crews, track maintenance, signalling, terminals, and rolling stock maintenance. In (3), variation of cost by traffic density would represent a major factor. For the bus and coach operator, life is much simpler in that a public road network is used, to which a contribution may be made through annual vehicle duty and fuel duty, whereas the railways, in providing their own infrastructure, also face the problem of allocating their costs to specific activities.

Table 6.1 An example of the CIPFA bus cost structure.

Category	Main components	Basis of variation
Variable costs	Crew wages, bus servicing	Time
	Fuel, tyres, third-party insurance	Distance
Semi-variable costs	Bus maintenance	Time
	Depreciation and leasing	Peak vehicle
Fixed costs	Administration staff and welfare	Time
	Buildings and general	Peak vehicle
Interest on capital debt		Peak vehicle

Derived from appendix A of *Passenger transport operations* (London: Chartered Institute of Public Finance and Accountancy, 1974).

Interest and depreciation

In general, interest and depreciation are treated separately from the categories of operating cost described above. This is not to deny their importance, but to acknowledge their different nature, being often dependent upon accounting conventions and historic conditions as much as current operating methods.

Depreciation

This is the process of setting aside funds during the life of an asset, such that it can be replaced by an equivalent asset without additional capital being required. Transport operators generally use the straight line method, in which the assumed life of an asset is divided into its cost to give a sum set aside each year. For example if a bus costs £75,000 and has a life of 15 years, then the annual depreciation charge would be £75,000/15, or £5,000 per year. An alternative is the reducing-balance method, in which the same percentage of the initial cost is set aside each year. For example, at 20%, £15,000 would be set aside in the first year, £12,000 (i.e. 20% of £60,000) in the second, and so on. This method is appropriate to those assets which may depreciate more rapidly in the first few years of their lives, and be resold for further use elsewhere. However, even in the coach sector, to which this does apply, the straight-line method is generally preferred.

If there were no inflation, then the historic price of the asset would generally be sufficient as a basis for depreciation. However, in practice the money thus set aside is inadequate for funding the replacement. Under such conditions, either additional capital must be raised to make up the difference (through equity or

107

fixed-interest loans), or replacement cost depreciation adopted, in which the sum set aside each year is adjusted in the light of inflation, so that the final total is sufficient to replace the asset at current prices. This approach also formed part of the concept of current cost accounting (CCA). During the 1970s and early 1980s it was encouraged in the public sector – for example, in the National Bus Company – but was not generally followed in the private sector. It has now been largely dropped, in favour of reversion to the historic cost method. The effect of relying on historic cost depreciation is that only the monetary value of assets is retained, and a serious danger of failing to make necessary replacement investment will arise.

The lives used for depreciation purposes correspond roughly to those found in practice, but may vary according to accounting conventions, treatment of depreciation and profits in company taxation, leasing, etc. For buses and coaches 8 to 15 years is common, but for rail vehicles up to 30 to 40 years. Certain assets may not be depreciated at all – this is true of most infrastructure, such as embankments, bridges or tunnels (whether road or rail), where periodic heavy maintenance and occasional rebuilding is adopted rather than complete replacement. A critical point may be reached when a major structure needs replacing, the subsequent additional investment then raising the question of whether the route should be abandoned. From 1992/3, British Rail changed its accounting basis by charging to capital some costs previously treated as current, notably on track and infrastructure renewal.

The growth of leasing in recent years also raises complications. In "operating leases" an annual charge is made by the lessor to the operating company (sometimes also including maintenance of the vehicle), and the assets are not shown on the balance sheet, nor in depreciation. In "finance leases", the assets do appear on the balance sheet, and depreciation may be provided. This practice has been adopted to some degree in the bus and coach industry, and is becoming significant in the railways following privatization, in which leasing companies take responsibility not only for the existing BR fleet, but also the supply of all new stock is likely to be on this basis.

Interest

These charges are often influenced by the capital structure of the business and historical factors rather than the current assets employed. Publicly owned businesses have generally been financed through fixed-interest loans, interest on which has been treated as a "cost". Conversely, a private company financed entirely through equity – or dividend – capital, would not incur such a "cost", but be able to regard all its surplus after covering operating costs, depreciation, and taxation, as "profit". Thus, in comparing profitability of businesses one should assess carefully their capital structure. In addition to bearing fixed interest, much of the capital in public sector operations was repayable, imposing a further cost burden on the operator that would not be faced with equity capital.

However, in some cases, the historic capital debt has been wholly written off.

London Transport and its subsidiaries have virtually no fixed-interest debt. For railways, interest charges on the current capital value of their assets could represent a very high charge indeed, and very few meet this requirement (the intention to do so for the Hong Kong Mass Transit Railway is virtually unique among urban systems). The requirement for Railtrack to provide a return on its assets may greatly increase the apparent rail subsidy in Britain (no equivalent valuation is attached to the road network, funded purely out of current revenues). Within the bus industry in Britain, NBC and SBG were funded wholly from repayable fixed-interest debt. Since privatization, individual bus companies now have an element of equity capital, but in many cases (especially management buy-outs), a substantial proportion is in the form of fixed-interest borrowing. Since companies were often sold for more than their share of total NBC or SBG debt, they may in many cases face a similar or even higher debt burden than before.

Table 6.2 Effects of varying assumptions on vehicle replacement and capital structure, for a small bus company (£ million per annum).

Case	A	B	C	C	E
Revenue	2.00	2.00	2.00	2.00	2.00
Operating costs	1.70	1.70	1.70	1.70	1.98
Surplus	0.30	0.30	0.30	0.30	0.02
Depreciation	0.08	0.12	0.08	0.12	–
Interest	–	–	0.16	0.16	–
"Profit"	0.22	0.18	0.08	0.02	0.02
Return on initial investment (%)	16.3	13.3	5.9	1.5	13.3

Notes:
A   All capital as equity, historic depreciation
B   All capital as equity, replacement depreciation
C   All capital fixed-interest, historic depreciation
D   All capital fixed-interest, replacement depreciation
E   Fleet on operating lease; only capital investment is that in depot (£0.15 million), financed as equity.

The differences are shown in Table 6.2. This illustrates a notional bus company set up in 1986, running 20 vehicles. They were purchased at £60,000 each. The depot and office accommodation cost £150,000, giving a total initial investment of £1.35m. Annual revenue from all sources (i.e. including concessionary fare compensation, tendered services, etc., as well as direct passenger income) is £2.0m per annum, and operating costs (including administration, etc.) £1.7m. Vehicles are depreciated over a 15-year life, but their current replacement cost is now £90,000 each. Hence, depreciation per vehicle is £4,000 per year (historic), or £6,000 (replacement). No depreciation is charged on the depot or offices.

If the company were financed entirely through equity capital, then all the operating surplus after subtracting depreciation would be regarded as "profit". If funded through fixed-interest borrowing (assumed here at 12% per annum), then such charges would be deducted as a "cost" before arriving at profits. Also shown is a case in which vehicles are supplied on an operating lease, at £14,000 per vehicle per annum. This is charged as an operating cost. The only assets of

109

the company are then the depot and offices, represented by equity capital of £150,000. As can be seen, by varying these assumptions, the net profit can range from £0.22m to £0.02m per annum, for the same operating performance. The rate of return on the initial investment ranges from 16.3% to 1.5%. In the absence of replacement depreciation accounting as such the difference between historic and replacement costs could be reflected in provision of a separate account for this purpose. Another approach is to set a profit target as a percentage of turnover, to provide for the difference between historic and replacement depreciation, and to give a realistic rate of return on equity capital. For example, the Stagecoach Group have set a target of 15%.

Cost allocation methods

From this point, the specific features of the bus and rail industries make it appropriate to discuss costing techniques separately.

Bus industry

Until the early 1970s, the general approach in Britain was to estimate a total average cost per bus mile, by dividing total costs (all operating costs, and usually depreciation, and interest also) by miles run. Such an indicator is still produced (on a kilometre basis), and serves to describe trends. However, it is most unsatisfactory as a means of comparing costs between routes within a network, or between operators, since it is clear that most costs do not vary with distance, but with time. Demands for support to rural services made to county councils resulted in a questioning of cost allocation methods. This led to the formulation of the NBC/CIPFA system,

Standard unit costs for each cost centre – typically a depot – were derived for driver hours, fuel and tyre costs per vehicle mile, depreciation per peak vehicle, etc. Table 6.3 gives an example based on a fairly typical allocation of costs under the CIPFA system, where the cost centre is a single depot, running urban and rural services.

The grouping of costs in Table 6.3 slightly simplifies that in Table 6.1, by placing "variable" and "semi-variable" into one category, and grouping fixed costs at depot level (local administration, building maintenance, etc.) and a share of company costs (central administration, fixed interest charges), but enables the principal features of the CIPFA system and its underlying assumptions to be illustrated. Maintenance costs are treated on a distance basis.

For purposes of calculation, a bus life of 15 years is assumed. Depreciation is on a straight-line basis, at current replacement values, allocated to each sector (urban or rural) in proportion to the number of vehicles owned. Fixed depot

Table 6.3   Bus cost and revenue allocation (£).

		Urban	Rural
Annual fixed costs of depot		200,000	
Local share of annual company costs		250,000	
Bus variable operating cost per km		0.20	
Bus variable operating cost per hour		7.00	
	By type of service:	*Urban*	*Rural*
PVR		24	*12*
Buses owned		28	*14*
Total km per week		24,000	*16,000*
Total hours per week		1,500	*500*
Revenue per week		29,000	*8,000*
Replacement cost per bus		80,000	*65,000*
Variable cost per km		0.25	*0.125*

costs, and local share of company costs are allocated between sectors in proportion to peak vehicle requirement (PVR). An operating year may be taken as 50 weeks, allowing for bank holidays, etc.

Urban and rural cost differences
Prior to introduction of the CIPFA system, a crude average cost per bus-kilometre for the whole system would have been applied. From the above data, in this case it would be £0.88 per bus-kilometre. However, the urban and rural averages above are £1.00 and £0.72, respectively: this difference arises mainly from the fact that the rural services have a higher average speed (32km/h compared with 16km/h), and hence the hourly variable costs per bus-hour are spread over more kilometres. Just this simple modification produces a large difference, not only in costs but also the estimated profits or losses by each sector.

For example, the urban services have a revenue of £1.21 per bus-kilometre, and rural 50p per kilometre. Relating both to the overall average cost per bus-mile of £0.88 produces an apparent surplus on urban routes of 33p per kilometre, and a loss on rural services of 38p per kilometre. However, using the averages separately estimated for each reduces the urban surplus to 21p and the rural loss to 22p, cutting considerably the apparent cross-subsidy from one category to another.

The introduction of the CIPFA system thus produced a fairer allocation of costs, especially where urban and rural services were mixed. However, it was still a cost allocation system which retained a large amount of averaging. For example, urban and rural services were assumed to use the same type of bus, with the same variable cost per mile. In reality, the rural service might well use a single-decker, and urban a double-decker. The more frequent stopping on the urban route would not only reduce speed, but also increase fuel and maintenance costs. The differing replacement cost per vehicle, and variable cost per kilometre, shown in the last two rows of Table 6.3, might be more realistic. If these changes are made, then the rural cost per bus-kilometre becomes 71p (compared with revenue of 50p) and urban £1.06 (revenue £1.21), further reducing the degree of cross-subsidy.

These contrasts by vehicle type have become more marked with the rapid growth of minibuses. Where a lower wage rate applies (typically 20% less than for full-size vehicles), minibuses in urban service will incur about 70% to 75% the total cost per bus-kilometre of full-size vehicles (other factors being the lower fuel and maintenance costs per kilometre and slightly higher average speed which may be attained). For example, if minibus cost per kilometre is 70% that of full-size buses, then doubling the service frequency (a 100% increase in bus-km) would increase total costs by only 40%, i.e. if the service broke-even at existing fares, then an increase in ridership of 40% would match the increase in costs, corresponding to a demand elasticity with respect to service level of +0.40. The cost per passenger space-km is of course greater for minibuses than full-size vehicles (by about 50%), but given the low average load factors found on many conventional services, such a substitution is feasible.

Peak cost allocation

Another respect in which average unit costs are inappropriate is in peak/off-peak cost allocation. Not only are certain vehicles only used at peak times, making it appropriate to allocate their costs entirely to that period, but also the crew utilization on peak-only duties may be poor.

Suppose that, within the urban operations shown in the initial data, 8 of the 24 PVR operate only in the peak period, some 4 hours per day, Monday to Friday, each covering 64 km. Their crews perform no other work, and result in time-based variable costs of £42.00 per working day. If we assume that 10 buses are owned in total to cover the peak-only operations (for purposes of depreciation), then these operations incur an average cost of £2.10 per kilometre. If the revenue from them was £1.21, a loss of £0.89 per kilometre would be incurred. This implies a much greater cross-subsidy from other traffic than in the urban–rural case above. Although the average revenue – at the same rate per kilometre as over the day as a whole – may seem rather low for the peak-only services, one should bear in mind that they are often loaded in one direction only, and that much of the extra peak traffic in many towns comprises school-children (see Ch. 2), who may pay substantially lower fares.

The peak/off-peak cost allocation issue was examined in greater depth by CIPFA, and an improved method of cost allocation introduced. Nonetheless, it does highlight the contrast between cost allocation methods and those which determine avoidable costs. Even if an average unit cost per driver-hour for the peak-only buses were derived, this would be a poor guide. One peak-only bus might be covered by a driver who also drives on all-day buses to cover the meal-break reliefs of their drivers, and in this case it would not be reasonable to allocate his/her whole shift to the peak. Conversely, an off-peak journey might be added to the service, covered by a driver currently employed for the peak only, within his guaranteed shift, hence with a very low avoidable cost. As a basis for "fair" allocation between routes, the CIPFA system certainly represented an improvement on previous methods, and a good basis for negotiating with local authorities, but as a basis for managerial decision-making it remained very crude.

The determination of cross-subsidy within a network by time period is highly dependent upon crew cost allocation, which in turn depends on the local working agreements (for example, whether split-shift duties are worked) and the level of output in each period from which change is proposed. These were examined in depth by Leeds University in a study for NBC (University of Leeds 1984). Further comment on cross-subsidy is made in the discussion on pricing policy in Chapter 7. A further review of the effects of different peak/off-peak costing assumptions is provided by Savage (1989).

A common feature of bus costing is that the route forms the basis of both revenue and cost attribution, rather than market sectors (except, perhaps, when peak-only operations are considered). While this is convenient for the producer, it may not reflect market conditions very well. A single route may, for example, link two towns carrying town-to-town, village-to-town and intra-urban traffic, each with different pricing policies and elasticities, yet all would be grouped together under conventional costing procedures.

Rail cost allocation

Table 6.4 British Rail cost structure, 1992/3.

Component	£ (million)	% of total
Train crew	468	12.5
Fuel & electricity	212	5.7
Shunting, stabling and cleaning of trains	121	2.8
Operations control and signalling	288	7.7
Maintenance of locomotives, power cars, coaches and wagons	581	15.6
Terminals	464	12.4
Marketing and commercial services	99	2.6
Track and associated structures	420	11.2
Signalling and telecommunications infrastructure	204	5.5
Management costs	278	7.4
Other expenses	266	7.1
Depreciation and amortization	246	6.6
Train catering	50	1.3

Source: Derived from BR annual report and accounts 1992/3. Percentages may not sum exactly to 100, because of rounding.

Table 6.4 shows the composition of British Rail's total costs in 1992/93. It can be seen that the categories of train crew, fuel & electricity, shunting, etc., and rolling stock maintenance (totalling 36.6%) correspond broadly to those found in the bus industry, with similar issues of allocation arising – for example, the cost of peak-only services. However, over half the total costs are not related to train operation as such, but terminals (a term covering all stations and depots), track and signalling, and a large share of general and administration costs.

Allocating these to specific traffic flows becomes difficult and often arbitrary, despite attempts to improve this process over many years. One such was the "Cooper formula", used under the Transport Act 1968 until 1974 inclusive, to estimate the grants required for specific loss-making services. Although train service costs could be allocated to routes fairly clearly, allocation of terminal, track and signalling costs over common sections of route was arbitrary. They may be apportioned on some common basis, such as gross tonne-kilometres (for track and signalling), or number of passenger movements (for terminals), but these are very crude.

For example, wear and tear on the track itself may be correlated with gross tonne-kilometres, but is also associated with the maximum axle-loads (usually greater for freight stock) and maximum speeds (usually greater for passenger services) over the section in question. Cost and complexity of signalling is determined by the headway between trains, mix of speeds (see Ch. 9), and safety requirements, usually much stricter for passenger traffic.

Comparing the attributed revenue with the allocated costs for such traffic often resulted in misleading choices. For example, a freight service sharing track with passenger trains might well fail to cover its share of allocated costs, yet withdrawing that service might bring about very little reduction in track or signalling costs. If the freight service covered at least its specifically attributable costs, then it could be worth retaining. Likewise, an off-peak passenger service might be improved at low marginal cost, making better use of existing track and train crews, yet appear not worthwhile owing to the higher share of track, signalling and terminal costs which it might attract.

In recognition of these problems, the Railways Act 1974 abolished the specific grants for passenger services, replacing them with the PSO payment for the passenger network as a whole (see Ch. 1), and the payments from PTEs. However, the shift was a somewhat extreme one, making assessment of costs other than at a national level rather difficult.

The period from 1974 saw the development within BR of a system based on the "avoidable cost" concept. Each activity was required to make "contribution" to track, signalling and terminal costs based on those costs, together with covering its train operating costs. The "contribution" was based on the difference between attributed income and expenditure, after allowing for specifically attributable costs. However, this system left a very large proportion of costs not allocated to any specific activity.

It was followed by the development of sector management (see Ch. 1) in which financial targets were set for sectors based on InterCity passenger, and Network South East passenger, Regional passenger, Freight and Parcels sectors. In order to avoid the problem of arbitrary cost allocation described above, a specific sector was deemed to be the "Prime User" of a common resource, other sectors being required to meet only their specifically avoidable costs. In general, passenger traffic was regarded as the prime user of the system (reflecting the fact that it accounts for the majority of revenue, and justification for financial support). For example, on major long-distance passenger routes, the InterCity sector was the prime user, bearing responsibility for track, signalling and terminal costs. Other sectors making use of these facilities were charged only those costs specific to them. Thus, a local passenger service sharing an InterCity route would be charged its train operating costs, together with those of additional intermediate stations, signalling for closer-headway operation, etc., but InterCity would bear the great majority of track and signalling costs.

The concept worked much better than previous fully allocated systems, but suffered from the somewhat arbitrary definition of "Prime User". If it were proposed that an existing freight line be used to carry a new local passenger service also, then the passenger service would by definition become the "Prime User" of the track and signalling, and thus bear many costs now attributed to the freight sector. This could deter the re-opening, even if the revenue and other benefits of the proposed passenger service exceeded the avoidable costs of its introduction. A related problem occurred when some train operating costs were shared between sectors (although most were clearly specific to a single sector) – for example, parcels and InterCity passenger services, or locomotives shared between passenger and freight operations.

It has been the general intention of central government since the mid-1970s that freight and InterCity services should cover their costs (howsoever defined) from revenue, with the PSO and PTE payments directed largely toward other passenger services. InterCity and freight sectors have been required to also make a specified rate of return on current assets employed.

During the 1980s, the "prime user" concept was replaced by the "sole user" concept. This followed the same hierarchy of allocation by sector, but took a "bottom up" instead of "top down" approach i.e. instead of allocating the existing costs, it considered what resources were required to run the pattern of services currently offered. For example, an InterCity service might need a basic two-track main line maintained for high speeds. Additional freight traffic would impose higher axle loads, and possibly the need for specific sidings and loops. Additional local passenger services would impose additional signalling costs at intermediate stations, and the need for extra block sections, and perhaps require additional parallel tracks. The sum of these requirements could then be compared with infrastructure currently provided (which might include, for example, redundant freight loops). The method thus pointed the way toward reducing infrastructure costs.

The completion of "Organizing for Quality" in 1992 placed specific portions of track and signalling infrastructure under specific sectors, giving a closer link between managerial responsibility and costs incurred.

115

Comparative rail and bus costs

Some crude comparisons between rail and bus costs may be made by dividing total system costs (including track, signalling and other infrastructure costs) by train-kilometres run. Such averaging gives an indication of the much higher costs incurred per train-kilometre than for bus, and hence the difference in average loads required to break even.

Table 6.5 shows some examples, together with averages for bus services. The much higher rail figures are influenced by differences between train and bus size, and of course the inclusion of infrastructure costs (the "prime user" ranking of passenger services on the BR system may also exaggerate some of the differences).

Table 6.5 Examples of unit operating costs, and Railtrack charges.

System/year		Average operating costs (including depreciation and renewal) per train-km or bus-km	Railtrack average charges per train-km for 1994/5
London Underground	1992/3	£17.42	
Tyne & Wear Metro	1992/3	£4.78	
Glasgow Underground	1992/3	£11.42	
Docklands Light Railway (to nearest £)	1992/3	£17.00	
British Railways	1992/3		
- InterCity		£ 9.99	£8.53
- Network South East		£ 7.58	£6.10
- Regional Railways		£ 6.05	£5.16
Local bus services	1992/3		
- London		£ 1.73	
- rest of Britain		£ 0.94	

Sources:
Annual reports for years shown for London Transport (p. 56), Tyne & Wear PTE (p. 15), Strathclyde PTE (p. 61), British Rail (p. 63). Docklands Light Railway from *Transport statistics for London 1993* (London: HMSO, 1993), p. 36.
Bus service costs from *Bus and coach statistics Great Britain 1992/3* (London: HMSO, 1993), p. 23.
Railtrack sector costs from report in *Local transport today*, 3 March 1994, divided by passenger-train kilometres from *Transport statistics Great Britain 1992/3*, table 5.13b.

It can be seen that unit costs in the London case tend to be higher than elsewhere, both for rail and bus, although this is not necessarily true of unit cost per passenger-kilometre, due to the much higher loadings attained, for both modes.

The Tyne & Wear Metro clearly attains the lowest urban rail operating costs, probably due to high staff productivity, and treatment of capital costs.

Even if "track costs" for buses were included, on the basis of calculations shown in *Transport Statistics Great Britain 1993* (p. 56), this would only increase bus costs by about 6p per vehicle-kilometre.

The average charges imposed by Railtrack for 1994/5 are also shown. These approach total average costs in 1992/3, and are clearly much greater than the sum of infrastructure-related costs shown in Table 6.4, even allowing for inflation. A major factor is that Railtrack's assets have been valued at a replacement cost of £6,500 million, on which a return of 5.6% is initially required (i.e. £364 million per year), later rising to 8%; further comment on this issue is made in Chapter 10.

Statistical models of cost structures

In addition to the procedures for allocating cost categories to activities described above, statistical relationships can also be established between variables, and the resultant models used for purposes of allocation, or forecasting. In the latter they may provide a quick method of estimating costs of proposed service changes without carrying out a detailed analysis from the start. Thus a regression model for bus costs, incorporating bus-km, bus-hours and peak vehicle requirement could be used to estimate total cost of alternative service provisions, prior to more detailed assessment of preferred options.

Modelling of costs has been used in rail systems to establish relationships between traffic density and unit costs (especially in track and signalling) and to test whether overall economies of scale by network size exist. Fairly strong relationships with traffic density may be found but an uncertain picture remains on the question of economies of scale by network size (Preston & Nash 1993). There remains the danger that the variables included in the model themselves simply reflect judgements by engineers or accountants rather than fundamental relationships. For example, various standards of track maintenance are often set, associated with traffic density, based on engineers' judgement. These in turn will be associated with different levels of cost. A modeller would thus establish a relationship between costs and traffic density, but this may be a rather circular process. Improvements have been made recently however, notably the "MAR-PAS" model of BR (Hope 1992).

Within the bus industry, modelling exercises have been carried out to test whether economies of scale by fleet size exist. They have generally confirmed the earlier work of Lee & Stedman (1970), suggesting no economies of scale. Indeed, diseconomies may exist, although it is difficult to distinguish the effects of large fleet size from features of large conurbations such as greater traffic congestion and higher wage levels, the size of operator and size of city served often being correlated. As in the rail case, economies by route density may be found (Windle 1988). Although bus operators do not incur the fixed costs of infrastructure applicable to rail, in both modes higher traffic density permits larger vehicles to be used, and/or higher load factors to be obtained, thus reducing cost per passenger carried.

117

References and suggested further reading

A general review of costing and pricing models, and their relationship with demand models, is provided in Kenneth A. Small, *Urban transportation economics* (Reading: Harwood, 1992).

Chartered Institute of Public Finance and Accountancy (CIPFA) 1974. *Passenger transport operations*. London, 1974 (and *Peak/off-peak costing and revenue allocation supplement*, 1979).

Higginson, M. P. & P. R. White 1982. *The efficiency of British urban bus operators* (table 4.1). Research Report 8, Transport Studies Group, Polytechnic of Central London.

Hill, T. W., I. P. Wallis, M. W. Starr 1984. Bus service costing – an improved planning tool. *Traffic Engineering and Control*, 25(2), 54–9

Hope, R. 1992. MARPAS relates track costs to traffic' *Railway Gazette International* 148(3), 147–50.

Lee, N. & I. Stedman 1970. Economics of scale on bus transport: British municipal results. *Journal of Transport Economics and Policy* 4(1), 15–28.

Preston, J. M. & C. A. Nash 1993. European railway comparisons: lessons for policy. Paper presented at the Third International Conference on Ownership and Competition in Surface Passenger Transport, Mississauga, Canada.

Savage, Ian 1989. The analysis of bus costs and revenues by time period. *Transport Reviews*: Part 1 (Literature review), vol. 8 (1988), 283–99; Part 2 (Methodology review), vol. 9 (1989), 1–12.

University of Leeds, Institute for Transport Studies and the National Bus Company, London 1984. *Cross-subsidy in urban bus operations*.

Windle, R. J. 1988. Transit policy and the cost structure of urban bus transportation. In *Bus deregulation and privatisation: an international perspective*, J. S. Dodgson & N. Topham (eds), 119–40. Aldershot: Avebury.

CHAPTER 7

Pricing theory and practice

Introduction

One starting point in pricing policy is to establish links between prices and costs. An operator seeking to break even or make a small profit is taken as the initial case, with some simple average costing approaches described. However, provided that revenue at least exceeds the variable, or escapable, cost associated with a particular facility, it will be worth retaining, at any rate in the short-to-medium run. Simple average cost-price relationships should therefore be considered only as a guide to the principles involved.

The costs which an operator has to meet from passenger revenue will depend upon conditions already described. In addition to current operating costs, depreciation will have to be covered (historic or replacement), and interest charges (dependent very much upon the historic capital structure). Taxes and subsidies will also affect the "total costs" as perceived by the operator. For example, in Britain local bus services receive a rebate of most fuel duty, but in other countries fuel may carry a high rate of tax. The New Bus Grant, until 1984, partly offset the cost of replacing vehicles.

The term "revenue" may also be ambiguous. In addition to fares paid by passengers, this will also include income from advertising, work for outside bodies by engineering workshops, etc. Payments in compensation for concessionary fares offered to certain groups of passengers at the request of local authorities – the elderly, disabled, and in some cases children – are normally regarded by operators as "revenue" rather than "subsidy", especially as the aim of current policy is to ensure that the operator does not receive revenue totalling more than would have been obtained (after allowing for any specific extra costs) at the existing level of fares. Thus, if one divides total revenue (as defined by the operator) by passenger trips or passenger-kilometres (km) to get an average unit revenue, this figure may overstate considerably the average cost as perceived by the passenger. Unit revenues will also be affected by the mix of traffic (cash fares, travelcards, off-peak fares, child fares, etc.), and, where graduated fare scales apply, by changes in trip length over time. Rather than talking of an "average fare" (an almost meaningless concept), it is better to use the term "average revenue per trip", which conveys the sense that revenue received will vary according to the mix of traffic as well as changes in fare scales initiated by the operator.

Taking buses as an example, the simplest "rule" for average cost pricing would be to set the fare equal to the average cost per passenger (pax) trip:

$$\text{Fare per trip} \ = \ \frac{\text{Total cost}}{\text{Total passenger-km}} \quad \text{or} \quad \frac{\text{Cost per vehicle trip}}{\text{Passengers boarding per vehicle trip}}$$

The first version gives a flat fare over the whole system throughout the day, the second a fare which could vary according to the cost of running a bus under different conditions (for example, a higher cost in the peak) and passengers carried (for example, higher in the late evenings when poor loadings are found).

A pure flat fare as such is hardly ever found, lower rates usually applying for children or the elderly, but many systems in North America and Western Europe come close to it. In Britain, it is less common, but may be found in Newport (South Wales), together with services in small towns. Furthermore, the zonal bus fare structure in London is such that many users make trips within only one zone (notably the larger outer zones), and in effect perceive a flat fare, as do underground users in the central area.

Where a flat fare is charged each time a passenger boards a vehicle, the cost to someone making a linked trip becomes very high, increasing by the whole flat fare at each transfer. However, the simplicity of a flat fare system makes it easy to incorporate a transfer facility, by permitting unlimited transfers within a given period (such as one hour), the time of issue being printed on the ticket. In some cases, this can be superimposed on a graduated system for unlinked trips: West Midlands' PTE introduced a flat rate transfer (at 50 pence) in July 1985, utilizing the ability of its Autofare–3 equipment to print time of issue on each ticket. Another approach, found in some North American systems, is to offer a ticket permitting one transfer on cancellation at a slightly higher price than the unlinked flat fare trip. Reliable operation is clearly essential for such systems, so that the connecting leg can be made within the period allowed by timetabled services.

A second simple rule would be to relate the fare to distance travelled, i.e.:

$$\text{Fare per km} \ = \ \frac{\text{Total cost}}{\text{Total passenger-km}} \quad \text{or} \quad \frac{\text{Cost per vehicle-km}}{\text{Average load}}$$

Under the first version, a common fare per kilometre would be set over the whole system, while under the second it would vary with costs and loadings – for example, a poorly loaded early morning service would bear a high fare, a well loaded inter-peak service, a low one.

In practice, perfect graduation is not attainable. Although for railways station-to-station prices can be set, for bus services there are too many stops to make this practicable, and stops are grouped in fare stages, typically about one kilometre long. Fares are then set on a stage-to-stage basis, so that someone travelling from any point in Stage 1 to any point in Stage 4, would pay a four-stage fare (as explained in Chapter 2, this can lead to an over-estimation of passenger-km on a network when derived from distance paid for, rather than directly observed).

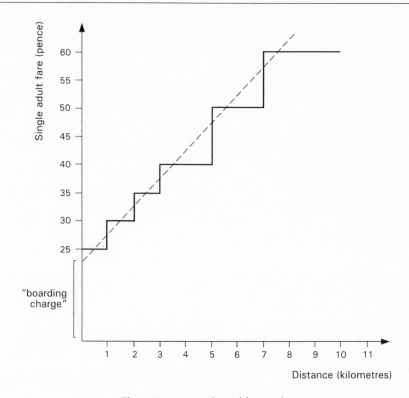

Figure 7.1 A graduated fare scale.

Another typical feature of graduated fare scales, as shown in Figure 7.1, is that the fare is not in linear proportion to distance, but has an initial step, followed by a given rate of increase thereafter. This can be represented (in some cases explicitly) as a "boarding charge", plus a rate per kilometre. To some extent, this is a reflection of costs, as each passenger boarding incurs the costs of ticket issue, and causes delay to the vehicle. However, it has often developed in a rather accidental fashion, as successive fare increases have caused a higher percentage to be applied to the lowest fares. As Figure 2.2 shows, the trip length distribution on urban bus services is such that relatively few trips are above 5–6km, even in a large conurbation, and the need to distinguish various categories of longer trips becomes less important. Wider "steps" in the fare scale are therefore applied as trip length increases. Traditionally, the graduated scale has been considered a "fair" reflection of costs, both by operators and passengers.

Yet it is evident that most costs are related to time, not distance, and that they will vary markedly by time of day, as described in Chapter 6. Nor, especially when passengers are charged in proportion to the distance travelled by the bus rather than the direct route to their destination (which may often be the case in rural areas), does the fare bear much relationship to perceived value of the trip.

Given the importance of time in determining costs, one could also set out as simple rule on a unit time cost, i.e.

$$\text{Fare per minute} = \frac{\text{Total cost}}{\text{Total pax-minutes}} \quad \text{or} \quad \frac{\text{Cost per vehicle-minute}}{\text{Average pax-load}}$$

There is virtually no case of such policies being directly adopted by public transport operators, although charging by taxis sometimes incorporates this. The taper on graduated fares scales may have similar impact, the rate per passenger-km for longer trips reflecting the lower operating per vehicle-km on longer services at higher average speeds.

Peak costing

As indicated in the earlier discussion on costs, a major determinant of cost is the level of peak provision. Not only are some vehicles used only at this time, but many crews may be needed for the peak and not fully utilized at other times. There are two main ways of looking at this. Either most costs are allocated to the day's services as a whole, on a time and/or distance basis, with only the extra peak output costed wholly to the peak. Alternatively, the peak output can be seen as the raison d'être of the service, with all the costs of providing it allocated initially to the peak (i.e. all vehicles, and a shift of crews), with extension of service to other parts of the day seen as an incremental cost. Neither can be seen as the only "right" option, but whatever basis is selected should then be used consistently for calculation.

The first approach (a) may be more appropriate where a fairly steady level of service is offered throughout the day, with some expansion at peaks. This is typical of many medium-size towns, of 50,000 or so. The minibus services introduced in such towns during the 1980s offer a case in which virtually no "peak only" working is found (except where larger vehicles have been retained to provide separate journeys for peak school travel). The second (b) would be appropriate where there is a very high peak, with which most costs are associated. For example, in rural areas the peak in demand associated with statutory provision for school travel often determines the number of buses operated, and other services can then be costed on an incremental basis. In large urban areas, rail services are geared very much to meeting the work journey peak, a very high share of their costs (rolling stock, train crews, scale of infrastructure, etc.) being associated with this. The extreme case is found in fully automated urban systems where, once peak capacity has been provided, the additional costs of off-peak service are confined to some energy and train maintenance costs, a very small proportion of the total.

A third approach to peak costing is to observe that some additional peak operation above a "base" level of all-day service may be desirable in any case, to provide drivers to cover meal-break reliefs of "straight shift" staff, and enable vehicles to be maintained largely during daytime hours. An optimal peak: inter-peak vehicle output ratio may be defined, dependent upon demand patterns, shift working practices, and vehicle maintenance procedures, typically around 1.2 (Higginson & White 1982). Only vehicles and crews needed above this level would then be attributable solely to the peak. Figure 7.2 illustrates these three approaches.

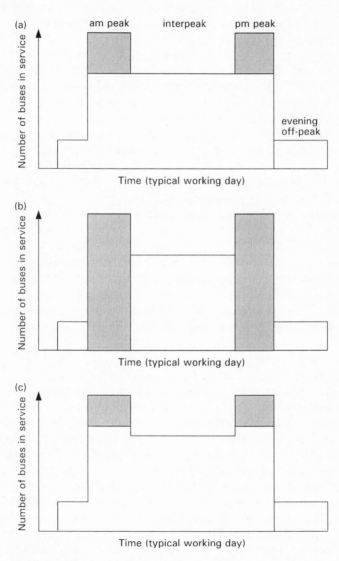

Figure 7.2 Peak cost allocation; the shaded areas represent costs allocated wholly to the peak.

123

Based on a simple assumption of a constant average revenue per single passenger trip over the whole day, the extent of cross-subsidy between different periods of the day may be estimated. An early attempt was the MAP study of the Hereford City network by NBC in 1976, using costing assumptions shown as (a) and (b) in Figure 7.2. On both, evening trips after 1800 made a large loss, but on assumption (a) other times of day generally covered their costs. On assumption (b), the morning peak made a loss (this being the more pronounced). If fares were to be varied around the existing average to reflect these costs (not allowing for elasticity effects), those in the inter-peak would be cut, and those in the evening increased by over 100%.

A subsequent study by Leeds University and the National Bus Company (1984) examined four towns: Runcorn, Bridgend, Cheltenham, and, from SBG territory, Hawick. Cross-subsidy by time of day emerged very strongly. The interpeak made a surplus, and early morning and evening services a loss, mainly due to poor loadings. The pattern for the peaks depended upon the costing assumptions employed (some five in all), being particularly sensitive to crew costs. It should be borne in mind, however, that the studies were based on the networks prior to MAP revised networks being introduced, which tended to reduce peak-only, and evening, vehicle output, thus reducing the extent of cross-subsidy. This study also showed that urban routes tended to be fairly close to break even as a whole, and inter-urban routes made a surplus. These subsidized rural areas, often to a much greater extent than direct revenue support received from local authorities.

A more detailed examination of alternative networks and costing assumptions was carried out for the Cheltenham town network, showing route-by-route costing and cross-subsidy results to be robust under many assumptions, but time of day costing and cross-subsidy to be highly sensitive to any assumptions made. (Note that, although costing estimates for cross-subsidy purposes prior to deregulation became increasingly refined, crude assumptions continued to be made about revenue. Furthermore, the single passenger trip formed the basis of analysis. Further comment is made on these issues later in this chapter).

The high cost of peak-only service provision generally means that it cannot cover its costs over the typical trip lengths found in local bus use. However, for longer journeys, peak-only services may cover their costs. The costs of putting a vehicle and crew into service for a peak-only return run are largely fixed, and increase only gradually with distance (the latter mainly fuel and maintenance costs). Figure 7.3 shows this case. The development of commuter coach services into London since the Transport Act 1980 illustrates the point well. With a 75% load factor, an operator can break even if the journey is about 50km or more each way. Shorter trips, or poorer load factors, may be viable if additional inter-peak work is found, such as tourist hire (Robbins & White 1985). Likewise, long-distance commuter rail services into London may cover their costs even for peak-only workings.

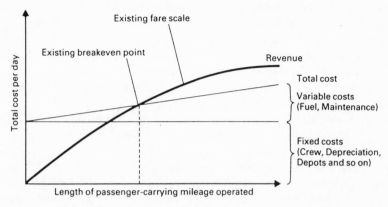

Figure 7.3   Break-even distance for peak-only operations.

Price elasticity

The elasticity of demand for a product (which may be defined very simply as the relationship between percentage change in units demanded – in this case trips – and percentage change in real price) will depend upon the degree of substitution by other products. In the case of local passenger transport, this takes five forms:

1. *Change of mode*   Although car driver/bus passenger comes first to mind, few perceive this choice. More likely, in the short run at least, are car passenger/bus passenger, and walk or cycle/bus passenger. Rail and bus, or coach, competition may be significant over longer distances, and rail may also be perceived as an alternative by the car driver more readily than is bus.
2. *Change of trip frequency*   Shopping, personal business and other non-work/education trips can be varied in frequency in response to a fares change.
3. *Change in trip destination*   If fares rise, alternative destinations may be sought. For shopping trips, this substitution may occur quickly. For work trips, it may become apparent over the longer term, as home and/or workplace are re-located.
4. *Change in activity*   Some marginal activities may be changed, such as watching a video at home instead of seeing a film at the cinema.
5. *Shift in activities within the household*   Trips may be combined: for example, a working member picking up shopping on the way home, instead of someone else making a separate shopping trip.

The above classification implies that demand for very short trips may be more elastic than long ones, since walking and cycling can be substituted easily. Some longer-than-average trips may also be more price sensitive, since locations can

125

be substituted – for example, a local shopping centre for a regional one. We would expect off-peak travel to be more price sensitive, owing to the greater chance to vary trip frequency and location for the type of trip generally observed at such times. Long-run price elasticities would be expected to be higher than short-run, as more opportunities for substitution occur.

Evidence available largely supports such thinking. For urban bus travel an overall average elasticity of –0.30 to –0.40 (changes in trips related to change in average revenue per trip) has been found remarkably robust, both in Britain and other countries (Goodwin 1992). This is greater for trips of about 1.5km or less where walking is easily substituted (around –0.7), and for bus trips over about 10km. Elasticities are generally higher in small towns – associated with lower average trip lengths, a high proportion of non-work trips, and lesser constraints on car use. Effects are illustrated in case studies on the Morpeth town service, and on the Morpeth–Newcastle route, in the mid-1970s (Heels & White 1977). Passengers with a car available also display higher elasticities (Transport and Road Research Laboratory 1980). Given the relatively large values found for very short trips, it is ironic that many bus operators in Britain adopt complex graduated fare scales, but nonetheless impose a very high fares per kilometre for the shortest trips, thus still deterring such trips much as a flat fare might do.

In the long run, opportunities for substitution might increase, and as a rough guide elasticities may be assumed to be about 50% greater than in the short run, i.e. the overall urban bus average rising to about –0.55 (Goodwin 1992).

Urban rail services display a somewhat different pattern. The work trip to the conurbation centre displays a low elasticity, probably around –0.15 to –0.20, since few alternatives may be available in the short run. However, a much higher long-run elasticity may be found. The introduction of commuter coaches may also increase the short-run elasticity, especially where the rail service is of relatively poor quality, and coach thus forms a more acceptable substitute.

Off-peak journeys on urban rail networks may be highly price sensitive, even in the short run, since many of them are for trips which can be relocated elsewhere (shopping in the conurbation centre, or in the suburbs), or generated by low fares (city-centre entertainment). Elasticities close to –1.0 (i.e. that at which total revenue is maintained when fares fall) may be observed. A very strong case may thus be made for offering cheap off-peak return fares, and perhaps even lower-priced evening returns, on urban rail services.

Furthermore, if full account is taken of long-run interaction between transport costs, network structure and land use – including both home and work location decisions – an "equilibrium" pattern may be determined, in which greater effects of fare changes are evident than in the short run. Mackett (1985) indicates values of around –1.0 or greater for commuting from Hertfordshire to London. Models taking account of such interaction over entire urban areas likewise indicate higher values than those derived in the short to medium-run by observing trends in one mode alone.

One can thus see a danger that, in the short-run, the relatively inelastic nature of urban public transport demand encourages operators to raise fares as a means of increasing revenue, but in the long term such revenue gains are much smaller, and for rail commuting, might even be negative.

In the long-distance market, even short-run elasticities are much greater – in the order of –1.0 (examples are given in Ch. 9).

Combined with knowledge of cost structures, a clear case can thus be made within urban networks for lower fares during the inter-peak period, with higher fares at peaks. The evening period is less certain, since although costings suggest that a higher fare is needed to break even, this could also be a very price-sensitive market, at any rate for those trips originating from the home during this period (a considerable proportion of evening trips, especially in large cities, represents homeward journeys by those who have gone in to work or shop earlier in the day, as discussed in Ch. 2).

Some operators have shifted from a standard fare scale applying over the whole day to one differentiating by time period. For example West Yorkshire PTE introduced a low maximum off-peak fare in 1981, which proved very successful in stimulating traffic. A much higher elasticity than normally expected was found, around –0.85 (Grimshaw 1982). Although PTEs no longer have power to set fare scales since local bus deregulation in 1986, most operators in West Yorkshire have followed this structure subsequently. Evidence from price competition in Southend during 1992 also indicates a high sensitivity to the off-peak "Summer Fares Bonanza" introduced by Thamesway (a Badgerline subsidiary, in competition with the municipal operator), enabling total revenue to remain approximately constant (Office of Fair Trading 1993). In both cases, simplification at off-peak times may have increased the impact.

Note also that the concessionary fares for elderly and disabled, whose range was increased rapidly in the early 1970s (see Ch. 1) often act, in effect, as an off-peak fare, being confined to such periods. Their holders may account for 20% or more of all trips on urban bus networks, and up to 50% of the trips made at certain off-peak periods. Since the operators regard the compensation payments on their behalf as "revenue", this income is attributed to the off-peak, contributing to the apparent cross-subsidy from the interpeak to other times of day. In practice, the fare perceived by the passenger – such as a half fare – may thus be a pretty close reflection of the actual average cost at such times.

Conversely, many peak bus users are school-children who may be carried at half fare, or a low flat fare. Thus, revenue per passenger in the peak may be considerably lower than over the day as a whole. The cross-subsidy to the peak may be considerably greater than estimated from studies using a simple overall average revenue per trip, or the peak work journeys, at full adult fares, may cross-subsidize school trips during the same period.

127

The form of the demand curve, and its implications

The discussion on elasticities so far has been based on the form of demand curve generally applied by economists, as shown in Figure 7.4. A smoothly sloping concave curve is shown, with the price (in this case, fare per passenger trip) on the vertical axis, and volume (number of passenger trips) on the horizontal. The slope of the curve will depend on the elasticity value, being steeper as elasticity falls. That in Figure 7.4 represents a fairly high elasticity, as might be found for off-peak travel, or long-distance users. At an existing price (P_1) a given volume of traffic will be found (V_1). However, some additional users could be attracted at a lower price (P_3), and if it were possible to discriminate so as to offer them this without loss of revenue from existing users, additional revenue could be attracted (the darker shaded area). Likewise, some of the existing users could still be retained at a higher price (P_2), owing to the consumer surplus they enjoy, and if it were possible to do so, additional revenue corresponding to the lighter shaded area could be obtained.

In practice, such clear discrimination is not possible, and a mixture of effects is likely, e.g. the higher price aimed at existing users willing to pay it would also hit some more price-sensitive users within the short distance urban market. It is generally impracticable to aim for discrimination of this sort with present pricing

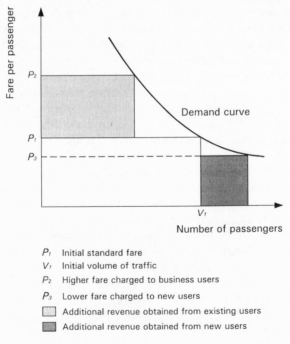

P_1	Initial standard fare
V_1	Initial volume of traffic
P_2	Higher fare charged to business users
P_3	Lower fare charged to new users
	Additional revenue obtained from existing users
	Additional revenue obtained from new users

Figure 7.4   A demand curve, and scope for price discrimination.

systems, although some shift to peak/off-peak differential pricing may achieve part of the same effect, while mainly intended to reflect costs. Those travelling in the off-peak may be assumed to be more price-sensitive, and thus extra trips be stimulated from lower fares. Within the less price-sensitive peak there is often a need to raise fares in any case, simply to reflect costs, let alone discriminate by extracting a higher surplus of revenue over costs from such passengers. Scope for discriminatory pricing is generally much greater in the intercity sector, as outlined in Chapter 9.

Although a single elasticity value may be assumed at the existing price/volume level, this is likely to vary as prices change. One would expect elasticity to increase as price rose, since users would be more likely to seek substitutes for a product of given quality, and may experience budget constraints. Price would also rise as a proportion of generalized costs (for a given value of time). Likewise, if price fell, elasticity would be expected to fall. One simple assumption is that elasticity is proportional to price: thus, if the price rose by 50% elasticity would increase by half. This is probably a rather extreme assumption, and for most price changes a constant elasticity may be assumed as a fair approximation, although the principle of elasticity varying with price remains valid. It should also be borne in mind that elasticities used in existing models are themselves derived from a range of past experience, and may only be valid within that range.

One may question, however, whether the traditional form of the demand curve is necessarily correct, or the most appropriate in all circumstances. As with much micro-economic theory, it assumes that consumer behaviour takes the form of many small incremental changes. Is this so, especially when modal choice is concerned? An alternative formulation is shown in Figure 7.5. Here, conventional scientific notation is followed, rather than that of economists. Thus, the causal (x) factor, price, is shown on the horizontal axis, the dependent (y) factor, quantity, on the vertical. Quantity is in turn represented as a probability of choosing between two options – for example, between rail (1) or car (0) – an approach analogous to that adopted in disaggregate mode choice modelling.

An individual, faced with the choice between two modes, will experience a critical threshold point at which the perceived advantages of the mode now used will be offset by a price increase, and a shift to the other mode take place. Thus a rail user with car available might shift back to car, despite problems of congestion and parking, at a certain price increase. The "demand curve" for an individual would thus be represented by a discontinuity, from a probability of 1 to that of 0. In aggregate form, it is likely that this value would vary between individuals. If, for example, it were normally distributed, then an aggregate curve of the form in Figure 7.5 would result, the point of inflection being at the average threshold value for the group.

This logic leads clearly to the S-shaped curve in Figure 7.5, in which elasticity is low at either extreme, but very high in the centre, in contrast to the constant, or gradually changing, value generally assumed.

Another feature of the traditional demand curve is that it is held (if only

129

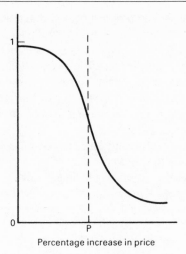

Figure 7.5 An S-shaped demand
curve, around a threshold value (*P*).

implicitly) to represent demand levels among one group of users at one point in
time, yet in practice aggregate elasticity values have been derived from observa-
tions over time. Given the high turnover in the market (Ch. 2), we are not
observing behaviour of the same individuals.

This analysis is most appropriate for those demands where an "all-or-noth-
ing" change is likely, such as a shift in modal choice for the journey to work, or
between different forms of public transport pricing, such as single cash fares and
travelcard, described further below. For the cash-paid off-peak journey, given
the quality of data available, there may be little difference in practice between
the S-shaped and traditional demand curves, the latter continuing to be a valid
approximation.

What product are we selling?

The structure of this chapter has so far, largely followed the conventional
assumptions made by transport economists. The supply of services is analyzed
in terms of output by route, and/or time of day, and the demand in the form of
individual passenger trips. However, the passenger is concerned with getting
from one activity to another, not with rides in vehicles. At the very least, we
should consider the linked trip as the basis for analysis and pricing structures.
Furthermore, relatively few users are making only an occasional one-way trip
(taxi journeys are perhaps the main example of this): most normally make a
return journey, based on the home. Even if return tickets are not sold, this should
surely be the base for analysis.

Thus in considering cross-subsidy, comparison between different groups of users is certainly valid (off-peak shoppers and peak-only workers or schoolchildren, for example), but does it really make much sense to consider how far a worker on "flexitime" travelling to work late morning and returning mid-evening is "cross-subsidizing" one leg of his or her return journey from the other? In some cases, more complex trip chains (as defined in Ch. 2) may be the product purchased: for example, the ability to go from home to work, make some journeys within the city centre during the day, and a return home evening journey. On public transport systems, these are generally found in the larger cities, such as London.

Looking at private transport modes, the "product" being purchased may be defined even more widely. Leaving aside an intrinsic benefit from purchase of a particular type of car, we see that the user is purchasing the use of a transport system (car, and road network), largely through a few large transactions (car purchase, annual maintenance check, insurance and tax disc), while costs varying with use (fuel, parking charges) account for a small proportion of the total. There is evidence for petrol price elasticities affecting car use, analogous to those for local bus travel: around –0.16 in the short run, and –0.33 in the long run (Goodwin 1992). However, for local travel in the very short run, individual trips may be perceived as having a zero money cost. Although various policy options exist to make more costs proportional to use, and place taxation of benefits on a similar footing, the greater part of car user costs is still likely to be invariant with distance in future.

Traditional selling of public transport, especially bus, has been based on a transaction for each single trip, heightening the perception of costs vis-a-vis another mode and also operationally cumbersome, especially on one-person-operated buses.

Some exceptions to this have applied for many years. The station-to-station rail season ticket provides a convenient form of prepayment, and gives unlimited travel between points specified during a defined period (week, quarter, etc.). On buses, some operators have offered multi-ride tickets, i.e. tickets prepaid for a given number of journeys, of fixed value, and cancelled on each trip. These reduce the number of transactions, and change perception of cost. There are few examples in Britain, the principal one being the "Clippercard" of Greater Manchester PTE (for flat fare concessionary travel). However, such tickets have been widely used elsewhere in Europe for many years and form the basis of a nationwide system in the Netherlands (the "Strippenkaart").

The travelcard concept

Overall development

The most important development has been the "travelcard", used here as a generic name (and also as the trading name "Travelcard", in London and the West Midlands): a season ticket or pass which permits unlimited use of a network, or zones thereof, usually for all public transport modes, during a defined period. The user is normally identified by a photocard, with a renewable portion indicating zones and period of validity. Such cards have been in use in German cities for many years, and in Edinburgh (Lothian Region) since the 1950s. However, their major growth began with the Stockholm monthly card introduced in 1970, followed by most other large cities in Europe, including West Midlands in 1972, Paris in 1975 and, rather late in the day, London in 1983.

The initial effect of such a card may be seen as giving a "discount" (i.e. a lower average cost per trip) to existing travellers, especially those who make many and – where graduated fare systems apply – longer journeys. At the same time, new users may be attracted, especially from car, by the lower cost and convenience of the travelcard, and existing users are encouraged to make more trips, especially in the off-peak.

In common with traditional rail seasons, the travelcard has been criticized for the "discount" given, which might be seen as inequitable and not reflecting the higher marginal costs of peak capacity. It is important to distinguish the question of a "discount" given to frequent travellers through prepayment, and that given to peak travel as such. A travelcard price may be set so as to attract users now paying in cash – with benefits for the operator (in speeding boarding times, reducing operating costs, and cash flow), and the user's own convenience. At the same time its price can be differentiated so as to reflect peak costs (for example, a separate off-peak travelcard at lower price might be offered, as in London, or cheap multi-ride tickets to off-peak users). Indeed, to regard any fare other than the full single cash rate as being offered at a "discount" becomes unrealistic when, as in many European cities, the great majority of travellers are on some form of prepaid ticket, and the cash fare is in effect a penalty price (hence my preference for the term "average revenue" rather than "average fare", since the latter carries connotations of the cash single fare being the norm).

More important are the long-run, versus short-run, effects of the travelcard. Following an introductory phase at a low price, to gain market penetration, with operating benefits (but revenue loss), the price may be later increased (while maintaining a differential with cash fares), taking advantage of the threshold price effect depicted in Figure 7.5. Within a certain range (probably around 10% on any one increase), relatively little traffic loss may be experienced, as the price change occurs along the relatively "flat" part of the curve. Provided that the price increase is not around or above the threshold level, much of the traffic generated in the initial, phase may be retained, with increased revenue.

There is also evidence of an underlying growth in the travelcard market over time, as the convenience of use becomes more widely appreciated This can be seen in the Lothian Regional Transport case, where market penetration of the travelcard grew steadily during a period in which the relative price vis-a-vis cash fares was unchanged (White 1984).

These effects have been analyzed with respect to the West Midlands and London, documented in more detail elsewhere (White 1984, London Transport 1993). In the West Midlands, Travelcard use grew rapidly from its introduction in 1972. After an initial price freeze, both real and money fares rose from 1975. Using a time-series demand model of the type discussed in Chapter 2, it can be shown that, for the same net revenue target, about 7 to 10% more passengers were retained than might have been the case had cash-only fares applied. A cost-benefit analysis, including operating benefits (such as faster boarding times), and the cost of additional retained peak period capacity, also showed a net benefit. In 1984–85, the Travelcard accounted for 31% of all unlinked passenger trips, and the concessionary pass for free travel 24%, leaving only 45% paying cash on bus. Similar proportions were found in Tyne & Wear.

The London Travelcard experience

The sequence of events in London was somewhat more complex. A traditional pattern of cash-based graduated bus fares applied until 1981, apart from the introduction of a bus pass (a bus-only travelcard) in 1974. On the Underground, a form of graduated fare was adopted for station-to-station singles, with route-specific season tickets also offered. In Spring 1981 a flat fare was introduced for suburban bus routes, following successful results from earlier experiments. This was soon followed by the then Greater London Council's "Fares Fair" policy, in which bus and underground fares were reduced by about 25% in money terms in October 1981. A zonal structure, based on concentric zones around the central area, was also introduced, although bus and rail pricing remained separate. Following a challenge to the legality of the "Fares Fair" policy, a House of Lords appeal decision resulted in a 100% cash fares increase in March 1982. However, the zonal structure was retained.

Following clarification of the legal position, a fares reduction was introduced in May 1983 (19% on buses, 28% on the underground), together with the LT bus/underground Travelcard, which effectively superseded most rail season tickets and much bus pass use (although a separate bus pass remained on sale). Growth in sales, and also in total travel on the system, was very rapid. Between December 1982 and December 1984, passenger-kilometres on the underground rose by 44%. This growth continued to a peak in 1988–89, in which year underground passenger-kilometres were 72% above the 1982 level, and bus passenger-kilometres some 13% higher. Car commuting into the central area fell. The growth in both bus and underground usage was much larger than would be expected through a simple application of traditional price elasticities. Work by London Transport (1993) indicates that specific effects attributable to the Travel-cards as such (i.e. quite apart from its impact in reducing average cost per trip made) may be identified:

Table 7.1   Impact of the London Travelcard.

	Underground	Bus
Growth in passenger-km	33%	20%
Growth in real revenue	16%	4%

Note that revenue also rose, albeit less rapidly than volume. In 1992/3 total bus revenue in London was 1% higher than in 1985/6, compared with a drop of 14% for the rest of Britain (despite the sharp fare rises in some metropolitan areas). This contrasts with the impact of "across the board" fare reductions on traditional cash-based systems as a means of stimulating public transport use (such as the policy followed in South Yorkshire between 1976 and 1986). Apply-ing a standard –0.3 elasticity, a 10% real fares reduction would indeed stimulate bus use by about 3%, but at a revenue loss of about 7%.

The most recent LT analysis (1993) also indicates differences between "own mode" and "conditional" fares elasticities, i.e. if the price of one public trans-port mode was raised while that of another remained constant, a significant switch of trips between the public transport modes would occur, as well as a net overall reduction in travel (the "own mode" effect). If, however, prices were raised simultaneously (the "conditional" elasticity) the effect would be limited to the net reduction in public transport use as whole. In the London case (in which a substantial proportion of public transport users would have a choice of modes), the "own mode" elasticity for buses is estimated at –0.62, but the "conditional" elasticity at –0.35 (corresponding figures for the underground are –0.43 and –0.17 respectively). In other cities, such effects may be harder to distinguish, due to the much more limited rail networks.

The convenience of a travelcard is particularly noticeable in a large city, in which many more opportunities are opened up by removing financial penalties of interchange. One large benefit, which cannot be quantified easily without good O&D data, is the extent to which the same trip can be made more quickly, by optimal choice of route, and reduced waiting time. One estimate by Shon (1989) evaluated such opportunities for a corridor in north east London, equiv-alent to about 10p per trip.

Elsewhere in Britain, travelcard market penetration prior to deregulation tended to be somewhat lower, especially in many smaller towns, where much less interchange occurs, and the card had not been promoted through an initial period of low price to gain market penetration.

Is there a case for premium pricing?

Most urban public transport provision is priced according to distance, time, ticket type and user type, rather than directly reflecting service quality. In the long-distance sector, wide variations exist (first and standard class, for example), but they are largely unknown in the urban sector, except for the significant rôle played by taxis, which represents a much larger share of user expenditure than of trips made (see Ch. 2).

In many developing countries, for example, "paratransit" services often operate at premium fares 100% or more above standard rates. However, where there is little overcrowding, as in Britain, the evidence to support such price differentiation is very weak. Splitting the urban market by class of service requires accommodation to be provided in separate vehicles, hence effectively lowering the frequency of service to each user group (the past operation of first-class coaches on the Paris Metro being the only significant exception). Since waiting time is important, particularly to those with high values of time, the effect could easily be self-defeating.

It is sometimes suggested that a higher frequency of service could be justified at higher fares. Users with high values of time, in particular, might be willing to pay for the reduced waiting time thus incurred. However, the overall elasticity of demand with respect to service level (vehicle-kilometres) very rarely exceeds +0.4 (as in more successful minibus conversions, for example), and is often much lower. It is thus of the same magnitude as that for fares. Hence, if a conversion to a higher-frequency service, with a pro rata increase in costs, generated extra demand, an attempt to "price up" to reflect quality would simply be self-defeating.

For example, if a doubling of frequency (100% bus-kilometre increase) took place on a +0.4 elasticity, demand would rise by 40%, but costs by 100%. If a premium fare of 100% was introduced on a –0.4 elasticity, demand would fall by 40%, although revenue would rise by about 60%. In other words, demand would simply return to its initial level, and load factors would halve, as twice as many vehicle-kilometres were operated to serve it. In reality, the position would be worse still, as a further fare increase would be needed to cover the increase in total costs, lowering demand below the initial level.

In practice, almost all minibus conversion in Britain has been based on the same fare levels as initially charged for full-size vehicles, the economic case resting on lower unit cost per vehicle-km of minibus services (for example, if minibus unit costs were 70% of those of full-size buses, a doubling of frequency would only entail an increase in total costs of 40%. This would match the revenue growth resulting from a 40% passenger increase, at the same fare level as charged before). However, it would be true to say that some of the most extensive minibus service conversion has occurred in parts of Britain which were charging fairly high real fares for low-frequency full-size bus services (parts of the South West and South Wales, for example), and hence the minibus's higher

135

frequency could be seen as giving better value in relation to fares already imposed.

Premium fares do apply to urban light rail schemes funded under section 56 criteria, in which such fares are charged to reflect the improvement in service quality (as seen on the Manchester Metrolink, for example). Here, quality is reflected more in the overall image and speed of the service than frequency per se (the Metrolink being less frequent than parallel bus services). However, the imposition of a premium fare makes it difficult to offer a reasonably priced bus/ rail through travelcard, and hence to maximize use of the public transport network as a whole.

An area for possible premium pricing yet to be fully explored is that of taxibus and shared taxi operations. Although legalized under the Transport Act 1985 they have had very little impact to date, yet could offer attractive services to fill a "niche" market (for example, direct late evening services), at prices between those of conventional public transport and single-hirer taxis.

Fare collection methods

Approximate revenues per trip by mode are as follows:

local bus journeys	40–50 pence
London Underground	70–80 pence
taxi	£2
National Express coach	£10
InterCity Rail	£15
British Airways (whole network)	£160

In the intercity sector, a complex price structure is justified in terms of relatively large price elasticities (around −1.0), and the wide range of ticket types and service quality offered. This is often associated with pre-booking of capacity, notably through pricing policies such as "Apex" fares. Increasingly sophisticated "yield management" systems, pioneered by airlines, are now being applied to rail also.

For urban public transport use, the very low revenue per trip makes the present typical means of collecting revenue – cash transactions on the vehicle – very cumbersome. It incurs direct operational costs (through slowing down a service, the majority of whose costs are time-based), and worsens service quality by extending boarding times, affecting both average speed and its variation (not only those paying in cash, but also those paying by other means are affected by such delays, both in extending in-vehicle travel time, and increasing waiting time at stops through more erratic running).

The user also requires information about the service (exact timetable, and/or frequency; likely in-vehicle time) in order to judge the door-to-door duration of a journey. Uncertainty may be increased by the need for information on timing and feasibility of connecting and/or return journeys, and need for fares information in order to produce the exact fare, or avoid penalties for over-riding.

In contrast, the uncertainty faced by a user of alternative modes for short-distance urban trips is much less. For the shorter trips (up to about 2 km) walking and cycling are alternatives. Here, the user is involved in no cash transaction specific to the trip, and has no need to consult a timetable. If the alternative is the car, then again cash transactions are generally avoided (except where parking must be paid for), and no timetable information is needed, although some uncertainty about travel times under congested conditions may apply. The recent Chartered Institute of Transport working party report on the bus industry (1993), in reviewing market research evidence, notes that "Finding accurate information can be time-consuming and deters the casual user. People who have to use buses will persevere, others will not . . . . Attention was drawn to difficulty in paying for fares if passengers were expected to have the right change".

It could be argued that road pricing, if introduced, will impose a need for car users to incur a transaction for each trip made. However, any money transactions will be made electronically at regular intervals, rather than physically handled for each trip.

If we can reduce the information needs of the bus user, we can thus reduce the uncertainty about use of this mode. Real-time information systems and electronic ticketing technology can then be used to provide assistance and reassurance, rather than adding complexity to the process. This can be achieved by reducing the need for timetable information (through high frequency, and reliability), together with the need for cash transactions and fare information (by using simple off-bus systems).

From the user's point of view, possession of a travelcard also reduces the need for information. Provided that zones and any other validity conditions are clearly understood, their use does not require information on specific fares for the journey being made, or to handle cash.

However, the travelcard in its present form may be criticized in that checking for validity is often rudimentary, and management information is reduced. In principle, each occasion on which a travelcard or pass holder boards a bus may be recorded by the driver pressing a button on an electronic ticket machine (ETM), such as the "Wayfarer". These data are then recorded on a data module along with that for cash-paid fares, so that the number of pass holders boarding in each fare stage for each bus journey is recorded. In comparison with the data collected on cash-paid journeys no information on trip length is recorded, whereas for a cash-paid fare the maximum number of stages paid for is known. One might add, however, that in practice bus management rarely seems to use ETM data for detailed analysis, and the quality is often variable.

Nonetheless, errors may occur in checking the validity of a travelcard or pass as a passenger is boarding, especially at peak times. Drivers may fail to record manually such boardings on their machines. The need for all pass holders to show their pass to the driver on boarding offsets some of the savings in boarding time that might otherwise be found if multiple entrances could be used, as common elsewhere in Europe (although on safety grounds, a single entry adjacent to the driver is to be preferred).

Some form of automation for the validation stage of travelcard use may thus be of assistance. Recent developments in contactless smart cards no longer require the user to pass the card through a device. Hence validity (by zone, card type, renewal date etc.) may be checked automatically, and a record of boardings obtained. Unit costs of producing such cards are now acceptably low. The fundamental marketing concept of the travelcard is unchanged.

It has been argued that we should go one step further, to a smart card (or magnetic card) system in which the cost for each trip could be deducted for each occasion it is used, through re-encoding. Typically, a discount may be offered for such use vis a vis cash fares (e.g. £5.50 worth of travel for £5 card) – assuming that "discount" is a meaningful term (see above). Travelcard holders making a much greater number of trips than the average might be asked to pay more. A further benefit may be that occasional users for whom travelcard is not worthwhile could be encouraged to switch to cashless payment through such a system.

A further factor encouraging such development is the apparent need to attribute trips and revenue collected in much greater detail than before, under deregulated systems, in which precise allocation of revenue between routes and operators becomes much more important from the viewpoint of separately owned and financed undertakings (although it is not a matter of interest to the passenger).

Where a flat fare is deducted for each trip (e.g. for some types of concessionary fare in Britain), this adds little complexity or delay. However, incorporating fares graduated by journey length continues to cause difficulties. Technology is available (from Scanpoint, for example), which permits an inspector to check validity of a stored value card in terms of the journey length for which a deduction has been made on boarding the bus. In some cases, a paper ticket may be issued (as on the Milton Keynes network), corresponding to the value of the smartcard deduction made. However, at this point the basic benefits of off-bus systems – reducing boarding time – are being negated.

At this point it may be helpful to distinguish between "journeys" and "transactions". The former are the trips made by users (defined either as single bus rides, or linked trips to the ultimate destination), the latter the handling of money. Under traditional cash-based systems these are the same. With Travelcards, the transaction is recorded at the point of sale (such as a local shop): clearly, good records of this are needed to combat fraud. The journey is then recorded separately, perhaps through the driver actuating an ETM (see above), or through on-bus surveys estimating the overall volume of car or pass use.

The latter do not produce the apparent precision of ticket machine data, but may enable estimates of total use to be made within a high degree of accuracy (for example, plus/minus 1% at the 95% confidence interval). Such surveys may also enable data to be collected on exact origins and destinations of trips, trip purpose, etc. To what extent is it worthwhile installing a more sophisticated system in order to increase this degree of accuracy, in terms of the overall economic benefit obtained, especially from the user's point of view? In particular, where automatic validation is applied, then a record of the number of boardings is obtained. Sample surveys could then be used to determine average trip length and its distribution, without imposing more complex fare and ticketing systems on the passenger as such.

These issues currently arise in London, where a system of "net cost contract agreements" is favoured by central government, in place of the "gross cost contracts" under which most tendering took place until 1993. While in theory, the net system gives incentives to operators, the much greater complexity incurred in terms of revenue allocation causes substantial administrative costs.

The development of the "contactless" smart card offers a convenient technology for quickly validating a travelcard and, where required, re-encoding a stored value variant. These cards can now be produced for £5 or less each, with a life of about five years or more (or over 10,000 read/encode operations). The smart card experiment launched in the Harrow area in February 1994 on local bus services by London Transport provides a large-scale test of this technology. Validation of Travelcard, bus pass and concessionary pass use can be speeded-up and recorded with greater accuracy, enabling the corresponding revenue to be attributed under net cost contracts. The technology can also be used for operation of stored value pricing, and this may also be developed by LT as part of the Harrow experiment.

Experience since local bus deregulation

Deregulation of local bus services in 1986 was effectively preceded by removal of much of the fares control traditionally enforced by the Traffic Commissioners, following the Transport Act of 1980. However, price competition has been limited in practice. Apart from occasional "fare wars", most competitive action has taken the form of variations in service level. Outside London, fares have generally risen marginally in real terms (excluding some metropolitan areas where they rose from a very low level after abolition of the metropolitan councils in April 1986). Most operators have also tended to retain a traditional graduated fare scale applied over the whole network, although more opportunity now exists to vary fares by time of day, and between routes according to traffic density, etc.

The explanation lies largely in the elasticities of demand already mentioned. Given the fairly small price elasticities for bus use (–0.3 to –0.4), a fare reduction by a single operator would cause considerable revenue loss, unless very substantial transfers from other operators took place. Insofar as users typically board the first bus to arrive, only those with a low value of time would find it worthwhile waiting for a "low fare" vehicle. For example, if existing operators

139

charge 50p per trip, and the users' value of waiting time is 4p per minute, then a large differential would be needed. If a new operator charged 35p per trip, then it would not be worth waiting more than 4 minutes for the lower fare buses. Given that timetable information is often poor, quiet apart from variations in service reliability, most users will tend to board the first bus to arrive, even with this price differential of 30%. Hence, the logical strategy for a new operator in most cases is to charge the existing fares: this is discussed further in Chapter 10. The rôle of travelcards outside London has tended to diminish. In some cases, these became the preserve of a single operator (since competition policy condones this practice, but requires inter-operator travelcard price agreements to be submitted for approval). Where competition has developed, operators have sometimes offered their own travelcards, but these carry the disadvantage that users cannot board the first bus to arrive. Hence, a shift back to cash fares may be seen. For example, a low proportion of off-bus ticketing is now reported in Oxford (about 10%), following development of competing networks by two operators.Although each offers a travelcard, users prefer to board the first bus to arrive, and hence pay in cash in order to retain this freedom. While reducing waiting time, this has the unfortunate effect of increasing boarding times on the buses themselves, thus contributing to lower average speeds and greater variability.

References and suggested further reading

Chartered Institute of Transport 1993. *Bus routes to success* (report of a bus working party). London: CIT.

Higginson, M. P. & P. R. White 1982. *The efficiency of British urban bus operations*. (Ch. 7). Research Report 8, Transport Studies Group, Polytechnic of Central London.

Goodwin, P. B. 1992. A review of new demand elasticities with special reference to short and long run effects of price changes'. *Journal of Transport Economics and Policy* **XXVI**(2), 155–69. (Fuller details of the examples discussed may be found in *An annotated bibliography of demand elasticities*, P. B. Goodwin, T. H. Oum, W. G. Waters, J. S. Yong: Report 682, Transport Studies Unit, University of Oxford, July 1992).

Grimshaw, R. F. 1982. *The effect of maximum off-peak fares on bus patronage and revenue*. Development Report D19, West Yorkshire Passenger Transport Executive, Leeds.

Heels, P. & White, P. R. 1977. *Fare elasticities on interurban and rural bus services*. Research Report 4, Transport Studies Group, Polytechnic of Central London.

London Transport 1991. Fares Policy Statement. December.

London Transport Planning Department 1993. *London Transport traffic trends 1971–90*. Research Report R273, London Transport, London.

Mackett, R. L. 1985. Modelling the impact of rail fares increases. *Transportation* **12**(4), 293–312.

National Bus Company 1977. Data from the Hereford Market Analysis Project, as quoted in *Innovations in rural bus services* (Eighth Report from the Select Committee on Nationalized Industries, Session 1977/78).

National Bus Company/Institute for Transport Studies 1984. *Cross-subsidy in urban bus operations*. Institute of Transport Studies, University of Leeds.

Office of Fair Trading 1993. *Thamesway Limited: the operation of local bus services commencing in, terminating in or passing through Southend-on-Sea (an investigation under section 3 of the Competition Act 1980)*. London, August.

Robbins D. K. & P. R. White 1985. Combining scheduled commuter services with private hire, sightseeing and tour work: the London experience. In *Proceedings of the 26th Annual Meeting of the Transportation Research Forum*, Jacksonville, Florida, 273–81. November. Arlington, Virginia: Transportation Research Forum.

Shon, E. 1989. *Evaluation of public transport fare integration in London*. PhD thesis, Institute for Transport Studies, University of Leeds.

Transport and Road Research Laboratory 1980. *The demand for public transport: results of an international collaborative study*. Crowthorne, Berks: TRRL.

White, P. R. 1981. Travelcard tickets in urban public transport. *Journal of Transport Economics and Policy* **XV**(1), 17–34.

— 1984. User response to price changes: application of the "threshold" concept. *Transport Reviews* **4**(4), 367–86.

CHAPTER 8
Rural public transport

Defining "rural"

The term "rural transport" appears to conjure up immediately an image based on remote rural areas of very low-density population, such as the Scottish Highlands or central Wales, in which low frequencies of service are found, "unconventional" approaches such as the post-bus are widely used, and high levels of financial support required. While such areas may characterize the extreme case, they are highly untypical. Concentration on such conditions as "rural", and likewise those of the very large cities as "urban", leads to a large and growing proportion of the population being ignored.

The 1991 Census shows that the population of England and Wales was then 51 million. Of this, Greater London accounted for 6.8 million (13%), the metropolitan areas 11.1 million (22%) and the "shire" (non-metropolitan) counties 33.0 million (65%). The 1991 national total was 3% above that for 1981, being static in Greater London, but falling by 2% in the mets. The shires increased by 5% during the decade, with increases of up to 8% in "resort, port and retirement", and also in "remoter, mainly rural" areas (OPCS 1992). Some of the growth is, in effect, the suburban fringe of larger centres, but other growth is in free-standing settlements, as patterns of employment and population structure are changing.

Only the most remote rural areas continue to lose population in absolute terms, although the traditional rural occupations such as those based on agriculture, continue to decline in numbers employed. In many regions, new residents have been attracted – either urban commuters, or those retiring to such areas. While this movement is mainly based on high car availability, it also has implications for public transport use. The "traditional" rural population, characterized by lower income and car ownership, may be displaced to towns. At the same time, those retiring to rural areas may subsequently become more dependent as their age makes car driving difficult. Working-age newcomers may make little use of rural public transport themselves, but may depend upon school buses to transport their children.

For purposes of analysing rural transport use in this chapter, the definition of "rural" employed by the Office of Population Census and Surveys (OPCS) will be used, – all those resident in areas with a population outside those defined as "urban" (i.e. a continuously built-up area with a population above a certain value). Following this reasoning, the National Travel Survey 1989/91 regards all settlements of below 3,000 population as "rural". On this basis, about 11% of the population can be classified as "rural".

Somewhat broader definitions have been adopted by other bodies, which are often more appropriate when defining patterns of public transport services, For example, the definition adopted for the Rural Transport Development Fund (RTDF) under the Transport Act 1985 by the Rural Development Commission for funding innovations is that of areas containing population centres of less than 10,000. Thus, many small towns and some lower-density parts of metropolitan areas are included. This is a realistic reflection of current network structures, in which village-to-town and town-to-town movements are often served by the same routes. Services within small towns are often very limited, and facilities may be provided largely by longer routes picking up local traffic. Even in larger towns, rural and urban services are often inter-mixed, being provided by the same operator and forming part of the same cost centre. For purposes of the transitional grant to rural services paid in the same manner as fuel tax rebate under the 1985 Act, a wider definition based on 25,000 population was used, further acknowledging these relationships.

More broadly, the activities within public transport of county councils outside the metropolitan areas, and Scottish regions beyond the main cities they contain, have often been equated with "rural transport". In this case, some larger settlements clearly are involved, but prior to the 1985 Act much of the emphasis in revenue support by such counties, and the planning framework introduced under the Transport Act 1978, was with the rural areas, urban routes in larger centres often being expected to break even or, where a district council bus operator existed, to be mainly the responsibility of that district.

The great majority of scheduled public transport in "rural" areas as defined above continues to be provided by so-called "conventional" bus services, using full-size vehicles. In addition, similar vehicles employed on school contract services play a major rôle. The "unconventional" modes such as community minibuses, car lift-giving or post-buses still account for a very small share of the total rural public transport market, but as described below, may be very important in certain localized areas, or for particular functions, such as hospital visiting. Also important within rural regions are some limited-stop and cross-country bus and coach services, linking smaller towns with large cities, and those rail services which did not close during the "Beeching" era of the 1960s and early 1970s. Often, traffic has been retained or increased, sometimes assisted by new stations and rolling stock.

It should also be borne in mind that certain "unconventional" modes such as those operated under the Minibus Act 1977 (and, subsequently, the Public Passenger Vehicles Act 1981), and community transport groups like the disabled, are by no means confined to rural areas. Although treated for convenience within

143

this chapter, they also play a significant rôle even within the largest urban areas for certain specialized requirements.

Public transport's market share and composition

As indicated in Chapter 2, the proportion of all motorized trips taken by public transport in rural areas is small, as one would expect from the low density of population, low level of service and high car ownership (all inter-related).

The 1989/91 NTS indicates (on the definition shown above) that rural residents travel about 50% more kilometres per year (by all modes) than those living in urban areas, the differences being particularly marked for rural children, who travelled over 70% further than urban children. Taking all trips over 1.6km, the average length of a journey in rural areas was 17.6km, about 40% higher than the urban average. Between 1985/86 and 1989/91, the average total distance travelled by rural residents grew by 30%, compared with only 21% for urban residents.

As might be expected, very much higher car ownership levels are found in rural areas, with 37% of households having two or more cars in 1989/91, and only 19% no car (compared with 21% and 35% respectively for urban areas). An even higher proportion of total person kilometres – 87% – than the national average, was performed by car. However, due to the high absolute distance travelled by all modes, the average total distance per person travelled by public transport for rural residents is not so markedly lower than the national average, as one might expect. The high level of travel per head (by all modes) and rural car-ownership rates are clearly correlated.

In 1989/91 the average rural resident travelled 311km per year by local bus (urban 456km), 498km by rail (urban 687km), and 198km by "other public" (urban 331km). Rural residents also made some 568km by "other private" (urban 349km): since works and, more importantly, school contract buses, come under this oddly defined category, the overall effect may be to produce a fairly similar overall total distance by all public transport modes in rural and urban areas. However, the public transport use is geared much more to lower-frequency, longer trips, and to school and college travel.

Table 8.1 shows the rôles of different trip purposes within the public transport market, from selected case studies. Note that these were undertaken some years ago, and will now overstate the overall proportion of trips now carried by public transport, but nonetheless provide a useful indication of the relative importance of different trip purposes. Note that the pattern obtained may vary substantially, owing to timing and coverage of the surveys in question, especially if they are confined to scheduled public services in areas where most schoolchildren are handled on separate contract services.

The importance of education and shopping trips is clear. However, certain

Table 8.1 Percentage composition of the market served by rural bus services.

Area/date	Work	Education	Shopping	Other	Notes
Devon 1971	15	64	12	9	a
Evesham 1976	28	32	27	13	b
Stratford 1976	34	31	21	14	b
Newbury 1979	29	23	23	25	b
Cotswolds 1979–81	10	4	52	34	c
East Sussex 1983	19	6	54	21	d

Notes/sources:

a. *Study of rural transport in Devon.* Report by the Steering Group, Department of the Environment, 1971 (including school contract services).
b. Market Analysis Project surveys by the National Bus Company subsidiaries (see also Ch. 5). These cover all services for the cost centre in question, including intra-urban and inter-urban routes.
c. Surveys by Kingston University students in an area west of Cheltenham; Monday to Friday averages (most school trips were carried on separate services). See "Deregulation in the Cotswolds", J. Smith & R. Grant, pp. 1–15, Twelfth Seminar on Rural Public Transport, Polytechnic of Central London, November 1985.
d. Data for the escort service between Lewes and Peacehaven, shortly after its introduction. See *Co-ordinated public transport in East Sussex: County Rider services 823 and 825*, Research Report 7, Transport Research Laboratory, 1985 (table 4).

trips which may not be very substantial numerically may be vital to users, notably medical journeys. The ability to make these when required without access to cars is very important.

Another characteristic of the rural public transport market is the large proportion of passengers who are children, working-age women or pensioners, with very few adult males. The Cotswolds study (Table 8.1) found that, on Mondays to Fridays, 28% of passengers were aged 60 or over, and 23% under 20. Most were from lower-income households.

In contrast to the intercity market, and trips to the centre of large conurbations, there is virtually no prospect of attracting car users to rural public transport. However, many public transport users do come from car-owning households, especially for school and shopping trips.

Types of service provided

Local bus services fall into two main categories:
- Those between towns, or large villages and towns. Here, traffic densities may be sufficient to justify regular-headway services, up to hourly, and use of large vehicles. Those villages fortunate to be located on such routes enjoy a good level of service which their own population would not justify.
- Those between villages and the nearest town, which do not have any "inter-urban" function, and experience low average load factors as traffic "tails off" to the end of the route. Frequencies may range from several journeys per day down to once or twice a week.

145

The first type of service may be operated at a relatively low cost per bus mile, owing to high average speeds attained (compared with urban services), especially where main roads are followed. Loadings benefit from the mixture of village-to-town and town-to-town traffic on the same route. There is a good chance that costs can be covered from revenue: indeed, such services may have cross-subsidized others, as indicated in the Leeds University/NBC cross-subsidy study (see Ch. 7). The second type suffers from poorer loads, and often high costs owing to lower speeds on minor roads. Cross-subsidy from profitable routes, and/or direct support from local authorities, will be required.

Both types of service have suffered a general decline in traffic as car ownership has risen and unemployment increased, factors which have also reduced the ability to cross-subsidize. In general, evening and Sunday services have largely disappeared, except on the busiest routes. Daytime frequencies have also been reduced, especially on Saturdays, formerly the busiest day of the week in many areas. However, given a peak demand on Mondays to Fridays, largely for school travel (statutory provision, and, in some areas, shorter trips on public services), services at these times have continued. Often a daytime shopping service can be continued at modest cost using the drivers and vehicles needed for the peak school facility.

An illustration of a network in a low-density area, which receives little financial support, is shown in Figure 8.1, covering north-east Lincolnshire (roughly corresponding to East Lindsey District) and part of South Humberside, as in 1985: an illustration of the same network in 1969 was provided in an earlier edition (White 1986). The main towns are Grimsby (population 95,000) in the north east, and Lincoln (70,000), to the south west.Market towns at Louth (12,000), Horncastle, Market Rasen, Brigg and Spilsby (all under 4,000) act as local centres.

It can be seen that wide disparities in service provision existed. In terms of Monday-Saturday daytime services, good frequencies were offered between Grimsby and Louth (hourly), and a slightly lower level between Horncastle and Lincoln. Services about 5 times per day (corresponding to 25 or more departures a week) linked Louth with Lincoln. A Grimsby–Caistor service continued westward to Market Rasen. Most other areas were served only three days per week or less, notably that between Louth and Horncastle, and those around Alford and Brigg.

An interurban route between Grimsby, Binbrook, Market Rasen and Lincoln offered about six journeys each way. Sunday services were limited largely to the Spilsby–Horncastle–Lincoln section. "Unconventional" transport primarily comprised a post-bus circular service the area south of Louth, and the "Bus Club" service twice weekly between Louth and Horncastle, supported by subscriptions in addition to fares paid on use. Car-sharing schemes also played a significant rôle, especially in the thinly populated areas south of Louth. The major rail link was provided by the Grimsby–Market Rasen–Lincoln service (connecting at Newark for London), Louth having lost its services in 1970.

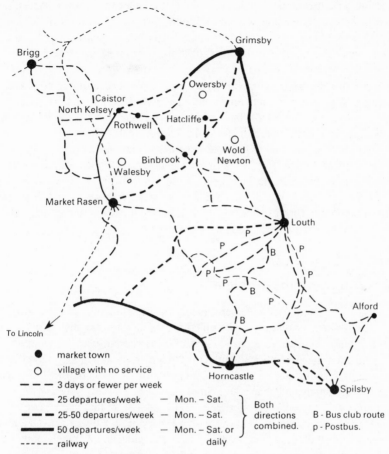

Figure 8.1 The rural bus network in northeast Lincolnshire and south Humberside in 1985.

The major services were operated by the Lincolnshire Road Car Company (now trading as "Road Car"), but most of the less frequent routes were run by locally based independents.

Following deregulation in October 1986, the overall scale of service provision has remained fairly similar, although with many changes of timetables and operators. The principal casualty was the Grimsby–Binbrook–Market Rasen–Lincoln service, withdrawn just before deregulation, and replaced by a limited service between Grimsby and Binbrook (the railway link provides a through service between the main towns). Road Car registered the Grimsby–Louth, and most of the Spilsby–Horncastle–Lincoln, and Louth–Lincoln services, commercially. A surprisingly high proportion of lower-frequency services provided by independents was also commercially registered. The "Bus Club" service was replaced by a conventional tendered service, although the post-bus remains.

147

Tendering was also used to maintain some of the other low-density routes, and the Grimsby–Louth evening service (a Sunday Grimsby–Louth service has also been reintroduced through tendering, after a gap of many years). The Road Car company was sold under the NBC privatization programme, becoming a subsidiary of another ex-NBC company, Yorkshire Traction.

To a surprising extent, competition has been experienced on the commercial services as well as for the tendered routes, notably a period of fairly intensive competition on the Grimsby–Louth route between the incumbent (Road Car), and the local municipal operator (Grimsby-Cleethorpes Transport).

Apart from the post-bus, minibuses have made very little impact. Innovative services assisted by the Rural Transport Development Fund (see also below) have been short-lived. A taxibus feeder from Louth to the railhead at Market Rasen operated for a few weeks. Somewhat longer-lived was an independently operated taxibus service to an area east of Louth (not shown on the map) which ran for about two years.

The "rural transport problem"

From the above example, the general nature of the problem is clear: a low frequency of service, providing very limited access to activities such as work, or entertainment. Even where a particular facility is served, such as shopping or education, the range of timings is limited: the length of stay in the market town for shopping may not suit all travellers, and statutory school contract buses usually give little opportunity for after-school activities.

Some would argue that the "problem" is overstated, in that many people live voluntarily in rural areas, and car ownership is very high. However, even among car-owing households, a significant demand for educational travel, and some weekday shopping trips, may exist by public transport. Essential workers in rural areas may be on low incomes.

Furthermore, if we see the problem as that of access to facilities, rather than provision of particular levels of service, it is clear that more travel is now required to gain access to the same range of facilities, as village shops and schools have closed. Smaller towns have also suffered losses, notably hospitals, making much longer journeys necessary. There is little evidence that mobile services – apart from libraries – have done much to offset these trends. They too, like local buses, have declined owing to high cost and low demand. They are more likely to serve larger villages, which in turn also tend to retain better bus services (Moseley & Packman 1983).

There is also a "problem" from the viewpoint of the bus or rail operator seeking to reduce deficits, or the degree of cross-subsidy, and the local authority seeking to reduce the costs of providing statutory school transport (although savings will generally be made from closing of small village schools even when these are taken into account).

Although support payments per trip may be fairly high, overall support levels for rural public transport are fairly limited, especially in the case of bus services. Much support to rural bus services has been on a basis of supporting the services as such, rather than users. Even before changes introduced by the 1985 Transport Act, expenditure to keep down the level of fares was considered inappropriate, and concessionary fares are more limited. Yet high fares may also limit mobility of those without access to cars, as well as low service frequencies. This is particularly evident in regions where long distances to the nearest major centre are found – for example, around Inverness (Stanley et al. 1981). Concessionary fares often take the form of tokens, or a reduced-fare pass, rather than the free off-peak travel or low flat fare found in some urban areas. Some rural districts, notably in south west England, do not give any concession to the elderly at all.

Some "solutions"

First, one should examine the scope for improving the performance of existing bus and rail services. The bus industry, in particular, has devoted little attention to marketing or product quality.

Some general changes in recent years have applied to rural services as elsewhere – improved cost-allocation techniques, and locally based management being given a greater rôle. As illustrated in Chapter 6, more accurate costing highlights the extent to which rural costs may have been previously overstated by use of overall network averages. Higher speed and better fuel consumption produce significantly lower costs per bus-km. The MAP techniques, as outlined in Chapter 5, originated in rural areas served by the Midland Red company in the mid-1970s. The re-examination of networks through the MAP surveys often indicated scope for retaining services to many villages, by using fewer routes to link them. Better use of peak vehicle requirement enabled costs to be cut – for example by greater use of double-deckers to handle the school peak while retaining a similar level of inter-peak service in many areas. However, evening and Sunday services suffered further cuts in the light of poor loads and high costs.

Although originally intended to identify "viable networks" to which local authorities could "add on" services with financial support, a more comprehensive approach was generally adopted, often retaining a considerable proportion of cross-subsidy in the re-designed networks. This was particularly true of the networks evolved through "Scotmap", in which little external support was received and a fairly good level of service retained in many areas.

The framework of the 1985 Transport Act led to something closer to the original "viable network" concept (i.e. those services that were registered commercially, with extra services specified by local authorities).

Pricing policy has received little attention in rural areas. During the mid-1970s in particular it was noticeable that steep real fare increases were often

149

applied. There is evidence that rural traffic may be somewhat more price elastic than in large urban areas, owing to the mix of trip purposes (other than school travel) and journey lengths: trips within small towns may be liable to walking and cycling substitution owing to their short length, and longer rural journeys to regional shopping centres may be reduced by less frequent travel and/or a shift to smaller centres. Pricing policy now displays more awareness of this, with cheap shopping returns now offered by many companies, especially over longer distances. The elasticity in this market segment is close to –1.0, making overall real price increases undesirable when off-peak capacity is available (Heels & White 1977).

The virtual decontrol of fares under the Transport Act 1980 was followed by greater variety in some rural areas. Operators are able to experiment easily, and standard fare scales over whole networks have become less important. However, this may have the consequence of increasing fares on low-density loss-making routes. While logical for the operator, this hits again those who already experience poor access.

Putting these changes together, one can see a continued rôle for conventional bus operation on many of the busier rural routes, and even some very low-frequency routes where services can be interworked with school or works contracts. However, few areas will have an evening or Sunday service, and some low-density areas a very limited frequency indeed. In addition, certain types of trip will not be handled very well – visits to medical facilities (especially where not centrally located), and journeys by elderly and disabled who may have difficulty using conventional buses.

A much more flexible approach to the operation of rural railways is now evident in Britain (Cordner 1989). This has included not only a willingness to adopt single-track working, and simpler signalling methods, as described in Chapter 9, but also extensive replacement of manually worked level crossings by automatic barriers, in some cases with local authority assistance, as between Skegness and Boston in Lincolnshire. Adoption of "paytrains" in the 1960s (in which the guard issues tickets as on a bus, replacing station booking offices) has been followed by general use of the "open station" concept where booking offices remain, removing manned ticket barriers. During the late 1980s, most of the earlier diesel multiple unit stock was replaced by "Sprinter" and "Pacer" units, giving savings in maintenance and fuel costs, and in the case of Sprinters, an improvement in quality. The creation of the Regional sector as part of BR's reorganization from 1982 also encouraged a positive view of such services, with specific policies for their marketing and investment being developed at national level.

Alternative solutions to the rural transport problem

Cars

The high level of car ownership and licensed drivers in rural areas means that many empty seats are available for those without access to cars – indeed, offers of lifts in such vehicles are one of the causes of decline in rural bus use. However, where public transport services are almost entirely lacking, or not available for specific activities (such as medical visits), lift giving can be organized systematically, through voluntary associations or county councils. This concept, generally known as social cars, developed on a limited scale in the late 1960s/ early 1970s in some areas, and has become more widespread as bus services have declined, and the legality of payment became generally established under the Transport Act 1978. Prior to this, the only form of payment was that from a sponsoring agency to the car driver, usually on a flat rate mileage basis, with no offsetting fare received. Provided that the service is not being offered commercially, and only the car driver's costs covered, such charging is now generally adopted, reducing the net expenditure, and removing some of the aspects of "charity" implied when a completely free service is offered.

Such schemes may be organized through organizations such as the Women's Royal Voluntary Service (WRVS) or through the county public transport co-ordinator. Local organizers are appointed, through whom bookings may be made, usually by telephone. They then seek to match volunteer drivers with trips requested. A fairly substantial pool of such volunteers is generally needed, to spread the commitment involved, and give a good chance of meeting specific requests.

In areas of very low population density, such schemes may serve most travel purposes. Elsewhere, bus services may continue to be used for many shopping trips, but the social car service acquires a more specialized rôle, such as taking patients and hospital visitors to medical centres – about two-thirds of the trips on the Shropshire scheme were for this purpose in the late 1970s. The first scheme in that county had been launched by the Bridgnorth Rural District Council in conjunction with the WRVS in 1971, initially with 50% financial support from central government under the 1968 Transport Act. Subsequently, the county took over most responsibility for financial support. Many more schemes were set up from 1977, encouraged by the county: some 6,084 passenger trips were made in 1979–80 (Fearnside 1980).

Social car schemes may also be organized through other agencies, such as area health authorities, to meet the needs of out-patients and hospital visitors. However, some of these have since been merged with general-purpose schemes administered through the county council, as in the area shown in Figure 8.1.

151

Post-buses

The comprehensive facility offered by the Post Office creates an opportunity for passenger service at low cost. Not only is mail collected 6 days per week from many points, but all addresses are served for deliveries. Post-van routes typically serve both purposes, running as loops based on market towns, where sorting centres are located. Two or three trips per day (less on Saturdays, and none on Sunday) can be provided with no additional staff or vehicles being needed, for the cost of running a minibus instead of a minivan, and marginally higher fuel and maintenance costs. The first post-buses appeared in the 1960s, but they extended rapidly during the 1970s, encouraged by availability of the New Bus Grant (at 50%, offsetting entirely the difference in capital cost), and fuel-tax rebate for local services (likewise offsetting extra fuel cost), In some cases, no support at all from counties was required, in others a very low figure.

Introduction of post-buses has varied considerably according to local initiative. Over 100 are found in Scotland – in some cases using vehicles as small as estate cars or Land Rovers – but a smaller scatter in England and Wales. The topography of some parts of Scotland – with most settlement concentrated in narrow valleys – is more appropriate for post-bus operation, and very low population densities in the Highlands encourage multi-purpose operation.

By July 1992 some 170 post-bus routes were in operation in Britain, with a plan to expand to 200: some 100,000 passengers were carried in 1991. A national post-bus manager was appointed by the Royal Mail in 1992. However, the impact of post-buses has been less than initially expected. Elimination of the New Bus Grant increased costs incurred and stricter costing has also stimulated higher demands on county support. While small in total these may be high on a per-passenger basis, and in some cases have resulted in withdrawal of post-buses (such as that into Petworth, West Sussex, replaced by a community bus in 1985). A more serious limitation is the fact that the post-bus routes are rarely varied to meet passenger needs. Journeys are often inconveniently timed, and indirect, such that return trips cannot easily be made. Often, a post-bus may be more useful in conjunction with another service, such as a school bus adapted to carry fare-paying passengers, each providing one leg of a return trip. Figure 8.2 suggests a possible re-shaping of mail-van routes, with one being re-routed to give a direct service into the market town, and an adjoining loop extended to cover other points formerly on this route.

In some other countries, post-buses play a much larger rôle, notably the well known Swiss network (Holding 1983). However, much of the traffic on such systems is often between village post offices and sorting centres, rather than to/ from private homes, and the network functions more like that of a large company – often cross-subsidized through other postal and telecommunication activities – rather than the type of post-bus found in Britain.

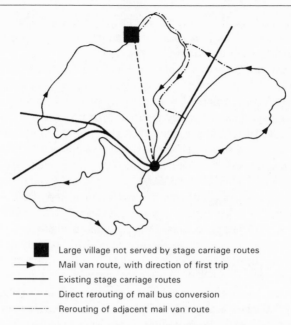

■   Large village not served by stage carriage routes
➤——   Mail van route, with direction of first trip
——————   Existing stage carriage routes
— — — —   Direct rerouting of mail bus conversion
—·—·—·—   Rerouting of adjacent mail van route

Figure 8.2   Potential rerouting of a mail van service to give a post-bus route into a market town.

Minibuses

Minibuses appear an obvious solution to rural transport problems, given the low demand and limited room for large vehicles on many routes. However, peak demands for school travel often require full-size vehicles, and a purely commercial minibus service (i.e. one with a paid driver) is unlikely to be justified in a rural area. The development of intensive minibus services since 1984 has taken place almost entirely in urban areas, relying on high utilization throughout the day. The one significant exception is the services operated by the Transit Holdings group in parts of Devon (by Devon General) and Oxfordshire (Thames Transit), where medium-size minibuses now operate most services, including interurban routes. Their capacity is sufficient for most purposes, although in some cases local authorities have found it necessary to contract in full-size vehicles to meet the school peak (highlighting its costs). Some other minibus operation by PSV O-licence operators is also found where small vehicles are used for specific contracts or minor routes, but remains much less common that full-size bus operation. Minibuses play a more significant rôle in most rural areas through voluntary or non-commercial activity.

Clearly, if the cost of a driver could be greatly reduced or even eliminated, the lower capital and running costs of minibuses could make them attractive for

153

rural use. In 1976 the Eastern Counties company launched a service in Norfolk, using a 9-seat Ford Transit maintained and supplied by the company, but driven by local volunteer drivers, trained to PSV standards. Weekly shopping services were provided, and private hire and excursion work undertaken at weekends. A high proportion of costs could thus be covered from passenger revenue at conventional fare scales. Some other areas adopted such schemes soon afterward. Under the Transport Act 1978 they were removed from the requirement for drivers to have PSV licences (a questionable change), provided that the vehicle used had not more than 16 seats, and was operated on a non-profit-making basis. The term "Community Bus" was applied in this Act, and has been adopted generally to describe such schemes. About thirty now operate, mainly in southern England. A fairly conventional pattern of local shopping services is provided, with weekend hire work (often greatly improving financial performance). Others provide services in smaller urban areas, especially those where many elderly people live, whom even a short walking trip may be difficult, notably those established in Hailsham and Bexhill, East Sussex, in 1981. A similar mix of shopping, medical and social trips is handled.

Many minibuses in rural areas are run through agencies for specific groups such as schools, churches, youth clubs, or voluntary bodies such as Age Concern. Their legal position in providing some form of regular service, but not as PSVs, was clarified in the Minibus Act 1977, under which permits are issued through county councils for each vehicle so operated. However various inconsistencies remain in terms of the safety requirements for both vehicle and drivers in comparison to those imposed on bus operators.

The Transport Act 1985 "tidied up" some of the inconsistencies in various forms of minibus legislation (PSV, community bus and permit services), notably through providing for the issue of permits to organizations, rather than in respect of vehicles as such, but specification differences remain, with implications for passenger safety. Some 4,600 "small bus" permits (i.e. for vehicles up to 16 seats inclusive) were issued in the year 1992/3 – of which 1,553 were issued directly by area Traffic Commissioners, 1,535 through local authorities, and 1,518 by other designated bodies (which include local education authorities). In comparison, only 108 "large bus" permits (i.e. vehicles over 16 seats, used for non-profit-making purposes), and 8 community bus permits, were issued in the same year (the Traffic Commissioners being the sole issuing authority for these categories) (Department of Transport 1993).

Taxis play a limited rôle in rural areas; indeed prior the 1985 Act, many rural districts did not exercise their permissive powers to licence them, making it difficult to trace their extent. Shared taxis were in any case not generally legalized until the 1985 Act, a by-product of which has been the requirement for all districts to introduce a taxi-licensing system. However, a shared taxi or hire car could clearly be a useful mode for rural travel where small numbers are found. Informal sharing often occurs in any case.

School buses

As mentioned at the start of this chapter, school buses play a major rôle in rural areas. These may be public services on which children are carried using season tickets, but in many cases special contract services are provided, not open to the public. Vehicles and crews are normally hired from PSV operators, although some counties, notably Lincolnshire, operate their own fleets, which do not have to meet PSV standards as no payment for their use is involved. Taxis and minibuses are also hired in by education authorities where smaller flows arise. Traditionally, there was little co-ordination between education departments hiring such vehicles, and co-ordinators responsible for public services, but the situation has greatly improved in recent years. The first change came through Section 30 of the Transport Act 1968, enabling permits to be issued for school buses to carry fare-paying passengers. From 1974, some county co-ordinators became responsible for school contract services, enabling greater co-ordination between their provision and the public network. The two are often merged, either through placing children on the public network through issue of season tickets, or converting the school bus service to PSV operation as a registered local service. Co-ordinators can also take into account the implications for school contracts of public service operations – for example, a market day shopping service may be provided at low cost, if the same operator has a school contract in the area.

Under the Transport Act 1980 councils running their own (non-PSV) school buses were able to receive permits for public services by such vehicles: these have been used in a few instances, generally to provide off-peak shopping services. However, another inconsistency in safety standards was created. Under the Transport Act 1985, counties are required to consider school and public services together, to obtain best value for money. This encouraged those authorities still handling school and public services separately to co-ordinate their planning.

Perhaps the most comprehensive type of innovative service is the ESCORT scheme, pioneered in East Sussex. Following the Lewes Area Rural Transport Study (Martin & Vorhees 1981), it was realized that many different agencies were used to provide specialized services at high unit cost, which could be merged. The first ESCORT service was launched in 1983, covering the area around Lewes and Newhaven. A 30-seat midibus, with wheelchair lift, provides a daytime shopping service to villages in the area. This is extended to serve an old people's day centre, and local schools, thus providing for several different groups of needs through the same vehicle. Local journeys within small towns are also provided as part of the service. Further routes have since been established, including one using community bus volunteer drivers to provide an evening/weekend service (Brown & Barnes 1985).

ESCORT can also be seen as an example of the "transport brokerage" concept, in which an attempt is made to draw together the many resources already available, and use them more efficiently, through putting providers and users in contact – these include social cars, taxis, minibuses and conventional bus operators.

Some counties have appointed "transport brokers" as part of their co-ordinating teams, the first such in Hampshire.

Another example of a multi-purpose operation is the "Border Courier" in the Peebles/Galashiels/Berwick area, in which a service is supported by health authorities and the regional council, carrying medical supplies to villages, as well as providing a general passenger service.

Impact of the 1985 Transport Act

At the time of its introduction, it was anticipated that the deregulation of local bus services under the 1985 Act would have particularly marked effects in rural areas, due to the pressure to eliminate cross-subsidy previously found, and removal of the comprehensive network planning rôle of local authorities in favour of a more limited rôle in "filling gaps" in commercially registered networks. In acknowledgement of this, a special rural service grant was introduced, as mentioned earlier in this chapter, at a flat rate per bus mile run (6p per bus mile in 1986/7, falling to 1p per mile in 1989/90, and discontinued thereafter). A special fund to encourage innovative services, the Rural Transport Development Fund (RTDF) was also set up, providing about £1 million per year in England, with parallel schemes in Wales and Scotland.

There is little comprehensive statistical data available on rural service levels and ridership since 1985. Although data for English "shire counties" is published (see further comment in Ch. 10), much of the operation therein is in fact within urban areas. Broadly speaking, a similar overall level of rural service has been maintained, as discussed in the north east Lincolnshire example. In some cases, a period of service expansion and competition on rural routes was followed by a return to a similar level of service to that applying before deregulation, as in the Norwich area (Harman 1989). A further review is provided by Astrop (1993), indicating an increase in bus-km in most cases.

One significant factor which helps to explain the relatively high level of conventional service retention since deregulation is the shift from national wage bargaining to local negotiations. In many rural areas, the wage levels paid by large operators were considerably above those applying in local labour markets. The expansion of service by smaller operators, notably for tendered work, has been followed by substantial reductions in operating costs by larger incumbents, in some cases enabling them to regain tendered services initially lost to smaller operators. This factor has undoubtedly been important in the area shown in Figure 8.1, for example.

The main problems arising from deregulation appear to be much the same in rural areas as in the industry as a whole: lack of investment in fleet renewal (Lincolnshire Road Car purchased no new buses between 1985 and 1992, for example), and the instability in service provision associated with frequent changes in commercially registered services, and consequent changes in tendered services.

The impact of the RTDF has been limited. Although many schemes have been set up in various regions, their overall contribution is small. One possible factor is the tendency of central government to set up initiatives parallel to those already taking place within local authorities through transport co-ordinators. Means are being sought to increase the attractiveness of the scheme (North 1992).

Overall policy issues

Rural transport has been the subject of many policy initiatives in recent years, often established by central government, which has been particularly concerned to stimulate the "innovative" or "non-conventional" services, as is evident in the 1977 and 1978 Acts. A research programme under the title "RUTEX" (Rural Transport Experiments) was launched in 1977, in which schemes in some areas were established, and subsequently monitored in detail, including community buses, hired cars, shared taxis, lift-giving, and flexible routeing on demand of a conventional bus service near Ripon, Yorkshire. They are described fully in a series of reports from the Transport Research Laboratory (1979, 1980). However, the subsequent impacts of such programmes have been limited, owing to the unique local conditions which affect each scheme. These will determine not only the likely levels of performance, but also the possibility of a scheme being set up in the first place: a community bus service, for example, depends upon a pool of volunteer drivers and an enthusiastic organizer.

Under the 1978 Transport Act non-metropolitan counties were required to publish annual Public Transport Plans (PTPs). These appeared from 1979 to 1985 inclusive, the requirement to produce them being dropped in the 1985 Act. Most local authorities have, however, produced general statements of policy, which have been subsequently updated.

In practice, the element of "planning" was fairly limited, given the short timescale on which many local authority budgets are based. Most, however, contained a very useful inventory of existing services, not only of conventional bus and rail operations, but also school contract, social service and voluntary schemes. This itself may have been a useful "self education" exercise in some areas, encouraging greater co-ordination between activities, especially school and public bus services.

The 1978 Act also required that counties, in preparing their PTPs, should review transport "needs", indicating criteria by which need would be defined, and an assessment of the extent to which each community's needs were met by public transport. Many counties made some attempts at definition, but few in a systematic fashion. One of the main exceptions was Kent, which devised and applied a method based on identifying people without access to cars, the needs

157

to which they are likely to require access, and the distribution of services to meet them. Thus, stress is placed on the activities which people need to reach (dependent in part on those provided in the local community) by public transport, rather than simply the level of public transport service as such. A description of the method is provided by Burley & Snell (1983). Similar methodologies have also been developed in Dyfed. Reviews have been provided by Banister (1981, 1989) and Bird (1981). More recently, an assessment for mid-Wales has been made by Moyes (1989). In any case, one level of "need" is defined by statute – school travel over 2 or 3 miles – and on this base some additional off-peak services can normally be provided.

Following local bus deregulation, local authorities have been unable to take a long-term view, being placed in a reactive mode as operators change commercial services. Nonetheless, some broad ranking of importance of different tendered service types is adopted, together with "rules of thumb" (such as the proportion of costs that a service might be expected to cover, or average loadings). A more systematic approach has been adopted by North Yorkshire (Bristow et al. 1993).

In the longer term, relocation of facilities may also alleviate problems. Although often suggested in principle, it has rarely been applied, except insofar as siting and catchment areas of schools can affect peak school transport demands. In other cases, such as village shops, it is not generally possible for local authorities to ensure their retention (planning powers being negative, rather than positive), although other bodies may do so, through setting up co-operatives, or giving financial assistance.

Perhaps the most critical problem is that of access to medical facilities. The continued shift to centralization into very large hospitals may be less evident now, but rural GPs continue to disappear, being replaced by group practices. Location of these in the centre of market towns, where local bus routes give good access may help, perhaps reducing the need for reliance on voluntary car schemes. Greater flexibility in opening hours would also help. Similar flexibility in shopping hours, and those of other facilities could be applied.

The range of concessionary fares offered also affects the mobility of those with access to cars, especially on low incomes. There has been little change in their scope since the 1985 Act, although the previous trend toward county-wide schemes may have been curbed. In the long run, a national scheme could still be possible, probably based on a half-fare. Schoolchildren travelling less than the "statutory" distances sometimes experience very high fares where counties are not willing to support the existing school-child fare as a form of concession.

Finally, the question of inter-urban travel should not be ignored. As stressed at the start of this chapter, rural transport is not only a question of getting to the nearest market town, but also of getting to regional centres, being able to make visits to hospitals, friends and relatives, and go on holiday. These trips are occasional but nonetheless important. Further scope may exist for upgrading existing inter-urban stage bus services with higher-quality vehicles (as recently adopted by the Stagecoach Group, for example). However, some lower-density express

158

coach services have been lost as a result of operators concentrating mainly on trunk routes after deregulation under the 1980 Act.

References and suggested further reading

Astrop, A. 1993. *The trend in rural bus services since deregulation*. Transport Research Laboratory Report PR21, Crowthorne, Berkshire.

Banister, D. 1981. The response of shire counties to the question of transport needs. *Traffic Engineering and Control* **22**(October), 488–91.

— 1989. *The reality of the rural transport problem*. Discussion Paper 1, Transport and Society series, Transport Studies Unit, Oxford University.

Bird, C. M. 1981. Six techniques for comparing transport needs. Transport Research Laboratory Report LR1017, Crowthorne, Berkshire.

Bristow, A. L., P. J. Mackie, C. A. Nash 1993. *Evaluation criteria in the allocation of financial support to bus operators – a survey of techniques*. Working Paper WP393, Institute of Transport Studies, University of Leeds.

Brown, C. & A. Barnes 1985. Experience with ESCORT. Rural Transport Seminar, Polytechnic of Central London, 16–25.

Burley, R. & J. Snell 1983. A method of identifying rural bus needs in Kent. Rural Transport Seminar, Polytechnic of Central London, 3–23

Cordner, K. 1989. South West Wales' low-cost railway. *Modern Railways* (November), 570–73.

Department of Transport 1993. *Annual Reports of the Traffic Commissioners 1992–93*, Appendix 4. London: Department of Transport.

Fearnside, K. 1980. Experience of lift-giving schemes in Shropshire. Rural Transport Seminar, Polytechnic of Central London, 44–74.

Harman, R. 1989. Bus deregulation – three years on. *Bus Business* (27 December), 8–9.

Heels, P. & P. R. White 1977. Fare elasticities on inter-urban and rural bus services. Research Report 4, Transport Studies Group, Polytechnic of Central London.

Holding, D. 1983. The Swiss post-bus system – a comparison with British rural operation. Rural Transport Seminar, Polytechnic of Central London, 44–74.

Martin and Vorhees 1981. *The Lewes area public transport study*. London: Department of Transport.

Moseley, M. & J. Packman 1983. *Mobile services in rural areas*. School of Environmental Science, University of East Anglia, Norwich.

Moyes, A. 1989. *The need for public transport in mid-Wales: normative approaches and their implications*. Rural Surveys Research Unit Monograph, Department of Geography, University College of Wales, Aberystwyth.

National travel survey 1989/91 (September 1993, section 10). London: HMSO.

North, D. 1992. Rural transport: time for a return to the policy agenda? *Local Transport Today* (1 October), 10/11.

OPCS (Office of Population Censuses and Surveys). Monitor PP1 91/1, October 1992.

Stanley, P. A., J. H. Farrington, R. P. MacKenzie 1981. *Public transport provision and access to facilities in East Ross and the Black Isle*. Research paper, Department of Geography, University of Aberdeen.

Transport and Road Research Laboratory 1979. Reports of RUTEX experiments: *Exe Valley Market Bus (SR427); Mid-Devon lift-giving scheme (SR525); Ripon Flexibus (SR491); Welsh schemes (SR507)*. Crowthorne, Berks: TRRL.

—1980. Rural transport experiments: proceedings of symposium. Report LR584.

White, P. R. 1986. *Public transport: its planning, management and operation,* 1st edn (Ch. 8). London: Hutchinson.

CHAPTER 9

Intercity public transport

Introduction

It is in the intercity, or long-distance, sector that the highest quality of public transport service can be found, and the most extensive use of public transport by those with cars available for the journey in question. On many routes improved quality of service has stimulated an increase in total patronage, despite rising car ownership. Another contrast with the short-distance market is that productivity has risen sharply, as vehicle size and speed have increased. Commercially viable opportunities for investment are also more numerous.

For example, in the late 1940s, an express coach was limited to a theoretical schedule not exceeding 30 mph (50 km/h), and seated about 32 passengers. Today the limit is 65 mph (60 mph on dual carriageways and until 1993, 70 mph on motorways), permitting a typical average of about 50 mph (80 km/h), and a double-decker may seat about 70. Seat-miles per hour have thus risen from about 960 to 3500, or by almost four times. In air transport, the change has been even more dramatic, from the 26-seat Viking averaging about 200 mph (320 km/h) to current jets seating about 120 (or about 190 in the Boeing 757), achieving around 500 mph (800 km/h), giving a productivity improvement per vehicle by a factor of ten or more. On the railways, there have not been any marked changes in seating capacity (around 350–400 per train), but increases in average speed from about 50 mph (80 km/h) to 80 mph (135 km/h), or higher on routes served by the high speed trains, coupled with much quicker turnround of stock, have improved utilization dramatically.

The present long-distance market in Britain

As described in Chapter 2, the National Travel Survey (NTS) gives a comprehensive sample of travel by residents of Britain. The 1989/91 survey indicates that only 2% of all journeys over 1.6 km in length were "long", i.e. over 80 km. However, these represented 29% of all kilometres travelled (an increase from 26% in 1985/6). In absolute terms, these "long" trips averaged about 18 per person per year (i.e. about one return trip every six weeks), of which 8 were as a car driver, 6 as a car passenger, one by "other private" modes, one by "non-local" bus (including scheduled express and other coaches), and two by British Rail. Car represented 80% of all "long" journeys (NTS 1989/91, section 9 "Travel by journey length").

The NTS also shows how journey purpose and distance are related. Of the journeys over 80km, about 12% were for commuting (almost wholly concentrated in the 80–160km category), while business comprised 17%, personal business and shopping 11%, social/entertainment 31%, and "holiday/other" 27% (no other category exceeded 1%) (Table 8A). The long-distance market is thus geared much more toward "optional" (non-work, non-education) travel than the travel market as a whole (see Ch. 2).

Within the public transport modes, a slightly different purpose split is found. For all journeys over 80km by rail, 22% were for commuting, (mostly associated with travel in the 80–160km range in the South East Region) and 11% for business (NTS Table 4E). Conversely, coach travel is geared largely to the "optional" purposes, with negligible "business" travel.

The ratio of car driver to car passenger trips implies an average occupancy of about 1.75 for "long" journeys: this is consistent with the higher occupancy for non-work travel (Ch. 2), and perhaps a greater tendency to share petrol costs which may be more readily perceived for long-distance journeys. Tickets such as the "family railcard" can be seen as one response to this by public transport operators.

However, because the frequency of long-distance travel is low, the one-week diary compiled by NTS respondents gives relatively limited information, many of them not travelling "long" distances at all during the survey week. The sample size is not large enough to give any meaningful data on domestic air travel, or for zones disaggregated below national level.

A more comprehensive picture was given by the Long-Distance Travel Survey (LDTS), undertaken from 1973 to 1980. Although then discontinued for economy reasons by the government, it gives the only data on a corridor-by-corridor basis in which all modes are covered consistently, and may therefore be taken as a starting point in such comparisons: comment on trends within each mode since 1980 is given later in this chapter. In the LDTS "long distance" travel was then defined as that over 25 miles (40km), somewhat shorter than the "long" definition now used in the NTS. As in the case of NTS, only journeys within Britain were considered. Hence, only those journeys by domestic air services originating and terminating within Britain were included, omitting the substantial "interline" traffic element (see further comment below).

We can also derive variations in travel by person type from the NTS and LDTS. Taking all modes and journey purposes together, the average distance travelled per person in 1989/91 within Britain was 10,170km, but notably higher for working age males (14,600 for those aged 16–29, and 17,070 for those aged 30–59). (NTS Table 8.3). This was associated with higher levels of commuting and business travel in particular, implying a greater tendency to make "long" journeys. A more detailed picture can be derived from the 1979–80 LDTS. On the definition then used of 50km, each person made 31 "long distance" trips per year. Men made twice as many trips as women, associated mainly with business travel. Those aged 65 or over made markedly fewer trips, about 11 a year. Students were also among the "economically inactive" groups, yet made 34 trips: the 18–24 age group made 2.5 times as many trips "visiting friends and relatives" as any other age group. Another critical factor is car ownership: those from households with cars available made 38 trips, those without, only 15. However, these differences were also correlated with variations in income, economic activity and area of residence. A fuller analysis is given by Rickard (1988).

Although the much higher total trip rates made by those with cars available are, naturally, associated mainly with car use, it is important to note that the average rail trip rate by both car-owning, and non-car-owning households was the same, at 6 per year. The absolute level of rail use does not necessarily fall with rising car ownership, unlike the urban bus market.

The LDTS also indicated the variations in modal share by route, as shown in Table 9.1. Taking major corridors from the London and South East region, the car share could be seen to fall as journey length increased. Thus, on the east coast corridor, cars took 72% of all travel within 192km (to the East Midlands, for example), but only 44% to points over 320km within England (such as Newcastle), and 36% of the travel to Scotland. The difference was represented by a growth in rail share, and, for the longest trips, air. Thus, on the east coast corridor over 320km, rail took 40% of trips, air 5%, but for Scottish traffic, the air share rose to 31%. If business traffic alone is considered, air became predominant in the market to Scotland, taking about 60%. Coach travel (including tour and private hire, as well as scheduled express services) took only about 9% of the long-distance market, although this was higher on certain corridors, notably between London and the North East.

Further analysis of the LDTS by British Rail showed that public transport took a higher share of the market to/from cities, in contrast to larger regions which car accessibility would be better. For example, between Manchester and the whole South East Region, rail took about 40% of all trips, but to/from London only, about 48%. As population moves outward from traditional cities, rail accessibility is thus worsened, and "city-centre-to-city-centre" journey times – important though they be for business traffic – may not be the major factor they were once considered. Feeder journeys by local public transport may be particularly slow vis-a-vis the trunk journey.

Table 9.1   Modal shares by corridor, mid-1974 to mid-1977 (%).

South East region, to/from (km)	Rail	Coach	Car	Air/other
West coast				
up to 192	30	9	60	1
192–320	38	10	47	5
over 320	32	9	57	2
Scotland	39	9	25	27
East coast				
up to 192	19	7	72	2
192–320	27	14	68	1
over 320	40	11	44	5
Scotland	26	7	36	31
South Wales and South West				
up to 192	20	9	70	1
192–320	20	9	69	2
over 320	26	11	62	1

Source: Long Distance Travel Survey, as quoted *Transport statistics Great Britain 1968–78*, table 32 (zones are illustrated in maps on pp. 25–6 of that report).

Current patterns and recent trends within each mode

Domestic air services

It is clear from Tables 9.2, 9.4 and 9.5 that parallels may be seen between domestic air travel and long-distance car and intercity rail developments during the 1980s, namely a static market in the late 1970s and early 1980s followed by accelerated growth from the middle 1980s, but hit by the impact of recession from 1990. Within the total shown, scheduled traffic represents the great majority, and charters (non-scheduled) only about 0.3 million trips per year. This very low market share (vis a vis international air travel from Britain) is partly as a result of effective surface competition in the leisure market, especially for family groups, and partly of the policy adopted by Channel Islands of limiting charter operations so as to safeguard year-round scheduled services. The pricing flexibility enjoyed by domestic airlines also reduces the need for non-scheduled services, since a variety of low scheduled fares is available on routes with a leisure component.

Table 9.2   Passengers uplifted by UK airlines (millions).

1978	1982	1984	1986	1988	1989	1990	1991	1992
7.0	7.4	8.6	9.4	11.6	12.6	13.1	11.9	12.0

Source: Transport statistics Great Britain 1993 (London: HMSO, 1993), table 7.2c.

Passenger trips thus grew by 62% between 1978 and 1992. Passenger kilometres grew by an almost identical 65% (from 2,900 million to 4,800 million), indicating no significant change in the average trip length of 400km.

The air total of 4,800 million passenger-km in 1992 may be compared directly with that for BR's Intercity Sector of 12,200 million, giving air a 28% share of the combined rail-and-air market thus defined. However, the domestic market is very small if compared with international scheduled traffic handled by British airlines, of 82,000 million passenger-km in 1992.

While there are many domestic air services, some operated with very small aircraft, the market is dominated by the routes to or from the London airports and cross-water routes. There are four distinct groupings, based on 1991 data (CAA 1992):

1. Domestic Trunk Routes between Heathrow and Edinburgh (1.2 million passengers), Glasgow (1.1 m), Belfast (1.1 m) and Manchester (0.8 m): a total of 4.3 million trips (36% of all domestic passengers). They are significantly denser than any other routes. Their share rises to 41% if the traffic on the parallel routes to Gatwick is included.

2. Other London routes are numerous but carry substantially lower volumes of traffic than the four trunk routes. Nevertheless, taking all the Heathrow and Gatwick routes together, including the trunks, they generated 7.2 million trips (65% of all domestic air traffic). The combined total for London City, Luton and Stansted was a further 0.5 million.

3. While several of the London routes, notably those to Belfast, Channel Islands and the Isle of Man involve water crossings, there are also several important cross-water routes not involving London. They reflect the journey time advantage enjoyed by air over surface modes when a sea crossing is involved. Most of these routes are from islands to the nearest port on the mainland, or from Belfast to major cities. The combined total for these cross-water routes (excluding those to Heathrow and Gatwick) was 3.0 million in 1991 (25% of the total).

4. Finally, it is noticeable that while there are many cross-country air services between points on the mainland of Britain, other than London, comprising the remaining 10% of domestic traffic, their individual passenger levels are low. Only two routes – Edinburgh, and Glasgow, to Birmingham – carried more than 100,000 passengers in 1991. Many such services are from airports in the Midlands to points in Scotland.

Much of the growth which occurred in the total domestic air market from 1984 onwards can be attributed to expansion on the four trunk routes. All four grew by 60% to 82% in the five years from 1983 to 1988 (White & Doganis 1990). This outstripped growth on most of the other domestic routes except a few thinner routes, usually involving a water crossing such as some Isle of Man, Channel Islands or Belfast routes.

Liberalization of domestic air services clearly had some impact on the trunk routes. In all four cases, the entry of new airlines onto the routes in the period 1983 to 1985 led to a major increase in capacity, the introduction of some promotional fares and a surge in demand. The latter, however, was insufficient to

165

compensate for the increases in capacity and passenger load factors generally declined, sometimes quite substantially as in the case of London–Belfast. Such liberalization coincided with an improving economic climate which was stimulating domestic demand on all routes and for all modes (CAA 1987). Thus it is difficult to isolate the impact of liberalization on traffic growth. In the case of London–Manchester growth was rapid even though the new entrant on the Heathrow route in the early 1980s, Dan Air, pulled out after a year or so.

On the non-trunk routes liberalization has had only a very limited impact because on most of them traffic volumes are too thin to support more than one, or occasionally two, airlines.

Journey purposes

While domestic air traffic is predominately for business purposes, well over a third is for leisure. At Heathrow in 1991 63% of domestic passengers, both UK and foreign residents, were travelling for business and the remaining third were on leisure trips. The domestic business/leisure split was fairly similar at Manchester but at Gatwick, leisure passengers were the majority, generating 53% of the domestic traffic, while business passengers were only 47% (CAA 1993). There are routes such as those to the Isle of Man or the Channel Isles where leisure traffic predominates.

A striking feature of the domestic network in Britain is the rôle of "interline" traffic, that is passengers using domestic air services in order to transfer to international or, less frequently, domestic services, notably at Heathrow and Gatwick.

On average, such interline passengers represent over 30% of the total traffic on routes to/from London, and for several their share rises to over half: in 1991 this was the case for routes to Heathrow from Birmingham, Plymouth and East Midlands. They also represented about 45% on major routes such as Manchester, and Newcastle, to Heathrow. This implies that such domestic traffic forms a very substantial part of the total passenger movements at regional airports. Such interline traffic is also significant for surface modes serving the London airports from the South West, South Wales and the Midlands (see also the section on express coach).

The importance of international interlining for domestic passengers has policy implications. Displacement of domestic flights from Heathrow or Gatwick because of runway congestion thus adversely affects many regional airports' linkages to foreign destinations.

Fare and pricing developments

Of the 11.7 million passengers carried by domestic scheduled services in 1991, the most common fare category was "economy" (45%), followed by "discount"

(26%), (CAA 1992). A detailed analysis by Dennis (1990) of trends in real fares between 1977 and 1988 showed two distinct developments. First, the basic economy fares, which are largely those used by business travellers, went up in real terms, typically by between 20% and 30%, though a few by less than this. Secondly, whereas in 1977, there where few promotional fares, apart from some small discounts on weekend flights, by 1988 there were such fares on virtually all routes. Their introduction led to a dramatic drop in real fares for eligible passengers, typically 25% to 40% lower than in 1977.

Such fare reductions became possible as a result of liberalization of fare controls by the Civil Aviation Authority and were aimed both at generating new demand, and meeting improved surface competition on certain routes. These lower fares were compensated for in revenue terms by increases in the real level of full economy fares, for which demand is less elastic. This, combined with improved yield management, probably meant that average domestic revenue per passenger changed little in real terms.

Competition

As a result of route liberalization, the dominant position previously enjoyed by British Airways on domestic routes has been reduced, its share of domestic passenger-kilometres falling from three-quarters in 1978 to just over half in 1988 (including the Gatwick operations taken over from British Caledonian). By 1990, it accounted for around 45% of domestic air traffic, although this share may have recovered marginally following takeovers of Dan-Air in 1992 and Brymon in 1993.

The most striking feature has been the emergence of British Midland as a "second force" domestic airline, stemming from the licences it was granted in the early 1980s to compete with British Airways head-on out of Heathrow on the trunk routes to Glasgow, Belfast and Edinburgh. Up to that point, domestic competition between British Airways and the former British Caledonian had been less direct, since the latter flew only from Gatwick. The former BCal domestic routes were taken over in 1988 by Air UK, which has also since developed a network of domestic routes feeding Stansted.

Express coach

The deregulation of express-coach services under the Transport Act 1980 (described briefly in Ch. 1) had immediate and dramatic effects, as Table 9.3 indicates. Taking trips the on National Express network, a steady decline from the mid-1970s was clear, with just over 9 million trips in 1980 itself. The early 1980s saw a rapid growth, peaking at 15.4 million in 1985. However, a subsequent decline returned the total to about 10.5 million in 1992. A combination of higher frequencies on trunk routes, greater motorway running to raise speeds, and fare reductions of about 50% immediately upon deregulation, together with increased public awareness of coach travel, explain much of the initial effect.

Table 9.3   National Express passenger trips 1980–92 (millions).

Year	1980	1982	1984	1986	1988	1989	1990	1991	1992
Trips	9.2	14.0	15.0	14.4	13.1	13.9	13.5	11.8	10.5

Source: National Express.
Note: Changes in some years are associated with changes in definition and scope. Totals from 1989 were increased by introduction of Scottish services.

Trends shown in Table 9.3 are for National Express, providing an extensive network in England and Wales. No data on express coach travel as a whole has been published since 1984, when 17 million trips were recorded (Department of Transport 1987), but given the market share of about 80% held by National Express in that year, it would seem reasonable to regard its trends as an indicator for the express coach sector as a whole.

From the first day of deregulation in October 1980 a rival consortium of independent operators, British Coachways, introduced competing services on the main trunk routes, but was unable to match the high frequency of service that National were able to offer. National also "saw off" the competition by cutting its fares to the levels of British Coachways, in some cases by 50%, notably on trunk routes to London, as shown in Figure 9.1, which shows indices for fares in real terms from just prior to deregulation to the mid-1980s. A fuller description is provided by Robbins & White (1986).

Price reductions were also made on major cross-country routes and other London-based services. National also benefited from their greater number of sales outlets, and access to coach stations, notably London Victoria. They were already a nationally known name which could take advantage of the publicity given to coach travel as a whole, whereas British Coachways was not. The independent consortium gradually broke up, and ceased in January 1983.

Substantial independent competition has continued on some corridors, but no single operator has been able to establish a competing network as such. By Autumn 1993 significant all-year-round competition was reduced primarily to the London–Poole, London–Bristol–Somerset, London–Birmingham, and London–Leeds/North East corridors.

Within the National Express network, the initial phase of low-fare competition against British Coachways was followed by a strategy of improving service quality, notably the "Rapide" service standard now offered to most towns from London, major cross-country routes, and airport feeder services, giving lower seating densities, refreshments, hostess service, toilets and video television. This type of service had in fact been pioneered by independents – Trathens from Plymouth to London, and Cotters from Glasgow and Edinburgh, in the autumn

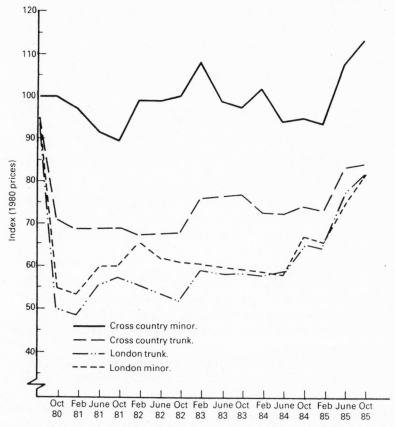

Figure 9.1 National Express period return fares, 1980–85

of 1980. The name "Rapide" was introduced for a joint service from Plymouth by Trathens and National in November 1981, and then adopted generally for this type of service.

The largest single source of traffic growth has been rail, and some of the coach growth of the early 1980s may simply have represented a recapture of traffic lost to rail in the late 1970s, when BR was able to introduce a range of pricing innovations aimed at traditional coach users such as students and the elderly, which coach operators could not match initially. Surveys undertaken by postgraduate students and research staff at the then Polytechnic of Central London (now University of Westminster) on both independent and National Express services, indicated that "visiting friends and relatives" was by far the most important single source of traffic, about half the total. Shopping/personal business, and holidays (with the obvious seasonal variation) are also significant. However, despite the service quality improvements, very few firms' business trips have been attracted to coach.

At coach deregulation in 1980, National Express was the trading name for the network of coach services offered by regional bus and coach companies within the National Bus Company. National Express was subsequently set up as a separate company, and as part of the NBC privatization (see Ch. 1), it was privatized through a management buy-out in 1988. After a subsequent change of ownership, it was floated as PLC in 1992. National Express owns only about six vehicles as such, the remaining 700 or so vehicles in its white livery being contracted-in from other operators, on a distance-based rate. Although initially confined largely to sister companies within the NBC group, this process has now become much more open, with many smaller independents, and some municipal PTCs, also acting as contractors. From the passengers' point of view, a single network is offered.

A somewhat different pattern has applied in Scotland. At the time of deregulation, the Scottish Bus Group (SBG) traditionally operated trunk routes between London and major Scottish cities, while other cities in England were connected by joint National Express/SBG routes. Very little development of express coach services in Scotland had occurred, despite substantial motorway construction. Independent operators took a greater rôle, both on the London trunk routes, and in setting up new services within Scotland, notably on the Glasgow/Edinburgh–Perth–Dundee–Aberdeen, and Perth–Inverness corridors. SBG subsequently placed the trunk routes between London and Scotland, and within Scotland, under the "Citylink" company, which played a similar rôle to National Express in England and Wales. It was established as separate organization in 1982, and like National Express, came to contract in from a wider range of operators.

Competition between National and Citylink as such was negligible until 1989, when National purchased the express coach services of the Stagecoach Group, thus competing both within Scotland and on London trunk services. A period of intensive competition between the two major networks then followed. Citylink was privatized through a management buy-out in 1990. However, the degree of competition proved unsustainable. In May 1993 Citylink was acquired by National, and services rationalized. National thus exercises a remarkable dominance in a deregulated market. Following the merger between the National Express Group and Saltire Holdings (the holding company for Citylink), an enquiry was carried out by the Monopolies and Mergers Commission (1994). This concluded that the main competition lay between coach and rail, notably in pricing, and that the merger had enabled both operators to escape a loss-making situation on the trunk London routes. The report also contains much other useful data on the express coach market, not otherwise made public.

In addition to growth on long-distance services, substantial expansion has been seen in coach operation at the regional level, notably between London and Oxford on the M40 (where two operators run – each every 20 minutes, and one every 10 minutes at peak periods), and in Northern Ireland, where Ulsterbus has expanded its "Goldline" network.

In terms of competing directly with British Rail on trunk routes to London, the express coach is always likely to occupy a "second best" rôle, offering a slower service at a lower price. Taking a sample of 17 links between London and major cities in 1992, the average value of time at which a user would trade-off coach and rail travel (i.e. the value below which coach would be favoured) was about £4 per hour for full-fare users (or about £3 for those on reduced fares), a similar value to that for local bus passengers' time used in evaluating bus priority measures. This contrasts with £15–£20 per hour as the value of time applicable to business travel for which domestic air and intercity rail represent the choice open. The current average fare paid on National Express is about £9.

However, there is one market sector in which coach can compete more successfully with rail, namely airport access. Following deregulation in 1980, many services along the M4 corridor were diverted to serve Heathrow airport. Subsequently direct links have been established to Heathrow and Gatwick from many parts of Britain, and similar links to other airports. Coach can offer the convenience of a through service, and is less affected by congestion than on routes into central London. By 1984, coach had already captured about 30% of the land feeder market from the West Midlands and Wales to Heathrow, compared with about 5% using the rail-air coach link via Reading (Astill & White 1989). Increased emphasis has been placed on the airport market by National Express. Today, from Bristol and South Wales, a higher frequency is offered to Heathrow airport than to central London.

Private car and road traffic

No specific long-distance data are available, but indices of car traffic on major roads show the overall trends (Table 9.4).

Table 9.4 Indicators of vehicular traffic on motorways and main roads (thousand million vehicle-kilometres per year).

Road type	1982	1984	1986	1988	1990	1991	1992
Motorway	30.2	36.3	40.8	54.5	61.7	61.0	61.0
Non-built up major roads	64.8	66.1	68.5	74.6	78.3	79.4	78.3
All roads	284.5	303.1	325.3	375.7	410.8	411.6	408.8

Source: Transport statistics Great Britain 1993 (London: HMSO, 1993), table 4.9.

Of the "all roads" totals in 1982 and 1992, cars and taxis represented 80% of vehicle-km in 1982, and 82% in 1992, thus growing marginally faster than the total for all types of traffic. The growth of motorway traffic as such is slightly exaggerated by growth in the motorway network, notably in opening of the M25, and some reclassification of statistics from 1987.

As in the case of air travel, rapid growth in the mid to late 1980s was followed by stagnation, associated with the recession.

Rail

Table 9.5 shows trends in passenger-kilometres travelled on BR's InterCity and Regional sectors since 1978:

Table 9.5 Passenger-kilometres on BR's InterCity and Regional sectors, 1978– 92/3 (thousand millions).

Year	1978	1982	1984/5	1986/7	1988/9	1990/9 1	1992/3
Intercity	12.2	11.4	11.9	11.6	12.1	11.6	11.4
Regional	5.0	4.6	4.8	4.9	5.8	5.6	5.9

Source: Transport statistics Great Britain 1978–1988 (London: HMSO 1989), table 3.2 (1978 data), and *Transport statistics Great Britain 1993* (London: HMSO, 1993), table 5.12 (all other years).

Although the "Intercity" sector most obviously corresponds to the long-distance category, a good deal of Regional Railways' traffic in terms of passenger-kilometres also falls over 80 km, and changes in this category may explain much of the change in the figures shown above. Some substantial long-distance routes were also contained within Network South East (London–Salisbury–Exeter, for example), but variation in their use would be obscured by large variations in London commuter traffic.

About 66 million trips per year are made on the InterCity sector services as such (Green 1993), giving an average trip length of about 175 km. Total revenue in 1992/3 was £825 million (TSGB 1993, Table 5.11): an average per trip of £12.70 (or about 7 pence per kilometre).

The Intercity sector's total traffic has remained fairly stable over the period examined, although suffering a loss in the early 1980s, associated partly with recession, but also the impact of coach competition. Growth in the mid to late 1980s was followed by the impact of recession, as for other modes. Major speed improvements were concentrated in the early part of this period, associated with entry into service of the diesel High Speed Train (HST). The major quality improvements in recent years have been more evident in the Regional sector, with the adoption of "Sprinter" and class 158 stock on "express" cross-country routes.

Following the introduction of sector management in 1982 (Ch. 1) the Inter-City sector took responsibility for the major routes from London, together with the North East–South West route (Newcastle–Leeds–Birmingham–Bristol, etc.), and London–Gatwick (transferred to a shadow franchise in October 1993).

A market analysis (*Modern Railways* 1986) indicates that some 43% of the InterCity revenue is attributed to "leisure" travel (comprising visiting friends and relatives; holidays; days out; and sport/recreation); 37% to "business" travel; and 20% to "personal non-discretionary" (commuting to/from work; personal business; and to/from college). Although the business revenue per trip is higher than average, it is by no means entirely first class – the same analysis shows that 39% of business trips are by first class, but the majority (61%) by second. Prideaux (1989) identified about 15 million of the population as users of InterCity, some 10 million of whom use it at least once in any one year, and 750,000 "very frequently", suggesting a highly geared market. Users are predominantly young, only about 20% are travelling on business, and most common single reason for travel being "visiting friends and relatives".

Between 1978 and 1982 the average real revenue per passenger-kilometre on intercity fell by about 20%, associated with introduction of many low fare offers to respond to coach competition, and loss of business traffic during the recession at that time. It subsequently recovered to the 1978 real level by 1988 (White and Doganis 1990).

Elasticities of demand in the long-distance market

The long-distance market is characterized by substantially higher price and service quality elasticities than are found in the short-distance sector. This is associated with the predominance of non-business journeys, whose frequency and destination may be highly responsive to cost. Even markets assumed to be traditionally inelastic, such as commuting, and travel in course of work, are now considered to be more price sensitive than before, as the possibilities for substitution are explored in the medium-to-long term (for example, re-location of home or job, or stricter control of companies' travel budgets).

For the BR InterCity market the average price elasticity is around –1.0, but may be greater where strong coach or air competition is found (Wardman 1993).

For cross-country rail travel, elasticities of greater size than –1.0 may be assumed. A value of –1.3 has been obtained in work by Holt (1981). Experience of trends immediately after express coach deregulation in 1980, suggests an average price elasticity of around –1.0 for that mode also. A strong case for price reductions to maximize revenue and/or traffic thus exists, provided that significant extra capacity costs are not incurred.

In both rail and coach modes, a similar pricing policy is now adopted, in which highest fares are generally charged for the busiest day(s) (Fridays, and peak summer Saturdays or public holidays), while lower rates are charged at other times of the week. In the case of BR, there is also a marked business travel/commuting peak on Mondays to Fridays. For example, BR's Saver fares generally apply throughout the week, except at peak periods on busier routes, while "Supersaver" fares are not available on Fridays. BR has recently extended its policy further, adopting some of the airline industry "yield management" techniques. Apex fares (pre-bookable capacity of which a limited amount is offered) are now available on most main routes. Within the business sector, the full first class fare has been augmented by "Silver Service", offering an improved quality of catering service in standard accommodation.

173

National Express adopts a similar policy: its standard fare is applicable all days, but the lower "economy" fare not valid on Fridays or peak summer Saturdays. From November 1993 a common "advance" fare was introduced, offering substantial reductions on the normal fares, subject to a pre-booking period of at least 7 days. This was aimed at maintaining the typical 30% fare differential with BR, following the latter's Apex expansion (above). A discount "coach card" gives reductions of about 30% (except on "advance" fares) to those aged 60 upward, or between 16 and 25, in a similar fashion to BR railcards.

Demand is also sensitive to speed. Using data for specific modes, we can derive relationships with respect to in-vehicle speed. However, the user responds to door-to-door speed changes, which may be less marked when access and waiting time is taken into account. Speed elasticities of around $+1.5$, or journey time elasticities of around -0.7, may be applicable with respect to in-train journey times for rail services. These are likely to fall as speed increases, and access/waiting time accounts for a growing proportion of door-to-door travel time.

A further quantifiable element is frequency. Especially for short-distance travel, and business trips, this may be more important than speed. However, derivation of robust elasticity values is difficult, owing to the problem of separating cause and effect: does a high frequency service stimulate demand, or does its presence merely reflect the need to provide capacity to satisfy such a demand? For low-frequency services, around every two hours or wider intervals, high elasticities may be applicable (Jones & White 1994), but these will fall as frequency rises.

Much of the modelling work for BR has combined these effects into a generalized time elasticity, as reviewed by Wardman (1993). Typical values for intercity routes are around -0.9.

Although difficult to quantify, other factors may also be very important:

- Timing of journeys. Especially where frequencies are low, the timing of specific journeys will be critical. For example, is a day return trip for a business meeting practicable, or is a Friday evening/Sunday afternoon timing offered for weekend visits?
- Interchange. Although the time taken to interchange may be reflected in estimates of total door-to-door time, an additional inconvenience and uncertainty results, especially where inter-modal interchange occurs. Non-business journeys may be particularly sensitive to this. It may be worthwhile incurring additional operating costs to offer a through service, and in some cases passengers may choose a lower speed mode (for example, coach instead of rail) for this reason.
- Access to terminals. Provision of adequate car parking, as at the BR Inter-City "parkway" stations, may be a major factor, together with feeder bus, underground and taxi services.
- Comfort and convenience. Quality and cleanliness of seating, decor, availability of toilets, etc.
- Reliability of service, and helpfulness of staff.

- Ease of pre-booking tickets and seats, and/or ability to do so on demand without substantial queuing time (the author's recent experience of travel on TGV and British high-speed trains has included several occasions on which queuing time for tickets absorbed the entire in-train time saving associated with speeds over 160 km/h).

Increased emphasis is now being given to these features, for example, in the promotion of the Pullman travel concept by BR, in an effort to retain high-revenue business traffic, and other measures such as the ability to book tickets over the phone by credit card or "Telesales" (Green 1993).

Developments in technology

Rail

Although certain aspects of rail technology were discussed in the urban context in Chapter 4, many aspects of intercity rail technology are largely unique to this context, and recent developments offer further prospects for improving rail's market share.

Motive power

Diesel power is the most widely used mode of traction, both in locomotive and multiple-unit form, but lower operating cost and improved performance may be attained by use of electric traction. References are made in Chapter 4 to urban systems. For long-distance routes the standard voltage now adopted is 25 kV (25,000 V), ac, supplied via overhead catenary, at the standard industrial frequency of 50 cycles/second. However, the 3rd rail dc system at 650–800 V, adopted on the former Southern Region, is also used for long-distance routes such as London–Bournemouth–Poole and, somewhat anachronistically, the current route connecting the Channel Tunnel with London. Due to the close spacing of substations, this system is generally confined to urban networks, that of the Southern representing the cumulative extension of such a network. Elsewhere in Britain, the 25 kV system covers the Euston–West Midlands–North West–Glasgow corridor, together with the London–Norwich route, Anglia suburban services into London, Bedford–London, and the Glasgow suburban network. The East Coast Main Line (ECML), from London to Leeds, Newcastle and Edinburgh was recently converted, and some minor extensions are in progress.

The case for further electrification

The benefits from electrification have to be set against the capital cost of sub-stations, overhead or third-rail traction supply, and modifications to existing structures and signalling which may be required, in comparison with diesel operation. Low-density routes thus cannot justify such investment. However, the proportion of electrification in Britain – whether in terms of route kilometerage, or passenger train kilometerage – is low in comparison with similar European countries, notably France.

The major benefits include:

- Lower maintenance costs of locomotives.

  Data derived from the "Serpell Report" by the author show that in 1982 the average maintenance cost per locomotive-km for a diesel on BR was 125p, for an electric 50p, and for each High Speed Train (HST) power car, 95p. A review of evidence by the World Bank (Alston 1984) similarly suggests that electric locomotive maintenance costs are one-third to one-half those of diesel. These stem mainly from the much greater mechanical simplicity of the electric locomotive.

- Lower energy costs for equivalent output.

  In many cases, this is the second main factor. The thermal efficiency of burning oil in a power station, or on a diesel locomotive, is in fact fairly similar (around 25–30%), but the primary source for electricity can include many cheaper means, such as coal, hydro or nuclear generation. Use of regenerative braking – impractical with diesel –gives further gains.

  The first two factors taken together may account for 75% or more of the cost savings from electric traction. However, the substantial real fall in oil prices during the 1980s offset the underlying trend increase that was previously assumed to apply, reducing the net savings from schemes such as the East Coast main line electrification.

- Higher performance from a locomotive of given weight. This enables heavier loads and/or higher speeds to be achieved. The electric motor can also withstand greater output for short periods, considerably in excess of. its "continuous" rating, giving high rates of acceleration, or the ability to sustain speeds up gradients which would cause marked deceleration for a diesel. A benefit in terms of track capacity is thus given, which may avoid the need for additional tracks on busy routes (or, more typically in the BR case, enable a route rationalization).

- Higher availability of locomotives – typically about 85%, compared with 75% for diesel. Their service life is considerably longer – about 40 years rather than 25 years.

The third and fourth factors together imply that substantially fewer electric locomotives will be needed to produce the same output. Annual depreciation requirements are further reduced by the long life. One might expect, in addition, that the construction cost per locomotive would be lower, owing to their simplicity. However, on a world scale, electric locomotives are still produced in far smaller numbers than diesels, the latter thus gaining economies of scale in manufacture to give them a lower unit cost.

In the case of freight movement, differences can be compared largely in terms of costs. A break-even diagram as shown in Figure 9.2, can be drawn, in which the annualized "fixed" costs of electrification (interest and depreciation on the supply system, plus its annual maintenance – the last a very small item) are represented by a horizontal line. Variable costs, associated with locomotive-km, and/or train-km, are indicated by the sloping line. That for electric traction rises more slowly for the reasons listed above, and hence a break-even point may be estimated (usually in terms of gross tonnes per route-km per annum) above which electrification will be justified. This is usually in the range of 5–15 million gross tonnes, but varies widely according to specific conditions.

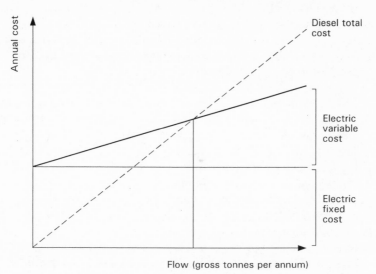

Figure 9.2 Break-even chart for rail electrification. Only traction-related costs are shown; those of signalling, terminals, administration, etc., are excluded.

In the case of passenger traffic, user benefits may also be significant, since a higher quality of service may be provided. Typically, this would include higher speeds (the HST is a notable exception to this, but at a high cost in maintenance). Higher frequencies may also be offered, as the cost structure of electric traction (with a much lower variable cost per train-km) favours this.

The initial capital cost of electrification has been reduced by adoption of simpler overhead structures and less rigid clearances for other structures (where 6.25 kV was formerly specified, 25 kV is now accepted). Nonetheless, it remains the major factor. It is difficult to isolate the costs of electrification infrastructure as such, since other track and signalling renewal is often undertaken at the same time, together with investment in rolling stock. The most recent inter-urban example in Britain, the extension from Cambridge to King's Lynn in 1992, incurred a cost of about £950,000 per route-km, although this was inflated by stricter safety standards introduced during the construction period. The other scheme currently in progress, the suburban electrification from Leeds to Ilkley and Skipton, has a cost of £1.2 million per route-km, but this includes a larger element of rolling stock due to the higher frequency provided (*Modern Railways* 1992).

Since the capital costs of electrification are incurred at the start of a project, while operating benefits will extend over many years, a long-term evaluation is essential. The break-even flow is highly sensitive to the discount rate selected (the two being roughly in direct proportion within the typical range of flows considered). The requirement imposed by the Department of Transport that projects be tested on an 8% real discount rate, thus has a significant effect on the scale of further electrification which may be justified.

Future expansion of electrification will also be affected by changes in unit costs, especially of fuel, and locomotives. Use of regenerative braking would also widen the energy cost difference.

Control and signalling

Reference has been made already to the concept of block signalling in Chapter 4. The same principle has been in use on double-track long-distance lines for over a hundred years, but owing to the much wider range of speeds encountered and lower densities of traffic, multiple-aspect signalling is used to indicate a range of likely stopping distances. In more sophisticated systems, such as the TGV, a form of cab signalling may be used to provide a continuous indication of permitted speeds, replacing trackside signals.

The use of multiple-aspect colour light signalling has been associated with the replacement of manually operated boxes (one to each block section) by area control centres, in which track circuits (as described in Ch. 4) are used to display the location of trains on a panel covering large areas. Substantial labour cost savings may also be made. As the reliability of computer hardware and software has improved, solid state interlocking (SSI) has replaced previous electromechanical systems.

In many areas, high labour costs are still incurred on low-density routes. The operation of level crossings has often remained manual, and only in the 1980s was a large-scale programme of conversion to automatic barrier operation carried out in Britain, although such methods have been commonplace in other European countries (such as the Netherlands) for many years. On single-track routes, several means of simplified signalling are provided, based on the general principle that only one train can occupy a section between two passing loops at one time. Former manual systems are now being replaced by radio electronic tokenless block (RETB) working, in which authority to occupy a section of track is transmitted electronically. As in the case of area signalling schemes for main lines, savings are obtained in manpower, and more effective control obtained over a large area. Examples include low-density routes in Scotland and East Anglia.

Although in Britain single-track operation is still considered very much a feature of low-density routes, the lower signalling and track provision costs associated with it, have encouraged conversion of some medium-density double-track routes – such as parts of the Carlisle-Dumfries-Glasgow route – to single track operation, often associated with elimination of manual boxes which formerly controlled each double-track block section. In many other countries, much of the network is single track, often accommodating high densities of freight traffic, both in the developing world, and other European countries such as Sweden. Centralized Traffic Control (CTC), based on data from track circuits and radio contract with drivers, enables the best use to be made of route capacity over large areas.

It should be stressed that the description of rail signalling given above is necessarily a highly simplified one, the technology being a complex subject in its own right. Only those aspects immediately relevant to cost and capacity have been considered.

Capacity and flow

The basic characteristics are in principle the same as for urban railways described in Chapter 4. In general, minimum braking distances are greater, acceleration rates lower, and hence minimum headways somewhat wider. As a practical scheduled minimum headway between successive fast trains, a figure of 4–5, rather than 2, minutes may be taken.

A major difficulty arises when trains of different speeds and characteristics are mixed over a common route: InterCity passenger, freight and local passenger, for example. Although – dependent upon the length of block sections – trains of similar speed can follow each other at close headways, this is not practicable when different types are mixed. This may be illustrated by use of a time-distance diagram, in which distance along a specific route is shown on the vertical axis, and time on the horizontal. The path of the train is represented by a line whose angle of inclination to the horizontal increases with speed, and in which an intermediate stop is represented by a short horizontal line. The "mix of speeds" problem may be alleviated by grouping trains of similar characteristics into "flights", so that empty paths occur only when one batch of trains follows another. Figure 9.3 shows the section of route between Birmingham New Street and Coventry, on which a basic half-hourly InterCity service, calling intermediately at Birmingham International, shares the track with local trains and some less frequent InterCity services. During the evening peak period, six InterCity and five stopping trains are fitted in by this means (one of the stoppers terminating at International).

The same concept may be applied to long-distance InterCity routes where speeds vary. For example, on the main line from Paddington, fast HST services are grouped within the same period in each hourly cycle. On the Euston–Rugby line, the basic all-day service is grouped into part of each hour, other paths then being available for slower passenger trains, special workings, etc. In the peak, a regular pattern, with an intermediate stop at Watford, is followed by all trains.

A graphical timetable of the type shown in Figure 9.3 can be used for scheduling purposes in several ways. On a single-track route, both directions of move-

179

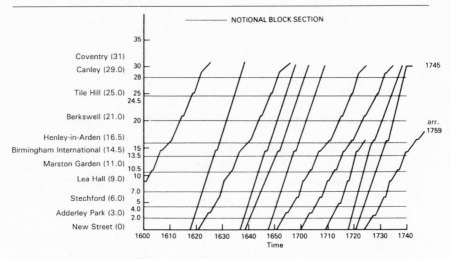

Figure 9.3 A "time distance" timetable graph, showing the scheduling of Intercity and local trains over the Birmingham–Coventry route (1983/4 timetable) between 16.20h and 18.00h on a weekday evening.

ment can be superimposed (i.e. lines sloping in both directions: where they intersect, passing loops will be necessary). On double-track routes, the constraint that not more than one train should occupy a block section at one time may be observed easily by marking off block sections on the vertical axis.

Track structure and route alignment

Conventional rail track is a flexible structure, in which the highly concentrated train weight (axle loads of up to 25 tonnes – or even 30 on some US freight lines) is distributed through rail and sleepers to the ballast (a layer of stone chippings) to the sub-base, embankment, viaduct or tunnel structure. Flat-bottomed, continuously welded rail (CWR) is fixed to concrete sleepers by steel track clips, replacing the former bull-head rail mounted in cast-iron "chairs" onto wooden sleepers. These changes have produced a smoother ride, lower costs and require less access time for maintenance. Ballast cleaning, "tamping" (placing of ballast correctly to support the sleepers), and rail replacement have been largely mechanized. At the ends of sections of CWR, overlapping tapered sections of rail have replaced the end-on joints, connected by "fishplates" around which fractures were liable to develop.

Heavier axle loads are accommodated through use of larger cross-section rail, up to 60–70kg/metre, although supporting structures, notably bridges, may continue to dictate axle-load limits.

A major constraint on alignment is the radii of curved sections. For a given speed, a minimum curvature will apply, and on open-country sections of many major routes (notably the East Coast main line) many curves have been aligned to permit higher limits. Use of super-elevation – raising the outer rail relative to the inner – also permits a higher speed for a given radius, but in practice, is restricted to a maximum of about 15cm.

In an attempt to reduce maintenance costs, some track is now constructed by use of a slip-form concrete paver, as for roads, forming a rigid base into which track clips are inserted. High capital cost results in it being confined to tunnels and other sections where reduced need for maintenance access is particularly useful.

Besides curvature, the other main constraint on alignment is gradient. Ruling limits of about 1 in 70 (about 1.5%) have been considered desirable on main lines, although on introduction of electrification, these have become less critical. The Paris-Lyon TGV route, used only by passenger trains, incorporates gradients as steep as 1 in 30 (about 3%), making tunnels unnecessary, and requiring few major viaducts.

Rolling stock

The basic layout of InterCity passenger stock is that of two four-wheeled bogies supporting a body of about 20m. Lengths have gradually increased as lateral clearances have improved. The traditional compartment layout has been replaced by an open-saloon plan, with centre gangway. Passenger capacity (standard class) has thus risen from 56 in the 1950s Mark 1 compartment and 72 in Mark 3 stock, the last-named 23m in length. Integral, all-steel construction is used to give a relatively low weight. As in the case of urban stock (Ch. 4), use of aluminium alloy extrusions can give further weight savings. The latest Mark 4 stock on the East Coast main line offers a similar capacity.

The 72-seat layout in the Mark 3 coach is based on the general pattern of seats grouped in fours facing each other. Given the acceptability of "front-to-back" seating on competing express-coach services, a higher-density layout has been placed in some vehicles, giving 80 seats.

The interior layout of long-distance stock has also been changed by reducing doors to the ends of the vehicle only, and providing luggage shelves at the ends of the passenger saloon. Air conditioning is now general, with much improved suspension. Air brakes have replaced vacuum to permit higher speeds. Curiously, exterior doors are still manually opened on Mark 3 stock, but automatic opening and locking is fitted to Mark 4 stock. Under financial constraints, little new stock is currently being built in Britain, but Mark 3 stock is being refurbished to offer a higher standard of interior accommodation.

Most high-speed trains are locomotive-hauled, or with a power car at each end (the HST, TGV and Eurostar). On the main electrified routes (East and West Coast) push-pull operation now applies, the locomotive placed at one end of the train for both directions of movement, with movement in the "reverse" direction controlled through a driving vehicle trailer (DVT).

High-speed conventional railways

A combination of track re-alignment, re-signalling and new stock enables maximum speeds to be raised to about 160 km/h on many sections. Up to 200 km/h is found extensively on BR, and other European systems. Uniquely for such speeds, much of the British network is based on the diesel High Speed Train (HST) technology, rather than electric traction. However, the IC225 stock on the East Coast Main Line is electrically powered, and, as its title indicates, has potential for operation at up to 225 km/h when resignalling work is completed. Apart from minor route re-alignment and re-signalling, the upgrading to 200 km/h has not involved any new infrastructure, except for the diversionary route between Doncaster and York on the ECML, required in any case to by-pass the severe speed restriction at Selby.

Elsewhere, entirely new infrastructure has been built on a much larger scale, enabling conventional rail technology to attain much higher speeds. The Paris-Lyon TGV (Train à Grande Vitesse) route, opened fully in 1983, permits a maximum speed of 270 km/h (160 mph), and an average of about 200 km/h. 25 kV power cars at each end of the 12-car train give some 6300 kW. Existing tracks give access to city centres and other routes for through-working. New construction has thus been confined to open country, and as mentioned above, use of the line by passenger trains only has enabled much steeper gradients to be accepted. A second route from Paris, the TGV Atlantique, opened in 1991 (with a maximum speed of 300 km/h) followed in 1993 by the "TGV Nord" between Paris and Lille, connecting to the Channel Tunnel from its opening in 1994, and subsequently with a high-speed route into Belgium and the Netherlands. The TGV technology has also been employed for the Spanish high-speed service (AVE) between Madrid and Seville.

The "Shinkansen" network in Japan began in 1964 with the opening of the Tokaido Line between Tokyo and Osaka, relieving the heavily overloaded 1067 mm gauge line between those cities. Subsequent extensions have taken this route to Hakata (1100 km) and new routes north of Tokyo (Joetsu and Tohoku) were opened in 1983. Traffic densities are very high, but so are construction costs, owing to the mountainous terrain, and high population density in lowland areas. Adoption of standard gauge (1435 mm) has limited the scale of the network, by making it necessary to build entirely separate routes, rather than utilising through-running over existing tracks to reach city centres, for example. Penetration of Tokyo city has proved particularly costly.

New high-speed routes have also been built in Germany (served by the ICE train), albeit at extremely high cost, and have been proposed for several city-pairs in the USA. The French conditions, of low-density, relatively flat, rural regions between major traffic nodes may be largely unique.

Attention has thus shifted back to upgrading conventional technology. If existing curvatures and braking distances imposed by signalling can be negotiated at higher speeds, then little infrastructure investment will be needed. Given the limits to super-elevation of the track described above, the body of the train itself may be tilted further to increase maximum speed for a given radius. The tilt may be passive (pendular) or active (with a mechanism activated by lateral acceleration of the train). One abortive attempt was BR's Advanced Passenger Train (APT), tested extensively in the 1970s and early 1980s. Tilting suspension is however, used successfully elsewhere, notably on the Swedish X2000, the Italian "Pendolino", and also on the 1067-mm gauge lines in Japan. In most cases, such tilting stock is used to raise relatively low speeds up to 160 or 200 km/h rather than match the very high speeds found on new main lines. The Mark 4 stock in Britain was built with a view to such use (hence the tapered profile), but this is now unlikely.

New modes for high-speed movement

It has been suggested that a gap exists in the range of modes available, between high-speed conventional rail, and short-haul air services, in the speed range 250–600km/h, for trips of about 400–500km: for example, to give a timing of one hour from central London to central Manchester. In the late 1960s, physical separation of train and track was considered necessary to avoid effects of oscillation, although subsequent experience of the TGV has proved that higher speeds are possible on rail.

The first approach to this problem was to apply the hovercraft principle, in the form of the British "Tracked Hovertrain" and French "Aérotrain", but both were abandoned in the early 1970s (the former partly on the assumption that the APT would shortly be available), perhaps on a short-sighted view, as magnetic leviation (Maglev) was already being developed as a more efficient alternative to the hovercraft principle. Maglev high-speed projects have continued to be tested in Japan and Germany, although commercial passenger operation still appears uncertain.

In any case the "gap" between high-speed conventional rail and domestic air services is being closed by the use of STOL (short take-off and landing) aircraft such as the De Havilland Canada Dash–7, or BAe 146 jet, as used on business services to the London Docklands' airport opened in 1987 (however, almost all its operations to date have been international, rather than domestic). Furthermore, much of the air journey time over such distances is taken up in access trips and waiting. Higher frequencies, unreserved services (such as the British Airways Shuttle), and better-sited terminals may prove more important than maximum speeds as such. Air traffic control delays are another significant factor for services to/from London

The current network structure and policy issues

Rail

Within the BR InterCity sector at 1993, the non-electrified routes were served by the HST fleet of 95 trains, and operated through-services such as projections to/ from Aberdeen and Inverness on the London–Edinburgh route. Even those regional routes that may appear "local" at first sight may in practice function largely as InterCity feeders. On the Barnstaple–Exeter branch, for example, about 75% of the traffic is for points beyond Exeter.

The major network development during the next few years is likely to be construction of the Union Railways' high-speed link between St Pancras and the Channel Tunnel, also serving north and mid-Kent, subject to finance being secured. This will supplant the current route on the 3rd rail network, and reduce journey time from about 70 to 40 minutes.

The West Coast Main line handles the greatest concentration of traffic in Britain – about 5 million journeys per year on the London–Manchester trunk section – yet is currently limited to 175 km/h. Several schemes has been considered for its upgrading, including completely new infrastructure on the TGV model, and a more modest "IC250" proposal, using technology similar to that on the East Coast Main Line. At present very little investment is occurring, but renewal of signalling and some rolling stock is becoming urgent. Some renewal, with modest upgrading, possibly through private finance, is now being examined. Green (1993) indicates that densities of traffic remain insufficient to justify radical high-speed technology.

Long-distance coach

Following impact of the 1980 Transport Act, as described above, the network has been re-oriented to provide fast high-frequency services (typically every two hours or better) between London and main centres, together with major cross-country services. "Hub" interchanges are provided at London Victoria, Bristol, Birmingham and other centres. Victoria Coach Station, now placed under the control of London Transport, has been substantially upgraded, and is now open to all operators (albeit some independents continue to use on-street terminals in central London to avoid resultant costs). However, its location is not ideal, a site in the Paddington/Marylebone area being more logical in terms of the main flows now handled. Unfortunately, a very hostile attitude toward coach terminals has been adopted by the local planning authority (Westminster) making such developments unlikely at present.

Further scope for express service improvement is curtailed by increasingly restrictive regulation on speed (although the safety rationale for this is unclear). Under ECE R66 regulations, specifying improved roof strength to reduce "roll-over" accident casualties, such new vehicles are limited to 100km/h. A similar limit applies to all new vehicles under EC regulations from 1994. Allowing for a tolerance of 5%, a 105km/h (65mph) limit is being adopted as a general standard in Britain (with all new vehicles from 1 January 1994 fitted with limiters at the new figure), so that older vehicles are also covered. It is also proposed to prohibit coaches from the "outside" (fastest) lane on motorways. Together with the effects of road congestion, the overall average speed of express coach services is thus likely to diminish, reducing the competitive advantage vis a vis rail.

Air

As indicated above, a very substantial part of the domestic air network is focused on Heathrow, and to a lesser extent, Gatwick. Interlining traffic forms a major element. However, the decision to open up access to Heathrow in 1991, coupled with limited overall capacity, means that use of runway slots for low-density domestic flights becomes increasingly less attractive. British Midland withdrew its Liverpool service in favour of Brussels flights in 1991. Services from Humberside, Birmingham, East Midlands and Norwich have also gone. While the major domestic trunk routes (from Manchester northwards) will continue to justify use of capacity at Heathrow, medium-distance services are being squeezed out. For direct access to London as such, rail offers a good alternative, but interlining passengers may find themselves suffering noticeably poorer access. In some other European countries, links to permit main-line rail services to serve major airports directly have been constructed (TGV services to Lyon Satolas, and Paris Charles de Gaulle; Netherlands' services to Schiphol, etc.). However, the Heathrow express link now being constructed will provide a link only toward central London, with no west or north connection to the intercity network.

References and suggested further reading

Alston, L. L. 1984. *Railways and energy*. Staff Working Paper 634, World Bank, Washington DC.

Astill, D. & P. R. White 1989. Express coach as an access mode to major airports. PTRC Summer Annual Meeting, September, Seminar D, 13–20.

Civil Aviation Authority (CAA). UK Airlines: annual operating, traffic and financial statistics 1991 (CAP606). CAA, London, 1992.

— Competition on the main trunk routes. Paper 87005, CAA, London, March 1987,

— Passengers at London airports in 1991 (CAP610). CAA, London, 1993.

Dennis, N. Analysis of air transport data, published in White &Doganis (op. cit.) 1990

Department of Transport. *Transport statistics Great Britain 1976–86*, Table 2.33. HMSO, London, 1987.

Green, Chris [Director of the then InterCity Sector]. The future of InterCity rail in Britain. Paper to Royal Society conference "Passenger Transport after 2000 AD", July 1993.

185

Holt, S. R. & P. R. White 1981. Modelling of inter-urban passenger demand on the Southern Region. Research Report 6, Transport Studies Group, Polytechnic of Central London.

Jones, D. E. S. & P. R. White 1994. Modelling of cross-country rail services. *Journal of Transport Geography* **2**(2), 111–121.

Modern Railways 1986. InterCity faces the future. January, 27–8.

— 1992. Data on electrification schemes. October, 548–9, 565–7.

Monopolies and Mergers Commission 1994. *National Express Group plc and Saltire Holdings Ltd: a report on the merger situation.* Cm 2468. London: HMSO.

National Travel Survey 1989/91. London: HMSO, September 1993.

Prideaux, J. 1979. How InterCity turned around. *Modern Railways* (August), 404–408.

Transport Statistics Great Britain 1968–1978 (data from Long Distance Travel Survey). London: HMSO, 1979.

Rickard, J. M. 1988. Factors influencing long-distance rail passenger trip rates in Great Britain. *Journal of Transport Economics and Policy* **XXII**, 209–33.

Robbins, D. K. & P. R. White 1986. The experience of express coach deregulation in Great Britain. *Transportation* **13**, 339–64.

Wardman, M. 1993. *The effect of rail journey times and improvements: some results and lessons of British experience relevance to high-speed rail forecasting.* Working paper 388, Institute of Transport Studies, University of Leeds.

White, P. R. & R. S. Doganis 1990. *Long-distance travel within Britain.* Discussion Paper 17 (Transport and Society series), Transport Studies Unit, University of Oxford.

Transport policy issues

In the first and second editions of this book, the last two chapters were devoted to transport policy issues, in the short and long run respectively. Writing again, seventeen years after the first edition, presents the opportunity to examine how some of the problems identified then have been resolved – or, in many cases, still remain critical. While the overall ideology behind central government policy over this period has itself been broadly consistent, its short run application has often been erratic, and in many respects increasingly extreme. However, within the last year or two some significant changes in underlying policy have emerged, notably in the rediscovery of the link between transport and land use policy, and the importance of issues such as energy consumption and environmental impacts. Although this chapter is generally chronological, certain themes are traced through over a longer period when first introduced, such as local bus deregulation, to avoid an unduly fragmented style.

Policy prior to 1979

The railways

Following the drastic cut-backs in the rail passenger network during the 1960s, no major closures occurred after 1971. Under the Railways Act 1974, the BR Board was required to operate a network "generally comparable" with that then running. Much greater flexibility in pricing policy, and in the working of the freight sector, had been applied from 1968. However a rather slack approach to containing costs had also become evident, possibly accentuated by the shift from route-by-route grants to a PSO payment for the whole network from 1975. Productivity improvement had greatly slowed down, and there was perhaps tendency to blame external factors for many of the railways problem (illustrated in statements by the then Chairman, Richard Marsh) rather than a willingness to make internal changes.

In his book *The train that ran away*, Stewart Joy, the BR Chief Economist until 1972, had illustrated this with many examples. In *The rail problem*, published in 1975, Pryke & Dodgson had highlighted the extensive scope for productivity improvement. Many of the changes suggested are now standard policy (such as driver-only operation) although received in a very hostile manner by management at the time.

However, the books of Joy, and Pryke & Dodgson, also reflected a rather negative view of the rôle of secondary passenger services. Little attention was devoted in them to the rôle of service quality, marketing or pricing (other than scope for real price increases in inelastic markets such as London commuting, as a means of reducing deficits). Improved efficiency was equated largely with cost reductions, rather than maximizing traffic (or revenue) relative to the resources input. This rather limited concept of efficiency has also been evident in many central government reviews of public transport.

Conversely, many of those keen to support public transport were often unwilling to accept the scope for improving efficiency as a means of reducing financial support without loss of service or real fare increases. An unrealistic set of alternatives was thus offered – improved efficiency and reduced deficits but with loss of benefits to users; or a retention of the existing system with its user benefits, but also its inefficiencies and rigidities.

London

London Transport (LT) had been placed under the then Greater London Council (GLC) since 1970. This had enabled public transport policy to be linked with that for highways and land use, and encouraged a greater level of financial support to public transport. Even under the Conservative GLC administration of the early 1970s, for example, virtually all of LT's capital expenditure was met by outright grants, where not covered already by central government sources such as the New Bus Grant. Together with writing off LT's capital debt on handover to the GLC, this virtually eliminated interest charges, a very favourable position in comparison to other bus and rail operators in Britain.

However, the limited area covered by the GLC as designated in 1963 – not even the whole built-up mass of London, let alone the commuter catchment – resulted in some problems for the bus system (arbitrarily splitting the London, and country bus, networks), and also caused problems for those parts of the underground (all of which remained with LT) running beyond its boundary, resulting in higher fares and/or demands for local authority support for the sections concerned. Until the early 1980s, the regional management structure of BR (London being covered by the separate Eastern, Midland, Western and Southern regions) made it difficult to adopt coherent policies within BR itself, let alone in relation to other authorities or transport operators. The cross-London Thameslink service (re-using the closed goods tunnel between Blackfriars and Farringdon), now seen as a clear success, had to wait until the formation of the London and South East Sector (now Network South East) before its potential was accepted, leading to its opening in 1988.

188

London Transport also illustrated even more clearly than BR the rigidities of large organizations. Despite several changes of title, the organization was effectively that created in 1933, as the London Passenger Transport Board. Even by the late 1930s, Frank Pick, its chief executive, had noted this problem (Barman 1979). A very large engineering establishment had been created, yet not cut back with the drop in bus fleet size associated with loss of traffic from the 1950s or transfer of over 1,000 vehicles to London Country in 1970. The engineering organization found great difficulty in coping with the rear-engined bus design (much more so than other operators), resulting in large fleets of seven-year-old vehicles being disposed of from the late 1970s. There was even less willingness among management to accept the need for change than in BR, as the author discovered in producing some initial productivity comparisons in 1977.

The local bus industry

Elsewhere in the bus industry, the National Bus Company (NBC), established in 1969, had consolidated the networks inherited from the previous state-owned (Tilling) and private (BET) groups. In some areas, the two overlapped, leading to a sensible rationalization between them, with fewer depots and simpler networks (for example, the former United Welsh, and South Wales Transport company networks around Swansea). However, this process had also extended to the merger of substantial existing companies in the belief that economics of scale would result. Thus, the whole of the Western National, Southern National and Devon General companies' management, covering Cornwall, Devon, and much of Dorset and Somerset, was concentrated at Exeter. Even by the late 1970s, however, it was evident that some of the more successful units in retaining traffic and giving a good financial performance were among the smaller ones, such as Oxford and Southern Vectis. The consolidation within NBC also involved the application of uniform liveries of red or green, replacing distinctive local colour schemes, further weakening the loyalties of staff and customers to identifiable businesses.

On the positive side, NBC created central planning and market research units, leading to development of the MAP planning system (described in Ch. 5), improved costing techniques, and other innovations. In contrast, the Scottish Bus Group (SBG) pursued a highly conservative managerial policy, which retained existing company loyalties, but did little to stimulate innovation.

The bus industry as a whole benefited from increased financial support. The New Bus Grant paid by central government was set at 25% under the 1968 Transport Act, and increased to 50% in 1971. This enabled operators to fund their replacement programmes at about the same rate as before, and compensate for the inadequacies of historic depreciation (provided that vehicles purchased were potentially suitable for one-person operation). Many small operators were able to buy new vehicles for the first time in many years. The rebate of fuel duty

189

for stage carriage services was increased to cover the whole duty from early 1974 (remaining thus until the budget of November 1993), following election promises by both major parties, to offset the effect of rising oil prices.

The two central government grants had the merit of simplicity, and proved particularly valuable to operators in non-metropolitan counties who otherwise received little support, although they may also have distorted the cost structure through effectively removing most track costs for buses, and reducing the cost of new buses vis-a-vis re-bodying.

Concessionary fares

The 1968 Transport Act and subsequent local government policy changes had stimulated a major expansion in concessionary fare schemes for the elderly and disabled in the early 1970s, notably the free off-peak passes in some metropolitan areas (such as the GLC, West Midlands and South Yorkshire), and half-fares or flat fares, in most other urban areas. Rural districts were less generous, some offering no concession at all, and others only tokens rather than passes. The benefits of such concessions go primarily to the user rather than the operator, but they helped to improve load factors by stimulating off-peak traffic, and in the case of passes for free travel, reducing boarding times on one-person-operated services. By the mid-1970s the range of elderly and disabled concessions was fairly similar to that found today, although some counties were subsequently able to consolidate separate district council schemes into a common county-wide form, usually based on half the standard fare, as in Surrey.

A White Paper published by the Labour government in 1979 proposed the adoption of a common national minimum standard, based on a half fare at off-peak times, but this has not been pursued by any subsequent government. In some cases, owing to financial pressures, local authorities have had to revert to a less generous concession, notably in Edinburgh, West Yorkshire and Tyne & Wear, where free off-peak travel has been replaced by a flat fare.

Public expenditure on local public transport

Direct "revenue support" for bus services – i.e. payments to support specific routes and/or entire networks – has been general since the 1950s elsewhere in Europe, but was not introduced in Britain (apart from some deficit financing of local authority undertakings and London Transport) until the 1968 Act, which enabled "rural services" (undefined) to receive support, and for the PTAs to set precepts on their constituent authorities. Rural grants were based on a 50:50 contribution by the local authority (district or county) and central government, provided that the service supported met at least 50% of its costs from passenger revenue. Rural authorities, whose previous rôle in public transport had been confined largely to school buses and objecting to rail closures, began to take a more active rôle in public transport provision.

Under the Local Government Act 1972 this was broadened to give the county councils a mandatory duty to promote a "coordinated and efficient system of public transport" (Section 202). Under the Local Government Act of 1974, they were empowered to receive the Transport Supplementary Grant (in England and Wales) and the present non-metropolitan local government structure was introduced. Counties then established "transport co-ordinating officers" (or posts of equivalent rôle), who were responsible for co-ordinating the services operated, especially those to which specific support was given. In many, this has also come to include co-ordination of school and social-services transport along with the public scheduled network, as described in Chapter 8.

By the late 1970s fairly clear distinctions could be drawn between the approaches taken by counties, which have generally continued through radical changes in central government policy. Thus some, such as Norfolk, adopted a minimalist approach, providing support for specific loss-making services and initiatives such as community minibuses, but not becoming involved in planning of the network as a whole, or fares policy. Others adopted a much more interventionist approach, based on higher levels of revenue support, such as Surrey and Hertfordshire. Here, the initiative was taken by counties in comprehensive passenger surveys and network planning, prior to the introduction of the MAP system by NBC. Service levels in general were substantially higher than a purely "commercial" approach might imply, and overall fare policies were also adopted.

Until 1975-6, a separate system of grants for road construction had been applied by central government, and in addition an allowance was made in the estimation of rate support grant (RSG) for road maintenance costs (for example, the relatively greater burden faced by a low-density rural county). Central government capital grants were also applied to major urban transport projects under Section 56 of the Transport Act 1968 and other specific grants also existed, such as those for rural bus services.

These were replaced by a comprehensive system in which all local authority transport spending (except for schools and social services) was included, both current and capital, on roads and public transport. Each county (or, in Scotland, region) was required to submit to the Department of the Environment (DOE), via the regional office, a Transport Policies and Programme (TPP) document, outlining expenditure plans for the following financial year (and up to five years for capital spending). The DOE then determined the total expenditure which it was prepared to approve (a rôle which in some ways limited the freedom of local authorities in contrast to the previous system), this being financed by a mixture of Rate Support Grant (RSG), the council's own revenue, and by the Transport Supplementary Grant (TSG), a grant introduced from 1975-6 which corresponded roughly to the national amalgamated total of the specific grants prior to that year.

The effect of amalgamating the various forms of grant was to enable author-

191

ities to switch from capital to current expenditure, especially in the metropolitan areas, where road capital spending was reduced in favour of current support to public transport, thus permitting lower fares and/or higher service levels. This was clearly not to the liking of central government (Labour or Conservative), who made several efforts to reverse this trend (culminating, one might suggest in the abolition of the "mets" in 1986). In many metropolitan areas the proportion of transport spending devoted to public transport current expenditure reached around 50% or more in some cases, compared with a typical range of 5–10% in "shire" counties and regions.

The application of the programme set out in the TPP of a county did not necessarily match the proposals as initially submitted, or later approved. Much of the expenditure covered by RSG was in activities other than transport, such as education, and there was no compulsion to spend money approved for transport on transport as such, or within the transport sector as originally set out. It was also possible for local authorities to spend above the accepted total, the difference being made up by rate income (for example, in the South Yorkshire case, to cover its low fares policy). In some cases, this could result in complete loss of TSG. Central government attempted to deter such policies by introducing "clawback" arrangements (under which local authorities lost RSG as their total spending rose above levels which the government found acceptable), and subsequently, through "rate capping", where the maximum rate was set by central government. In Scotland, from local government re-organization in 1975, TSG was not introduced, and only RSG was paid (although TPPs were submitted).

Planning and policy in the major cities

Within the larger urban areas, a network-wide approach to public transport planning and finance was adopted from the early 1970s. The PTEs' rail schemes set out in their development plans, stipulated under the 1968 Act, provided the basis for rail investment projects, although most of these were not completed until the late 1970s. The immediate change on formation of the PTEs was the merger of existing municipal bus systems into single fleets, and in two cases (West Midlands and Greater Manchester) acquisition of most NBC services in their areas. Comprehensive network planning and marketing became possible, although in the short run a common livery and (cash) fare scale were the most evident. The benefits of integration – bus/rail interchanges, and extensive travelcard use – generally came later.

In the short run, some diseconomies of scale may have been produced by the formation of very large fleets, although greater planning and financial expertise was also introduced. Following the election of Labour-controlled authorities in many metropolitan counties in 1974, general low-fare policies were adopted, often involving a fares freeze (maintained until 1985–6 in South Yorkshire), thus aggravating conflicts between central and local government.

192

The early 1970s also saw a marked shift to provision of the
measures to favour public transport – of the types described in
of which were installed at this time. In some cases, these were
decisions to abandon costly and intrusive urban road schemes, no
don, Nottingham and Southampton.

The most marked shift of this type occurred in Nottingham, where
donment of urban motorway schemes was followed by a large increase
bus services, extensive bus priorities in the central area, and the "zone a
lar" scheme, in which bus priorities and urban traffic control on radials int
city were to be used to directly constrain car flow, as well as aiding bus
Park-and-ride services for car users were also introduced (see Ch. 5), but the
effective diversion from car to bus was very small, in part owing to the high proportion of private non-residential parking in the centre, but also the very
short-lived nature of the zone-and-collar scheme, which was hastily abandoned
after an adverse public reaction.

Monitoring of other schemes at this time by Heggie (1976) and others also
showed that, in the short run at least, the scope for diverting car users to
improved public transport services appeared small, most of the increased traffic
from schemes such as the Stevenage "Superbus" coming from existing bus users,
non-motorized modes and newly generated traffic. Little effort was made to
introduce comprehensive bus priority or traffic-restraint schemes after 1976,
some of the less successful (or more controversial) ones being abandoned. Ironically, some of the more radical changes in public transport systems which have
attracted significant numbers of car users, such as the London Transport Travelcard, and Tyne & Wear Metro, did not arrive until the early 1980s, when the
car-diversion issue had temporarily become less important, owing to much lower
rates of traffic growth than previously anticipated.

Policies of the Conservative administration since 1979

The Conservative government elected in 1979, and its successors elected in
1983, 1987 and 1992, have implemented a general policy of privatization, deregulation, and containing public expenditure. In transport, this has partly rein-
forced previous policies – notably to reduce rail deficits, and contain local
authority spending – but also introduced radical change at national level. In public transport this has also been marked by deregulation of certain sectors, and
privatization. The former has had much greater impact on the pattern of service
to the user. This can be seen in the deregulation of express coach services,
described in Chapters 1 and 9, which resulted in very rapid growth in total traffic, together with innovations in pricing and service quality. Contrary to the
expectations of the government, the principal nationalized operators succeeded
in increasing their total patronage substantially, often with much greater success

.an independents. Managerial policy and (de)regulation, rather than ownership
.s such, thus emerged as the predominant factors.

Early phases of policy

In addition to deregulation of express coach services, the Transport Act of 1980
also liberalized regulation of "stage carriage" (now, "local") bus services, to an
extent greater than often realized. Price control virtually disappeared, and it
became somewhat easier to obtain road-service licences for new routes, resulting
in cases of direct "on the road" competition (Savage 1985), and rapid growth in
commuter coach services competing with rail into London.

The early stages of privatization in transport were applied to BR shipping services (Sealink), and hotels; the National Freight Corporation (NFC); and the
nationalized ports (now Associated British Ports), but with much less effect on
service levels and the customer. These undertakings already operated close to
profitability in highly competitive markets. The most interesting outcome was
perhaps the success of employee shareholding in NFC (initially created almost by
accident), which set a precedent for other industries, notably local bus operations. Powers were also introduced in the 1982 Transport Act to enable the introduction of private capital into NBC, but without effect until its complete
privatization under the Transport Act 1985.

The Transport Act of 1983

In the light of continued conflict between central and local government over the
appropriate levels of current expenditure on public transport, especially in the
larger urban areas, the government introduced the Transport Act 1983. This gave
central government control over the permitted expenditure of London Transport
and the PTAs, following uncertainty caused by the GLC "Fares Fair" policy (see
Ch. 7), and the subsequent legal challenge to the amount of revenue support thus
required. A "protected expenditure level" (PEL) was set, which could not be subject to legal challenge. The Act required the metropolitan authorities to evaluate
their proposed public transport current – as well as capital – spending. The PTEs,
and London Transport, were required to submit annually three-year plans, containing estimates of traffic, service levels and revenues under various options,
and an evaluation of them using social cost–benefit analysis.

A guide to the methodology was produced by the Department of Transport
(1982; see also Glaister & Searle 1983), the technique being popularly known as
the "Glaister model" after work undertaken by Dr Stephen Glaister of the London School of Economics. It was not, perhaps, entirely to the wish of the government, that the method generally showed a net benefit per £ of public
expenditure, low fares often providing a higher return than enhanced service lev-

194

els (see the discussion of the fares/service level trade-off in Ch. 7). The first round of plans by PTEs indicated that net benefits could often be estimated at subsidy levels substantially higher than those they themselves already received, let alone those desired by the government in their Protected Expenditure Levels (Turner & White 1985).

Using cost–benefit analysis, a similar approach for both current and capital investment appraisal could thus be adopted (the selection of a consistent discount rate forming the link between them). For example, user travel time may be reduced both by investment (in new reserved track systems, for example), but also higher service frequencies, and use of simplified fare structures to reduce boarding times. However, central government has maintained its emphasis on treating capital expenditure, especially roads, as a separate issue. The PTEs are still required to produce the three-year plans set out in the 1983 Act, despite the abolition of the metropolitan counties in 1986, but they are now confined largely to financial planning and broad statements of policy, following the removal of powers to influence overall fares and service levels under the Transport Act 1985.

Local bus deregulation

However, before the new system was fully established, the Conservative Election Manifesto of June 1983 proposed abolition of the metropolitan counties, whose policies in public transport were the main bone of contention between central and local government. The resultant local government structure from April 1986 has been described in Chapter 1. This was followed by a much more extreme interpretation of the declared manifesto policies to further deregulate the bus industry than many had expected, set out in the "Buses" White Paper of June 1984 (Cmnd 9300). Despite widespread opposition, the proposals were very largely enacted in the Transport Act 1985, creating the present structure of regulation and ownership of the local bus industry as described in Chapter 1.

Local services (excluding those in London and Northern Ireland) were deregulated from October 1986. Table 10.1 summarizes the main outcomes since 1985/86 (the last financial year before deregulation came into effect) and 1992/3. The main trends in ridership and bus-kilometres run were established within the first three years after deregulation, the differences between London and other areas (especially the Mets) becoming ever more noticeable in following years.

The striking feature is the absence of correlation between the sharp growth in bus-kilometres run, and the changes in ridership. While specific examples have occurred in which high-frequency minibus replacement of full-sized bus services has undoubtedly stimulated growth in ridership, these have been swamped by the absence of growth elsewhere, and negative effects such as those in instability of services and poor passenger information.

Much of the growth in bus-kilometres run outside London has been in the

195

Table 10.1 Trends in local bus ridership and bus-kilometres operated since deregulation: percentage changes, 1985/86 to 1992/93 inclusive.

Area	Passenger trips	Bus-kilometres
Metropolitans	−33.0	+18.2
English Shires	−17.6	+22.7
Wales	−20.9	+24.2
Scotland	−20.7	+21.4
Average for deregulated areas	−25.3	+21.2
London	−2.1	+20.8
Northern Ireland	−9.9	+19.0

Source: Bus and coach statistics Great Britain 1992–93 (London: HMSO, 1993), tables 1.1 (bus-km) and 2.1 (passenger trips). Northern Ireland data are derived from the combined total for Ulsterbus and Citybus, supplied by the operator.

Table 10.2 Effects on ridership and bus loadings of vehicles being transferred from a low-frequency to high-frequency route.

	Route 1	Route 2	Total/average
Initial case:			
Passengers per hour	504	52	556
Buses per hour	12	2	14
Passengers per bus round trip	42	26	39.7
After switch of operator B to route 1:			
Passengers per hour	504	0	504
Buses/hour	14	0	14
Passengers per bus round trip	36	–	36

form of competing services, often on routes fairly well served initially. Hence, the effective gain in frequency from the user's point of view is often marginal. Consider the example shown in Table 10.2. Two routes are shown, each with a round trip time of one hour. Operator A runs route 1, an intensive urban service requiring 12 full-sized buses to provide a five-minute headway. Each bus picks up 42 passengers on each round trip (this would correspond to an average of 21 each way – a reasonable average load, but most unlikely to result in any overcrowding). Total ridership is thus 504 passengers per hour. Operator B runs route 2, a local suburban service, requiring two buses to provide a 30 minute headway. Each bus picks up 26 passengers per round trip. Thus, 52 passengers per hour are carried in total.

If operator B, operating under a deregulated environment, were to shift his two buses to route no 1, it is unlikely that a significant overall increase in ridership on that route would arise, since a good level of service is already offered, and, at best, the extra two journeys per hour would fall in the middle of two of the five minute intervals on route 1 (implying a unlikely degree of timetable coordination in practice). In reality, operator B could maximize revenue by running just ahead of operator's A existing journeys. If all passengers used cash fares (and/or travelcards, etc. were interavailable between all operators), passengers on route 1 would tend to choose the first bus to arrive.

Hence, as operator B provides 2 of the 14 buses per hour now run on route 1 (14.2% of the departures) he would obtain about the same percentage of the passengers. If total ridership remained constant (the most likely outcome), his two buses would secure about 14.2% of the 504 passengers per hour, i.e.72 passengers, or 36 passengers per round trip – a clear gain from the 26 passengers on route B (an increase of 38%).

However, total passengers carried by all 14 buses (those of operator A plus those of B) would fall from 556 to 504. Hence, average passengers per round trip (taking both operators together) would fall from 556/14 (39.7) to 504/14 (36), a drop of 3.7 (by 9.3%). For operator A, the outcome is somewhat worse – average passengers per round trip would fall from 504/12 (42) to 36, i.e. by 14.3%. Withdrawal of route 2 would cause significant loss of benefits to consumers, if passengers had to walk long distances to an alternative, or were not able to travel at all. It might be necessary for the local authority to introduce a replacement tendered service, increasing total public expenditure.

One could also envisage this situation from the viewpoint of a new operator B, faced with the option of introducing a new service for which he saw some long-run potential (i.e. route 2), or taking the easier course of simply running his buses along route 1, and gaining ridership from the existing operator.

Although simplified, this outcome describes fairly well much of the aggregate change since deregulation. Additional competitive bus-kilometres have been run largely on existing routes, with very little impact in terms of generating extra passengers overall. Average passengers boarding per bus-kilometre in the deregulated areas fell by 38% between 1985/86 and 1992/3, matching the drop in real cost per bus-kilometre, leading to no significant change in real operating cost per passenger carried. For further discussion, see Chartered Institute of Transport (1993, appendix D), Fairhurst (1992) and White (1993).

Note that competition generally takes the form of expanding service levels, rather than lower prices. While some examples have occurred of price competition, they have often been short-lived. This contrasts with the express coach case, in which relatively large elasticities (around –1.0) encourage price competition as a means of diverting users between operators, and stimulating the overall market. In contrast, the small price elasticity for urban bus travel (–0.4 in the short run) means that a fares reduction is unlikely to attract sufficient extra ridership to maintain total revenue, unless very large transfers occurred from other services (see Ch. 7).

One could view the long-distance passengers as "shopping around", comparing price and quality before making a purchase decision (as one does in retail shopping), whereas the urban user will tend to board the first bus to arrive. The latter represents a perfectly rational decision when the "cost" of making the comparison (extra waiting time) is borne in mind. For example, if the disutility of waiting time is around 5p per minute, then a user would only be willing to wait two minutes for a bus offering a fare 10 pence less than their first choice (and assuming a high degree of certainty that the cheaper bus would, in fact, arrive within that period).

Such estimates for waiting time are borne out by the evidence from minibus replacement of lower-frequency full-sized services. A detailed examination of service 282 in north west London showed that passengers switched from waiting for a specific timetabled journey at a 20 minute headway, to random arrivals for a 10 minute minibus headway. The resultant demand increase corresponded to a service level elasticity of about +0.4, and to a waiting time value of about 4p per minute (White et al. 1992).

The sub-optimal outcome of urban bus competition (high frequencies, low average loads, and no reduction in real fares) is thus perfectly consistent with the economist's belief that rational expectations (by both customer and supplier) will determine behaviour. However, short-run rationality does not necessarily produce an optimal long-run outcome.

Returning to the example shown in Table 10.2, the same type of comparison may be made with respect to operation at different times of day or week. A new operator is tempted to run extra services during the busiest times of day (typically, 0800 to 1800, Monday to Saturday), rather than augment services at evenings or Sundays, when, although loadings per bus may be lower, additional bus-kilometres are more likely to expand ridership on the bus network as a whole.

In contrast to the sharp fall in ridership in the deregulated areas, ridership on the London Transport bus network (including tendered services of all operators) rose slightly to 1988/9,but even after a subsequent reduction was only 2.1% below the 1985/86 level in 1992/3 (Table 10.1). A major explanation for this much better performance lies in the rôle of the Travelcard (see Ch. 7). Bus-kilometres run increased by almost exactly the same percentage as in the deregulated areas as a whole, some 21% (see Table 10.1). Although the average real cost per bus-kilometre did not fall quite as much in London as elsewhere (by 28% rather than 38%), the number of passengers boarding per bus kilometre fell by only 19%, leading to a drop in real cost per passenger carried of 16%. The improvements in service level in London have been associated with conversions to "midi" sized operation (notably using the Dennis Dart vehicle), giving frequency improvements similar to those of minibus conversion elsewhere, but without the wasteful competition on trunk routes associated with deregulation.

This conclusion could be considered ironic in view of the comments on the rigidity of the LT organization made earlier in this chapter. A somewhat fortuitous combination of events may provide the explanation. On the one hand, the high level of funding provided by the Labour-controlled GLC in the early 1980s enabled the revenue risks to be taken that permitted a more successful fare structure to be introduced. The efficiency targets, and introduction of competitive tendering, following transfer of the control of LT to central government in 1984, provided the cost reduction. The precedents of cost reduction and minibus operation in the deregulated areas also played a rôle. Subsequent initiatives have come from both a more sophisticated approach to central planning (see Ch. 5), and those through individual bus operators.

Other factors in the decline in ridership outside London include the underly-

198

ing growth in car ownership, and some real fare increases (primarily in the Mets, where fares were raised from a low base, especially in South Yorkshire and Merseyside). The recession since 1990 is a further element (however, until that year, employment was in fact rising from a low point in the early 1980s, and would, *ceteris paribus*, have been expected to stimulate a growth in traffic). Even after allowing for all such relevant factors, the level of demand is significantly less than would have been expected, were typical elasticity values to be applied (Tyson 1992, White 1990). Broadly speaking, the level of ridership is that which might have been expected in the absence of any growth in bus kilometres run.

The main benefits to emerge from deregulation appear to have been in stimulating a sharp reduction in cost per bus-kilometre, and the growth of minibus operation (although it is not invariably applied in an optimal fashion). However, much of the cost reduction benefit may also be obtained through a system of competitive tendering, as applied in London. There is also evidence that the gross tendering system (in which the operator bids on a basis of costs incurred, with all revenue passing to the tendering authority), produces better value for money than the "net subsidy" method commonly found outside London (Tough & White 1993). This is attributable to the greater number of bids forthcoming, especially from low-cost smaller operators, when the revenue risk associated with net subsidy (in which the subsidy bid is for the difference between cost and revenue, rather than total cost), is removed.

Until April 1993, the system of tendering in London was based on the gross cost method, being applied on a route-by-route basis. About half of the London network was then operated in this form, with both London Buses Ltd own subsidiaries, and private sector operators, successful to a similar degree in winning bids. From that month the remaining half of the network, still operated directly by LBL's subsidiaries on a "block grant" basis, was transformed into a negotiated net cost contract (akin to the "net subsidy" method of tendering found outside London).

In November 1993, the government announced that the previously planned deregulation for London was to be postponed (in effect, abandoned for the foreseeable future), while privatization of LBL subsidiaries would proceed, and the net cost contract method would be applied to the whole London network. At the time of writing, however, some issues remain to be resolved, notably in the application (and desirability) of the net cost contract concept, and the relationship between central planning and operator-led initiatives in reshaping the future network. A phased programme for shifting gross cost tendered routes to the net cost system is now proposed, based partly on the development of improved information required for accurate revenue allocation. However, the better overall results from the policy adopted in London to date are clear.

Elsewhere in Europe, concerns regarding high cost levels are also evident, but these are likely to result in a system of competitive tendering (as found in Copenhagen, for example) rather than the complete deregulation attempted experimentally in Britain.

The privatization concept

As indicated above, the first phases of privatization policy were applied to the freight and ports industries, in the form of NFC and ABP. The road freight sector was in any case predominantly covered by private sector operators, the NFC companies (partly inherited from British Rail) being an exception to this pattern. From the mid-1980s, the policy was greatly accelerated, both in the transport sector (notably British Airways and the British Airports Authority), but also in manufacturing (British Aerospace, for example), and much larger organizations elsewhere in the economy (notably British Telecom). Within the transport sector it was applied to much of the bus industry under the 1985 Act, and is being applied to the railways under the Railways Act 1993.

It is appropriate to consider the various meanings of the term "privatization":

- Private ownership throughout the history of the business – for example, almost all taxi operations, and the traditional "independents" in the bus and coach sector. Some rail examples are found outside Britain, notably intensive local passenger networks in Japan.
- The transfer into private ownership of assets previously under public ownership – either through sale of shares to the public at large (as in the British Airways and BAA plc cases), or sales direct to other companies or management/employee buy-outs (as in the case of the bus industry). In the case of the railways, this is currently proposed for the train operations as such, but could eventually apply to the infrastructure (i.e. Railtrack) as well.
- Contracting-out certain activities as a means of improving efficiency, while retaining overall public control – either entire services (such as the tendering of bus services in London), or specific inputs (for example, maintenance work).
- Permitting access to a publicly owned network by other, private operators, while not transferring the whole operation to private ownership. Examples on the rail network in Britain include the minerals traffic handled by Yeomans and ARC with their own locomotives and wagons, the former Charterail freight service, and Stagecoach's former London–Scotland overnight passenger operation. At the international level, it has been introduced from 1 January 1993 through EC Directive 440/91, requiring separate accounting for (but not management of) infrastructure, and access for other operators, including railways from other countries, international combined transport companies, or "international groupings of railway operators".
- Private sector funding of infrastructure for public use. Current examples in Britain include the Heathrow Express rail link, and the private sector contribution to the Jubilee Line Extension. A private sector scheme for modernizing the West Coast Main Line is also under examination.

A substantial part of the bus industry has now been privatized, including all of the former National Bus Company (NBC) and Scottish Bus Group (SBG) regional companies; National Express; and all seven former metropolitan PTCs (the last being Manchester). Strong encouragement has been given to the sale of the remaining local authority-owned bus companies. The ten bus operating subsidiaries of London Transport are now following. During the financial year 1992/3, only 28% of total bus and coach kilometres run in Britain were performed by public sector operators, although this figure will since have fallen due to transfer of further local authority undertakings.

As described in Chapter 1, the sector management structure of British Rail has been replaced from April 1994, with track and infrastructure passing to a new organization, Railtrack, while passenger services are being franchised in about 25 groups, and freight services privatized directly.

Privatization experience on railways prior to 1994 was of an ad hoc form. Most substantial was the operation of "roadstone" minerals traffic from quarries to the main demand areas, i.e. Foster Yeoman from the Mendips to the South East, and ARC from the East Midlands. However, it remained restricted to a few high density flows. BR provided heavy maintenance and train crew. Similar operation could, in principle, be extended to other heavy freight flows, such as oil and coal. The market for general freight traffic in Britain is very weak, associated with short length of haul, and strong road competition. Even on the London – Scotland route, the private sector operator Charterail was unable to meet all costs and went out of business in 1992.

In passenger traffic, leaving aside historic preserved lines (mainly steam-operated, using volunteers), the Stagecoach experience has been the only major example to date, in which, from May 1992, a private company mainly known as a bus and coach operator, marketed the overnight seated accommodation on London–Scotland trains operated by BR. Despite a revised structure for this market from October 1992, the arrangements did not prove successful, and operation reverted entirely to BR from October 1993. Poor information and publicity may have been a factor, especially at the London end (parallels may exist with the experience of smaller coach operators under express coach deregulation).

On the passenger side, it is ironic that such fragmentation pressures should exist when in most respects BR was the most business-focused railway in Europe. The sector management structure evolved in the 1980s (see Ch. 1) placed responsibility both for infrastructure and operations with the same managements (Freight, Parcels, InterCity, NSE, Regional). Market-led considerations replaced the previous emphasis on engineering and operational leadership. In Regional Railways in particular, attitudes associated with previous regional boundaries were overcome to identify considerable potential of upgrading major cross-country routes with improved rolling stock and through service, such as Portsmouth–Cardiff–Brighton, Liverpool–Manchester–Sheffield–East Anglia, etc.

Experience in the bus and coach industry

As indicated above, bus usage outside London has shown an alarming drop since 1985/86, with no overall benefit gained from the substantial growth in bus-kilometres run. This period has coincided with the rapid privatization of NBC and SBG companies. However, it would be too early to draw any specific conclusions regarding effects of privatization *per se* on ridership or performance, the negative impacts probably being due to deregulation as such rather than ownership.

Privatization of the bus industry has taken the form of a mix of management/employee buy-outs, and purchases by large companies, consolidating into bigger groupings in some cases. However, some of the earlier management/employee buy-outs have decided that a better future lies in selling out to larger groups, a process which accelerated rapidly in the early part of 1994, with the switch of PMT (of Stoke of Trent) and Yorkshire Rider (of Leeds) to Badgerline, and the Western Travel Group (operating in the South West Midlands and South Wales) to Stagecoach.

Whereas the privatizations of British Airways, and of the British Airports Authority, were in the form of a public sale of equity shares, the bus privatizations have taken the form of private sales. In the absence of public equity share issues, a large element of finance has often come from fixed-interest bank borrowings. This carries the danger that the resultant interest payments pre-empt much of the operating surplus, and leave little flexibility in a period of recession (conversely, an improvement in the profitability of many companies since 1990/91 has often been associated with a reduction in interest charges, reflecting overall trends in interest rates, rather than operating performance as such).

It is noteworthy that much of the equity capital raised in the Stagecoach Group floatation in 1993 was used to reduce capital gearing (the ratio of interest-bearing debt to equity). The same objective can also be seen in the November 1993 Badgerline floatation, in which £36 million new capital was raised from sale of shares, principally to repay £22 million of existing debt. Three other parts of the bus and coach industry have also been floated on the Stock Exchange: National Express, the Go Ahead Group, and GRT Bus Group.

In privatizing bus companies, the state has sought both to maximize sale proceeds, and also stimulate inter-operator competition. However, these objectives may be in conflict with retaining a "sustainable" bus industry. Given the poor average profits in the industry (typically, around 2% to 4% of turnover), and instability often associated with excessive levels of competition, sustained competition may make it difficult for the privatized operators to make a sufficient profit to meet a reasonable return on assets, and fund vehicle replacement (let alone other investment in depots, stations, etc.). High sale proceeds may involve high borrowings to finance a management buy-out, with consequent pressures on profitability, and inadequate funding of vehicle replacement. These issues are considered in greater depth elsewhere by the author (White 1994).

Public financing of transport, and the relationship between central and local government

As described above, the TPP and TSG system which was developed in the 1970s was based on an attempt to plan for road and public transport systems together, with a common system of funding, based on an overall plan (the TPP), funded through a mixture of local authority revenues (at that time, the rating system), general government support to local authorities, and the Transport Supplementary Grant (TSG). Some conflict was inevitable in respect of the large sums devoted to revenue support in the metropolitan areas and London, leading to the Transport Act 1983 as described above. In Wales, TSG was applied only to capital spending (in effect, mainly roads) from 1982/83, and from April 1985 the TSG in England was restricted to road schemes only, in this case to those used by a high proportion of through, rather than local, traffic. For major public transport projects, scope for grants under Section 56 of the 1968 Act remained, but was subject to more stringent criteria from 1989 (see below). The pattern thus partly returned to that of the 1960s, with specific grants aimed largely at road schemes, together with a much greater degree of central government control on total local authority spending through the SSA mechanism as described in Chapter 1.

Investment criteria

Within the public sector in Britain, a fairly complex set of investment criteria for road schemes has been developed. Costs and benefits are discounted at 8% per annum in real terms. The principal benefits are usually in the form of time savings, together with other factors such as accident savings (which may increase in importance following more realistic valuation of serious injury casualties). Costs are primarily the capital costs of initial construction.

Within the public transport sector as such, a good deal of rail investment is funded on the rationale that it provides replacement of existing assets – for example, rolling stock, and signalling – and is not subject to such explicit criteria (although cost-effectiveness comparisons may play a major rôle). In terms of new infrastructure investment, however, a curiously complex procedure has been followed through the "Section 56" criteria applied under that section of the 1968 Transport Act, following removal of public transport's eligibility for TSG, to provide a means of funding public transport schemes, notably light rail projects in cities outside London. To date, it has been used for the Manchester Metrolink and Sheffield Supertram projects, and many other studies have been conducted on this basis. Two rail schemes within shire counties are also supported through this mechanism – the "Robin Hood" line from Nottingham to Newstead which opened in 1993 (to be extended to Mansfield and Worksop), and the "Ivanhoe" line in·Leicestershire.

203

Unlike road scheme appraisal, in which all user time-saving benefits are counted in estimating changes in consumer surplus, section 56 criteria are based on the assumption that improved speed and other enhancement of service quality may to some extent be "captured" through higher fares. Hence, existing users might be expected to pay more to reflect the improved service they receive. Part of the gain in consumer surplus is thus transferred to the operator as a financial benefit, reducing the net requirement for public funding. It is normally assumed that the operating costs as such will be covered from user payments. Public funding is then justified through "non user" benefits, primarily reduced road congestion through diversion of some car trips, and "development" gains (Department of Transport 1989).

In order to capture the benefits of higher service quality, higher fares may have to be charged. These may discourage some existing low-income public transport users from travelling, and also offset the generalized cost saving that would otherwise be expected for car users diverting to public transport thus reducing potential diversion (see Ch. 7). Hence, the overall economic benefits from the scheme are reduced.

In the major example of applying this approach to date, Manchester Metrolink light rail, the private operating company has succeeded in covering all operating costs from revenue, and has obtained an encouraging level of off-peak ridership, together with significant diversion of trips from cars. However peak fares are very high. The fare structure is not integrated with local buses, making the service very costly for those using feeder buses at the suburban end of the trip, and discouraging service integration.

The government now appears to have accepted, at any rate in relation to London and possibly other "complex networks", that such differential pricing could create perverse effects, in discouraging the use of new high-quality links designed to relieve existing overcrowded sections of the public transport network – such as the "Crossrail" proposal (Department of Transport 1991).

The shift to a "package" approach for TPPs, pioneered in the West Midlands and now adopted by central government (Department of Transport 1993), provides a welcome change of emphasis, but, as yet, little change in substance. TSG remains valid only for road schemes and some associated expenditure (primarily bus priorities, and park & ride schemes which benefit major roads). Most public transport schemes of any magnitude remain subject to section 56 criteria. Detailed economic analysis is required for all public transport schemes costing over £2 million (Circular 2/93, para. 61), and although a full cost–benefit analysis is now requested (para. 63), there is no commitment to fund schemes on this criterion. European Regional Development Fund contributions are treated as substituting for DOT funding, rather than being additive. Credit approvals form the other major mechanism by which local authorities can fund transport projects, but they themselves are constrained by the overall financial position of such authorities.

A substantial proportion of authorities put forward package bids for the

1994/5 round, and more were received in the following round. However, overall TSG funding announced by the Department of Transport (the grand total both for authorities with package schemes, and those putting forward conventional proposals) showed a fall of 14.5% on the previous year. Priority still appears to be given to major road schemes, and the government's own trunk and motorway programme, rather than local transport investment.

Private sector funding may play a useful rôle in certain limited cases – for example, the Heathrow Express Link, or minor improvement schemes (perhaps including park and ride site provision). However, it may also have distorting effects, and could create a questionable set of priorities where the greater part of funding still comes through public spending. For example, the Jubilee Line Extension through Docklands, finally given the go-ahead in October 1993, will cost around £1,900 million. The initial private sector contribution (through the European Investment Bank) is only £98 million. While a further £300 million is promised (in money, not real, terms), giving an apparent 21% private sector contribution, this is spread over a twenty-year period. Discounting at 8% per annum one can see the effective private sector contribution only corresponding to about 13% or 14% of total capital cost (assuming zero inflation).

Population trends

The starting point for any transport forecast must be the population served, and its composition. Changes in trip rate may then be considered separately, as influenced by factors such as price, car availability or service frequency (discussed earlier in Chs 2 and 7).

Worldwide population is growing at about 1.7% per annum, and generally at higher rates in developing countries (around 2.0% per annum, compared with 0.3% in Europe). Coupled with rural to urban migration in the latter, urban growth rates of 5% to 10% may be commonplace. The main problem for the public transport operator in such cases becomes that of simply coping with demand. Conversely, in Britain, not only is total population virtually static, but that in urban areas, especially older cities, is falling.

A very slow growth is now envisaged, the United Kingdom total rising from 57.8 million in 1991, to 59.7 million in 2001, and 61.1 million in 2021, with an ageing structure as the birth rate remains fairly low and life expectancy continues to rise. The proportion aged under 16 is anticipated to rise marginally from 20.3% of the population in 1991 to 21.0% in 2001, but then fall to 18.5% in 2021. Those aged over 80 are anticipated to rise from 3.7% of the total in 1991 to 5.2% in 2021 (Central Statistical Office 1994: derived from tables 1.3, 1.4 and 1.19).

Spatially, a continued shift toward more prosperous regions, such as East Anglia, is likely, with a continued outward shift within each region from traditional major cities to suburban fringe areas, and self-contained smaller towns. However, the rate of city population decline slowed down in the 1980s and encouraging such outward movement is no longer an aim of land-use planning policy.

The implications for public transport are that greater efforts will be needed to sustain patronage, with more attention paid to the levels of service in medium-to low-density suburban areas. Inner city radial routes will not necessarily require their existing level of peak capacity (although scope for shift from conventional bus to busway or light rail on high-density corridors remains). Better inter-suburban links will be required. In the long-distance market, city-centre to city-centre travel may become less important, and the need for good suburban interchanges will become greater. Cross-city links, especially in the London region, will become relatively more important as movements take place between regions around cities: these elements can be seen in the Thameslink route's growing rôle since its reopening, and plans for Crossrail. Growing medium-size centres will require better cross-country links. Milton Keynes and Northampton, for example, are poorly served for towns of their size.

Linked with population as a demand factor is the economic activity rate. This fell significantly in the late 1970s and early 1980s, in part owing to a fall in the total working age population, but also an absolute loss of jobs, especially in manufacturing. Decline has taken place since 1990 due to the most recent recession. Some gradual recovery may now be expected, although at lower real income levels than previously envisaged. Insofar as future growth is in the service industries, this could be to the benefit of public transport, in that office employment in city centres may expand.

Energy

Despite the further sharp rise in oil prices in 1979, the importance of energy issues diminished during the 1980s, following the substantial fall in worldwide oil prices in real terms from the middle of that decade. Demand declined as a result of cuts in energy-intensive heavy industry and improved efficiency elsewhere – for example, in heating – have alleviated this problem for the time being. Further technical improvement in private car design is continuing, and scope for gains through measures such as reduced vehicle weight and regenerative braking systems in public transport modes have been outlined in Chapters 3 and 4.

Nonetheless, complacency would be ill advised, as finite limits exist to oil and other natural resources worldwide. There is also concern regarding the "greenhouse effect" arising from increased atmospheric CO_2 emissions, although the argument in this case has yet to be fully resolved. In addition to the improvement in vehicular energy efficiency, gains in primary resource use may be obtained.

Coal-fired thermal power stations currently convert, at best, 35% of the heat energy in coal into electricity, although the combined cycle gas turbine plants now coming into widespread use offer up to around 50%. Combined power and heat stations could enable much of the waste heat now produced to be productively used.

Although an increasing proportion of oil output is devoted to transport uses, constraints are developing: for example in the lower octane ratios which may have to be accepted as refinery output mix changes. Overall, electricity would appear to offer a greater flexibility through use of alternative primary sources such as nuclear or coal, or renewable sources such as wave energy. Despite recent improvements and promised gains, the energy density of battery vehicles remains poor. The weight of the batteries, and the need for frequent replacement, increases their costs. Electrically powered vehicles using a continuous external supply, such as trolley-buses or rail vehicles, thus offer substantial gains. Other fuels have been proposed for private vehicles, such as hydrogen, but these themselves would require considerable energy inputs to convert them into a convenient form for on-vehicle use. At present, few efficient alternatives to the internal combustion engine appear in prospect.

Such constraints should not be viewed as giving rise to some overnight catastrophe, in which public transport would gain windfall traffic from the demise of the private car. However, they do favour a long-run approach designed to discourage a very low density land-use pattern which becomes almost entirely dependent upon the private car. A planning policy encouraging higher densities would enable public transport – and non-motorized modes for short trips – to offer an alternative to car use, and in turn stimulate a greater level of public transport patronage.

Educational travel

A specific policy area of increased importance, especially under local government reform, is that of school and further education travel. As indicated in Chapter 1, expenditure on school transport by county councils (contract services, directly run vehicles, and season tickets on scheduled bus and rail services) is often greater than the direct revenue support to local bus services. Under the Education Act 1944, provision of free transport is obligatory for children living three or more miles from school (up to age 8, two miles). The increasing total cost of this provision, and arbitrary nature of the distance over which it applies, has led to alternatives being investigated.

One obvious solution would be to abolish the distance limit entirely, applying a common low flat fare for all school journeys (including those of "non-statutory" length made on public local bus services, and generally cross-subsidized). However the issue has not been tackled systematically, and anoma-

207

lies remain. Under the Education (No.2) Bill of 1979, powers to permit counties to introduce charges for free school travel – which could have varied widely – were proposed, but provoked strong reaction. Under the Transport Act 1985, an explicit provision for compensation of low fares for "non-statutory" school travel as a "concessionary" fare was introduced. However, if operators were to cut back sharply on existing ("commercial") lower fares for children, the extent to which local authorities could utilize this power under severe financial constraints remains to be seen.

A common flat fare has been introduced in the Isle of Man, albeit in a context where a high general level of support is given to public transport. The restructuring of the education system, increasing parental choice (especially in secondary education) is also likely to result in much longer trips to school, encouraging a further shift from walking and cycling to motorized modes (both public and private). A comprehensive review of the issues is provided by Thornthwaite (1994).

The structure of local government

As indicated in Chapter 1, the current organizational framework in "shire" county councils and Scottish regions encompasses most transport and planning functions at the same level – highways, educational transport, tendered bus services, etc. Districts retain significant responsibilities for taxi regulation and concessionary fares. In the metropolitan areas, however, a highly unsatisfactory situation now arises as a result of the abolition of the GLC and metropolitan counties in 1986. Residual co-ordinating bodies between the district/borough councils are cumbersome, and the PTAs and PTEs (outside London) have a rather limited rôle, especially in relation to financial powers. Within London itself, London Regional Transport has taken on a wider public transport planning rôle, and the Department of Transport has become more closely involved in road planning and traffic management through establishment of the "Red Route" concept and appointment of the Traffic Director for London. However, local accountability may be lost as a result.

The review of local government structure currently in progress may cause further fragmentation of those bodies currently responsible for transport planning and provision. It appears likely that much (although not all) of England will be placed under unitary authorities, encompassing the rôles of both existing districts and counties, although in some parts of England the "two tier" systems of counties and districts will continue (for example, in Lincolnshire). Within Wales, a specific framework for 21 new unitary authorities to replace the 8 existing counties and 37 existing districts now exists.

While a unitary authority might be of sufficient size to cover much local day-to-day movement (if matching journey-to-work catchment areas), the provision of longer-distance educational transport, and tendered rural bus services would suffer difficulties. The limited involvement of rural counties in rail provision would be further reduced. There may be need to create some new regional bodies with specific public transport responsibilities (in South Wales, for example), as the boundaries of unitary authorities in more complex urbanized areas clearly fail to match the structure of the transport network. There is a danger that, while mobility of car users continues to increase, the planning framework for public transport becomes restricted to ever smaller areas.

The other consequence of a very fragmented local government structure is that central government becomes increasingly involved in very specific local funding decisions, as well as setting the overall framework of policy. Under the Railways Act 1993, the Franchise Director has a great deal of power in relation to determining service levels and support payments to franchise operators, yet is unlikely to possess the detailed local knowledge required to make such decisions effectively.

Taxation, public expenditure and equity

Despite reductions in financial support to public transport in recent years, a substantial proportion of operating costs, around 30%, is met from public expenditure for both bus and rail systems (this figure includes payments for concessionary fares, specific services and school transport). So far as BR is concerned, this is funded almost entirely through central government directly, apart from payments via the PTAs (see table 1.1). The bus industry is supported partly through central government (the partial fuel tax rebate on local services), but largely through local authorities, albeit under strong constraints imposed by central government.

This proportion of support is somewhat lower than found elsewhere in Europe or North America, where around 50% would be typical. Nonetheless, it is important to ask how such expenditure affects the net incomes users and taxpayers thereby receive, in contrast to that if full-cost fares applied.

Recent concern has been mainly with efficiency and public expenditure, rather than the equity aspect. A general aim of reducing disparities in incomes is no longer necessarily that held by government. At the same time, however, the pressure to reduce spending makes it all the more important to identify losers and gainers.

Some shifts toward more equitable allocation *within* the public transport sector have probably occurred since the mid-1970s. Air transport now receives very little support, apart from some minor airports. PSO to the InterCity sector of BR has not applied since 1988, and in the last year of operation (1993/4) Network South East covered all of its operating costs from revenue, PSO payments being used solely for capital expenditure. Within the bus industry, explicit

209

cross-subsidy has been reduced, although it could be argued that expenditure on tendered services tends to be directed, within urban areas, to those parts which display higher income and car ownership levels, and hence cannot support reasonable bus frequencies (in parts of Merseyside, for example). However, it does not necessarily follow that the individuals dependent upon such tendered services are of high income themselves – users of a service within a low-density suburb are unlikely to be typical car owners, but those of lower incomes living within such an area, who need access to employment, schools and shops outside it.

At the same time, however, rail retains a major advantage over the bus and coach industry. Not only is operating support paid centrally for a largely unchanged network, but substantial investment has been maintained, whereas the bus industry's only significant capital grant – the new bus grant – was phased out entirely in 1984.

Marked variations in bus industry support also remain. Rural dwellers are less likely to receive concessionary fares, and in general levels of revenue support have been lower than in major cities.

While public transport support has been cut back, and cost-based pricing thereby encouraged, there is little sign of willingness to introduce road pricing in major cities as a means of similarly matching supply and demand for road space by private vehicles, although extensive studies both of the technology, and likely traveller response, are now in progress.

Britain has witnessed a much greater use than elsewhere of "company cars", i.e. those paid for wholly or entirely by employers, largely as a perk in lieu of taxable income rather than a genuine necessity for business trips. While the car provision as such is now more rigorously taxed, no taxation is applied to the substantial benefits provided through provision of free parking spaces at the place of work, which in central London could be equivalent to around £4,000 per space per year.

Another major contrast between Britain and other industrialized countries lies in the taxation of user benefits on public transport. In many, employers may provide a season ticket without the recipient being taxed upon the benefit thereby gained, at any rate up to a certain level. Japan is the main example, but the practice is also common in Europe, sometimes through employers contributing directly to a lower ticket price, as in Paris. Although some attempts have been made to market travelcards via employers in this fashion, the tax imposed makes it unattractive both to employer and recipient, in contrast to the benefits given through the company car.

National taxation structure also affects the ability of local government to pursue its policy objectives. The limited scope for raising revenue through the council tax, reliance upon central government grants, and more centralized imposition of limits on total spending of local authorities by central government, have left very little local autonomy (see Ch. 1). Elsewhere, local or regional income taxes may play a major rôle – as in Sweden – or specific taxes can be raised for transport purposes, such as the "versement transport" in most French

cities, or taxes approved through local referenda in the US. British local authorities have no freedom to establish such means of raising funds, and an increasingly centralized policy has been adopted by central government, in contrast with
decentralization of urban finance and policy making in many other countries.
One possibility, put forward by Travers and Glaister (Glaister 1991) would be
to create increments on the business rate in selected areas. A small percentage
increase in central London could provide a large annual cash flow to fund rail
schemes currently planned.

In practical terms, an appropriate policy would be to first provide compara-
bility between public and private-transport user benefits provided by employers.
Purchase of travelcards could be made non-taxable up to an upper limit. At the
same time, more stringent taxation of company car benefits would still be justified. Car users' perceived costs could be adjusted by reducing the annual duty
on each vehicle (apart from a nominal sum to cover record-keeping), and raising
it on fuel, thus increasing the share of costs perceived each time fuel is purchased, while also charging more for use of the road system to those with
above-average mileage.

Changes of this sort would go some way to restoring the balance of perceived
costs between public and private transport in urban areas, and at national level.
In addition, local authorities may well wish to pursue their own policies – for
example, in providing a higher level of service and/or lower fare than break-even
operation would permit. The cost–benefit evaluations conducted under the Transport Act 1983 indicated a net benefit per pound sterling at the then existing levels
of support, and often at higher levels also, as discussed in the previous chapter.

Such local decisions could be seen as a form of "collective purchase" of transport services, yet creating much closer links between the voters and those
affected than is the case in national policy decisions on the rail passenger network, for example. The question of equity would still remain, of course. Would
those on higher incomes benefit more than lower-income residents of the inner
city? An assessment by Turner (1985) suggests that this would not be the case
for London. Taking fare levels and rates (the form of local government taxation
applying at the time) in 1984–5, the higher rates paid by higher income groups,
and their lower off-peak use of public transport, offset the greater benefits a
longer-distance peak-period user might gain from a general fares reduction.
Were a progressive local income tax to replace the council tax as the main source
of finance for such public expenditure, the relative gains to lower income groups
would be further improved.

Any local income tax system would have to be based either on the home
or work location of earners, preferably covering areas in which a fairly self-
contained pattern was found of both, i.e. journey-to-work catchment areas. This
would imply, for example a somewhat larger area than the present area covered
by London Transport, and certainly larger areas than the proposed unitary
authorities.

Another major issue in the context of taxation and finance is the financial

211

regime under which the rail system is to be operated from 1994. In place of a block grant to British Rail for Network South East and Regional Railways services, individual negotiations will take place between franchise bidders and the Franchise Director. Given the charges levied by Railtrack, most franchisees will require a substantial payment from the Franchise Director to retain services. Scope for improved efficiency within the new operators may (as in the bus industry case) provide some reduction in operating costs provided that this is not offset through revenue loss due to network fragmentation, or the extra administrative costs of the new organizational structure, possibly enabling some reductions in public spending in the longer term.

As described in Chapter 6, it has been decided that Railtrack should be required to provide a fixed rate of return on the replacement value of its assets, a significant element in the high charge per train-kilometre to operating companies. Hence, additional sums of public money will be needed, through payments via the operating companies, to meet this "cost", clearly offsetting any efficiency savings. It could be argued that such an approach represents a more realistic long-run policy, in that other transport businesses also have to make a return on their assets (bus operating companies, for example). It is ironic, however, that the replacement cost concept should be introduced at a time when it has been abandoned by the bus industry, whose calculations of profitability are based on historic depreciation only.

No financial return (either on historic, or replacement, values) is required of the road system. While the current annual taxation (of all types) paid by road users exceeds the current financial costs of maintaining and extending the road network, any realistic valuation of the road infrastructure at replacement cost, and for a rate of return on that investment, would greatly increase the costs charged to road users: one recent estimate puts replacement cost of the road network at £100,000 million – on which a 5.6% return (matching that now demanded of Railtrack) would thus be £5,600 million. In the absence of such a policy change, a major burden is being placed on the public transport system which is not applied to the road network.

Department of the Environment policy

Following the organizational split between the Departments of Environment and Transport in the late 1970s, the former initially had little rôle in transport policy, except through the joint regional offices (Ch. 1). However, with the growing emphasis on environmental issues as such, notably energy consumption atmospheric pollution, from the late 1980s, the DOE has regained a significant rôle. An awareness of the link between transport and land use policy has re-emerged. At the time of writing, the DOE policy places much greater emphasis on public transport, and the need to curtail total transport growth, than that of the Department of Transport itself, which remains committed to a major road-building policy.

DoE thinking is set out in two main documents (in addition to those dealing with overall environmental policy) – PPG13: *Planning policy guidance on transport*, and PPG6: *Town centre and retail developments* (Department of Environment 1993, 1994).

The transport PPG followed work by the ECOTEC consultancy, identifying the scope for land use planning policy in encouraging the use of non-motorized modes and public transport, as a means for reducing energy consumption and pollution. The trend toward lower densities of settlement, and more dispersed activity centres, has clearly been to the detriment of public transport, and has further stimulated private car use. As argued in Chapter 5, higher densities would assist public transport in providing larger catchment populations within walking distance of a given route. Planning authorities are advised to bear such factors in mind in location of new development, and their response to proposals they receive.

Pricing mechanisms for fuel and vehicle use also play a rôle. From the March 1993 budget, a policy of raising fuel duty by at least 3% per annum in real terms has been applied (now set at 5%). A departure tax on air travel (£5 for domestic and European Union flights, £10 other international) has been introduced, with some exceptions for regional services. Virley (1994) estimates that if the commitments in the March 1993 budget were maintained, then about one-seventh of the carbon reduction required to meet the Rio target by the year 2000 would be attained, although mainly through improved fuel economy in private cars rather than reduced distance.

Within PPG13, development within existing urban areas, of higher densities, is encouraged. Activity centres should be placed near public transport nodes. New, lower-density development is discouraged. Retention of existing waterway and rail alignments is suggested.

PPG6 acknowledges the problems that have arisen through out-of-town "Superstore" development in terms of public transport access, private car use, and the impacts on traditional town centres. The rôle of local shops in providing access, and thus reducing the need for motorized travel, is also stressed. The rôle of out-of-town centres for bulk shopping is, however, acknowledged. Siting of retail development where it can be served by existing transport facilities is proposed.

However, much of the advice is of a rather generalized form. That on shopping, in particular, has come after a marked shift toward out-of-town centres during the 1980s and early 1990s. The ability of local authorities to influence land use is restricted both by the general shift toward deregulation in many aspects of the economy, and uncertainty regarding their future structure and powers. Further emphasis on energy and environmental issues is evident in statements issued by the Department of Environment in January 1994, as part of the government's overall environmental policy, following the Rio summit in 1992. An explicit critique of the rôle of the private car is becoming clear, but the resolution between DoE and DoT policy has yet to emerge.

213

The generalized nature of the British government proposals contrasts with the much firmer targets set in Dutch planning and transport policy, for example (Sturt & Bull 1993). A significant component of this is the "ABC" categorization of development sites, according to their use and public transport access (for example, an office development would normally be located near to public transport links, while a low-density warehouse development could be acceptable at a site with poorer public transport access).

The rôles of "planning" and "competition"

At present, a somewhat inconsistent approach is adopted toward long-term planning (or indeed, any systematic planning) in the public transport sector in Britain. On the one hand, long-term forecasts are made for road traffic (in terms of the National Road Traffic Forecasts, NRTF, as far ahead as 2025), and similar forecasts are required in the planning of major rail schemes. At the same time, bus operations work on a very short timescale, often less than one year. While this reflects in part the degree of flexibility inherent in the technology of the modes concerned, it also reflects a different institutional framework.

Attitudes toward "planning" became particularly polarized during the mid-1980s, notably in views expressed in ministers' statements in response to criticisms of the "Buses" White Paper in 1984. Planners were seen as people setting out almost perverse schemes, to suit their own purposes, in contrast to the market-based desires of consumers. At the same time, however, it is accepted that some form of strategic planning is required for the various sectors of the rail business, airports, roads and a Channel link. Yet all, ultimately, serve the same broad "market" – that of moving people and goods. The early 1990s has seen a shift back toward the realization of some need for a longer-term approach within the Department of the Environment (DoE), especially through the rediscovery of links between transport and land use, and an awareness of the need to reduce travel as such.

Added to this has been a belief that "the market" (in the sense of a mechanism for allocating resources through price, rather than demand for a specific product) will provide a solution to problems of resource allocation, the management of innovation and technological change.

It is desirable to distinguish three forms of planning:
1. Planning undertaken by a business, which often aims to anticipate and stimulate changes in the market. This thinking forms the basis of corporate plans and marketing strategies.
2. Planning in the sense of physical planning, mainly by local authorities, of land use, new infrastructure, etc.
3. "Planning" by central government, either of major pieces of infrastructure (such as motorways) or in the economy as a whole.

"Planning" has tended to acquire a bad name, at least in public, from the second and third categories. Local authority land-use planning has certainly succeeded in retaining some environmental benefits through retention of open space, control of advertising, and improvements to town centres. At the same time, it has been associated with the "brutalist" concrete architecture of the 1960s and early 1970s – especially in housing – now widely condemned. Some local authority land-use planning has also been seen as mainly negative in its rôle, preventing some types of commercial development, rather than stimulating change.

Central government planning, in the economic sense, has often been of limited value, given the uncertainties imposed by international economic constraints, and the domestic market. However, the frequent changes of government policy themselves are also often to blame, giving little chance for any sort of plan to be seen through to completion under consistent objectives.

One solution, clearly, would be to leave matters to "the market". Yet the "market" itself does not produce new products. At the risk of sounding trite, one must stress that they come from people who are motivated to produce them and possess the technical abilities to do so. Some may be private businessmen, in the classic sense of the "entrepreneur", who is motivated mainly by the prospect of profit. But others might be organizers of a voluntary project – such as a rural community bus scheme – whose motive is not profit. They also include local and central government, whose scale of organization permits them to make innovations which private business is not suited to undertake.

Examples of the type of innovation made by private business would include the commuter coach services into London since the Transport Act 1980. Innovation has come about through small-scale investment, and where this has proved profitable, further investment has occurred (although the majority of commuter coaches were initiated by operators then in public ownership, as part of NBC, or municipal enterprises, their behaviour was similar to that of private business in this sector). Examples of the innovation by public bodies include the travelcards in major cities, which only achieve substantial market penetration if valid for all or most of the network, and may require substantial public financial support in their initial stages, to support risks involved in gaining market penetration (see Ch. 7). Much of the technological innovation in public transport – for example, in real-time information systems, or smart cards – also rests on public bodies as the "purchaser", although many competing businesses may offer rival products to meet this demand.

What is happening is that new products (whether provided by the public or private sectors) are being tested in "the market" to establish whether they are successful. The criteria of success may simply be a commercial profit (as in commuter coaching), or achieving some wider benefits measured through social cost–benefit analysis, such as the evaluations in plans under the "package" TPPs. Clearly, an achievement aim must be set before a product is introduced, if unsuccessful products are not to be maintained unwisely.

The major rôle of "planning", therefore, may be seen as the devising of these

215

new products, or projects, so that they can be implemented successfully. It must therefore include a substantial element of "feedback" from monitoring, as well as planning prior to introduction of the product.

The network planning introduced by bus operators in the 1970s and 1980s (but now largely confined, within Britain, to London Transport, as described in Ch. 5) is a good example of this. Surveys establish existing customer behaviour and requirements. The plan aims to match these manifest demands with supply of services, at the same time identifying opportunities for innovations such as new limited-stop services, minibus conversion or cross-town through links.

The scale of such planning will depend upon the length of time needed for preparation – clearly greatest where new infrastructure is involved – and the scale of change. Where the change is mainly that of bus services using existing road networks, it could therefore be initiated at the level of an individual bus company, given a sufficiently large catchment area and expertise in network planning methods.

Duration and scale are not necessarily correlated. For example, creating new bus priority schemes of the type described in Chapter 3 involves little expenditure and only modest additional infrastructure (except for new busways per se) yet the timescale may be a fairly long one, as other changes in traffic management, access arrangements for shops, etc. may be required. Conversely, introduction of a city-wide travelcard may require only a short planning timescale (although prior attention to sales outlets is essential, and often overlooked), yet may involve very large cash flows. Here, the main requirement may be to monitor sales after introduction and take appropriate action.

It is striking that the Travelcard in London, an innovation with much greater impact than many schemes carefully planned over a long period, involved a planning timescale of no more than about two years (1981–3), although successful monitoring of the scheme has come about not only through the operators' routine data, but also the user surveys conducted by London Transport.

Within private sector firms of the size traditionally found in the bus and coach industry, planning and investment are typically on fairly short timescales, yet here also effective planning may be needed to ensure success. Many of the long-distance coach services introduced by independents after the 1980 Act had little impact, despite modest fares and high-quality vehicles, owing to lack of suitable terminals, and sales outlets.

Given the approach outlined above, "planning" can be seen as a process involving all sectors of transport, rather than one unique to the larger, public sector bodies. There are of course differences of degree – in timescale, and resources involved – but not necessarily of kind.

What framework does such a planning concept imply? Clearly, much of the system will be set up within the specific businesses concerned, but part also will fall in the public domain. This will include that dealing with large infrastructure projects only handled by the public sector, or in which the government is involved owing to the political implications even if some funding is from the private sector (the Channel Link is an obvious example). Most road and rail infra-structure schemes thus fall within the public sector.

Since 1986, local bus services have been operated largely through company structures, either in private ownership, or still in public ownership but with finan-cial responsibilities similar to those in the private sector. Here, much planning is internal, but public sector planning remains important in respect of infrastructure, traffic management and the implications of other types of planning (such as the location of new housing development) on the public transport operators. The recent report from the Chartered Institute of Transport's bus working party (Char-tered Institute of Transport 1993) proposes a "quality partnership", in which oper-ators would seek to improve service quality and renew their fleets, while public authorities would in return provide improved infrastructure for bus services.

Another issue raised in relation to "planning" is the rôle of competition. The two are often seen as inherently opposed, "planning" being associated with highly regulated systems, "competition" with decontrolled, unplanned systems. Here again, the fundamental rôles need to be questioned. Competition is not an end in itself, but a means to an end – of achieving innovations in greater effi-ciency of operation, and new product developments. A highly regulated system may discourage these. At the same time, however, long-term planning is needed for certain types of innovation to occur at all. A very fragmented industry, work-ing largely on a short timescale, may well succeed in keeping down costs, but is unlikely to produce innovations such as comprehensive through ticketing or inter-modal interchanges. It may also be poorly placed to undertake training or research work to support future innovation.

To compete effectively, an organization must plan systematically. This applies not only within a specific transport mode, but also between modes. In many respects, the greater competition is between public transport and the pri-vate car, and certain system-wide changes (such as taxation treatment of user benefits) are likely to be needed, as well as innovations arising from individual public transport operators' efforts.

One of the most critical areas for competition and planning is technical inno-vation. Electronic ticket systems, based on cash fares, have become fairly wide-spread: the next logical step is to use encoded cards (or other devices for prepayment), eliminating the cash transaction altogether. This is being sought in parking systems and retail shopping generally, as well as public transport. Com-petition may well produce rival systems. If one succeeds in ousting the others, through superior quality, then the competitive mechanism will have done its work through enabling the best system to come to the fore, but if many different systems persist, a highly unsatisfactory situation will arise. No one *sys*to gain sufficiently wide acceptance for all or most users to ⸜ it, and cumbersome cash-paid methods of coll⸜ 217

A great stress has been place⸜ years, notably in the bus indus⸜ of previous exemptions fror⸜

note that section 131 of the Railways Act 1993 does provide some exemption from the effects of the Restrictive Trades Practices Act 1976 for rail operators). In some sectors of activity, competition clearly provides benefits through competitive tendering to reduce costs and/or raise quality. A large degree of direct competition already exists within the transport sector, especially in Britain. In the long-distance market a wide range is offered, at any rate on trunk routes, between coach, rail, air and car. Within the urban market, car and public transport are clearly in competition.

As mentioned earlier in conjunction with fares policy, walking and cycling are also alternatives to public transport over short distances. There are also the choices to be made of activities and location. Journeys may or may not be made, dependent upon transport cost and availability. In the short run, this applies to journeys such as leisure and some personal business. In the long run, it can also apply to some aspects of work and education travel.

Recent policy has gone well beyond this, however, by encouraging a high degree of competition within the bus industry as the "norm", especially following the December 1992 House of Lords' decision upholding the Monopolies and Mergers Commission appeal in the South Yorkshire case. A relatively small area may be defined as "substantial" for purposes of inquiring into cases where one supplier holds more than a 25% market share, under the Fair Trading Act 1973. As mentioned earlier in this chapter, the intensive "on the road" competition within the bus industry has not produced an overall benefit. There has been little fares competition, and most of it takes the form of increasing supply on already frequent services. Average loadings have fallen sharply. A situation now exists in many areas where all operators are still able to cover direct costs, but none are able to make a long-run profit sufficient to cover vehicle replacement and other investment needs. In contrast, the latest MMC enquiry, into the National Express/Citylink coach merger (see Ch. 9), takes a broader view, seeing the competition on trunk routes as primarily between coach and rail, and the merger of the two coach companies as a means of enabling coach operation to remain viable under these conditions.

One may argue of course that the presence of intense, continuous competition is simply the situation found in nature, as supported through Darwinian theory. However, while competition obviously plays an important rôle, the degree of emphasis placed upon it is often overstated; indeed, the stress on the competition principle came first in early economic theory, predating that evolutionary theory of the later nineteenth century.

In the specific case of the bus industry, we can see a case in which users have a freedom of choice between operators on some routes, but this may be associated with the removal of a wider freedom. One can choose between an aged red bus, or equally aged blue bus, running over the same route at much the same time. Some reduction in waiting time may result, but perhaps at the expense of through ticketing (enabling the user to board the first bus to arrive with... and the availability of comprehensive information.

At times one gains the impression that the government is more concerned with the freedom of individual companies and managers rather than the users as such: for example, in the initial reluctance to compel participation in comprehensive timetable publication or through ticketing for privatized railway operators. In the earlier case of bus deregulation, requiring all operators in the same district to accept pensioner concessionary tickets on the same basis seemed to be stipulated more as a means of placing inter-operator competition on an equal footing, rather than widening travel opportunities for the pensioners themselves.

The Fair Trading Act criterion of a 25% market share in a specified area makes sense in the retail goods sector, in which production can be concentrated economically at very few points, but an extensive distribution system is used to supply a wide range of goods so that in each local area a wide choice exists (of foodstuffs, clothing, consumer durables, etc.). This is fundamentally different from a service industry, in which production and consumption occur in the same place at the same time. A seat-kilometre not consumed at the time of its production is a seat-kilometre wasted.

Furthermore, transport demand is essentially a derived demand – for access to activities such as work, education, shopping and so forth. The real freedom of choice lies in the range of such activities that an individual can reach within constraints of time and income. For example, in comparing trips by those with and without cars available, the former generally display much higher rates, as illustrated through the National Travel Survey (Ch. 2). Except in certain congested situations, the car will offer a faster door-to-door journey time and hence a wider range of activities over a larger radius within a given total time budget. Short run perceived cost may display similar features. There is, of course, a secondary aspect of "freedom" associated with car ownership, namely the choice of model, size and colour of the car itself. However, there is little if any correlation between this and the amount of travel (except for patterns of use of "company cars"), in contrast with the order-of-magnitude differences between trip rates of car users and non-users. The high level of car use does, of course, impose externalities in the form of congestion, pollution and energy consumption, and hence the need to improve public transport as an acceptable alternative.

Applying this to public transport, one might see freedom as being maximized through an extensive network of reliable services, accompanied by comprehensive information systems and simple through ticketing. In some cases, direct competition between operators, or – more likely – initiatives taken by local management – might augment the quality and range of services on specific routes.

Taking the current situation in Britain, this suggests that something like the approach we have in London produces better results than that in the other large cities. At the same time, a rather centralized network planning system exists within London Transport, which could be augmented (but not replaced) by local initiatives, through the managements of local bus operators.

These issues may be illustrated by comparing Britain with other advanced, industrialized countries: The less rigid regulatory system in Britain has encouraged innovations such as higher quality long distance and commuter coaches, new types of rural service, and high-frequency urban minibus operation. Yet in other respects, innovation lags behind that in more strictly regulated economies. The first automated urban railway, Docklands' Light Rail, did not come into operation until 1987, four years after VAL in Lille (see Ch. 4). Most bus revenue is still received in cash on the vehicle, outside London. Recent developments in regenerative braking, and thyristor/chopper control technology for urban railways, have been adopted very slowly.

Another aspect of the relationship between planning and competition is that some planning may be needed for competition to be effective. For example, the lack of adequate terminal facilities for long-distance coach services, especially in London, limited the impact of the Transport Act 1980, both by restricting total capacity, and giving independent operators few opportunities. Victoria Coach Station has now been substantially upgraded (although ironically, the reduced volume of coach movements after 1986 made it easier to find space for better passenger facilities), but remains poorly sited for the major coach flows.

"Mobility" or "access"?

What is the main aim of providing public transport services? As suggested in Chapter 2, the output may be measured most readily by passenger trips, passenger-km or revenue. These are all measures of "mobility" i.e. the amount of travel. Given a fixed pattern of land uses and activities, increased mobility will represent increased access: a wider range, and/or lower cost of activities. For example, a greater distance in commuting from home to work may represent a wider range of job opportunities, or of lower housing costs. Mobility as such is not a benefit, but represents a cost, which is offset by the benefits of activities made possible.

Although, broadly speaking, greater mobility represents improved access, and may indeed be essential simply to maintain access to the same range of facilities (for example, as village schools are closed), the standard of living enjoyed by an individual will not necessarily be in direct proportion to their mobility. Someone living in a small town with employment, shops and schools close at hand may well enjoy much greater access to activities than a person in a poorly served housing estate of a large city, despite the much greater mobility the latter may display.

Changing the location and timing of activities may also be a means of improving access rather than transport changes as such. The cases cited in the chapter on rural transport illustrate this: medical facilities could be more conveniently located, and their timings changed to improve access by users of existing bus services. School transport, in particular, is very costly to provide, and involves awkward duration and timing of trips from the viewpoint both of parents and children. A full evaluation of transport costs (both financial, and of the travelling time involved) could lead to smaller, more local, school catchment areas being defined.

However, it is important to direct doubts about the benefits of ever-growing mobility to their true target, i.e. the tendency of activities to be located further from the customer, and for many marginal trips to be generated as incomes and car ownership rise. Like many ecological or environmental arguments, they may be used all too easily by those now enjoying the high level of material wealth produced by the present industrial system while living in what remains of small-scale communities, and applied only to others. A television programme some years ago presented by a novelist portrayed one of her regular visits to a traditional village in Dorset – in a chauffeur-driven car with a nanny to handle the child – which was described with genuine feeling. But the villagers appeared largely as a backdrop to church garden parties or farming activities. Amid a string of unintentionally patronizing comments, viewers were informed that non-car-owning residents enjoyed a bus service once a week to Dorchester market. And after a few days' stay she returned to London in the same chauffeur-driven car. The same tendency might be seen in descriptions of rural life elsewhere in Europe (Provence, for example?).

Even at the present levels of centralization of employment, shopping and other facilities a substantial increase in rural public transport provision could be justified to improve the minimum levels of access for non-car-owners. In many urban areas, similar deficiencies are arising, especially as evening and weekend services are curtailed. Pressures on concessionary fares budgets are resulting in curtailment of free off-peak travel passes for pensioners, and restrict the ability to retain low fares for peak child travel, which could hit low-income households.

Concluding observations

A pessimistic view might see the public transport system in Britain as being in continual decline, faced with rising car ownership, and the negative impacts of local bus deregulation and rail privatization. Comparisons with other European countries, especially in respect of major conurbations, suggest that an approach based on a longer-run view of public transport investment has produced a much more favourable outcome. Project these trends on a few years, and an even greater disparity is evident.

However, this could be a somewhat naive view. There are some positive aspects to the experience in Britain in recent years, including increased staff productivity, the impact (where appropriately used) of high-frequency minibus services, and the growth of the domestic air network (often neglected as an element within the public transport system). An exchange of experience between Britain and other European countries could prove fruitful, in which the positive view of urban public transport investment and planning found elsewhere in Europe was "imported" to Britain, while more flexible working practices and small-scale innovations were "exported" to countries in which increased concern is being expressed about high labour costs and levels of public expenditure for operating support. The mix of tendered bus operations under a planned network, as found in London and in Copenhagen, could be seen as a sensible combination of the two approaches.

The "captive" public transport market in Britain, in the absence of any catastrophic changes in resources for private car use, is likely to continue declining. However, demand remains highly sensitive to service level, price and quality. Increased concern regarding the environmental and resources effects of high car dependence, together with that for the mobility of those without cars, create a major opportunity for an expanded public transport rôle. Further stress on the need to increase the share of travel taken by public transport is evident in the recommendations of the Royal Commission on Environmental Pollution published in October 1994. However, the extent to which this is take will depend on the appropriate response by both government and the transport operators. The bus industry currently as a poor public image, yet in most cases represents the main element of public transport provision. Improved rail networks in urban areas will be heavily constrained by high capital costs. The bus industry does possess the scope – through fleet renewal, busways, and improved information and ticketing systems – to change its image radically, provided that supporting policies are in place.

References and suggested further reading

Barman, C. 1979. *The man who built London Transport*. Newton Abbot: David & Charles.

Central Statistical Office 1994. *Social trends 24*. London: HMSO.

Chartered Institute of Transport 1993. *Bus routes to success*. London: CIT.

— 1994. *Whither the Clapham Omnibus? The Future for Buses in London*. London: CIT.

Department of the Environment 1993. PPG6 (revised): *Planning policy guidance: town centres and retail developments*. London: HMSO.

— 1994. PPG13: *Planning policy guidance 13: transport*. March. London: HMSO.

Department of Transport 1982. *Urban public transport: an economic assessment of value for money*. Technical Report, London, December.

— 1989. Local Authority Circular 3/89.

— 1991. The role of investment appraisal in road and rail transport.

— 1993. Transport Policies and Programme Submissions for 1994–95. Local Authority Circular 2/93, April.

Fairhurst, M. H. 1993. *An analysis of bus passenger traffic trends in England since 1982*. London Transport Planning Department Research Report R272.

Glaister, S. (ed.) 1991. *Transport options for London*. Greater London Group, London School of Economics.

— & G. Searle 1984. Estimating the economic benefits of public transport subsidy.

PTRC Summer Annual Meeting, July, seminar J, pp. 5–18.

Heggie, I. G. 1976. *Modal choice and the value of travel time*. Oxford: Oxford University Press.

Joy, S. 1973. *The train that ran away*. London: Ian Allan.

Pryke, R. & J. S. Dodgson 1975. *The rail problem*. Oxford: Martin Robertson.

Royal Commission on Environmental Pollution 1994. *Transport and the Environmnent*. London: HMSO.

Savage, I. 1985. *The deregulation of bus services*. Aldershot: Gower Press.

Sturt, A. & D. Bull 1993. Putting broad accessibility principles into planning practice. *Town and Country Planning*, **62**(10), 268–72.

Thornthwaite, S. 1994. *School transport*. Preston: Transport Advisory Services.

Turner, R. P. 1985. Rates fair? *An evaluation of revenue support, rates and bus/Underground fares in Greater London*. Discussion Paper 14, Transport Studies Group, Polytechnic of Central London.

— & P. R. White 1985. To plan or not to plan? Three-year plans under the Transport Act 1983, the buses White Paper and beyond. In *Implications of the 1985 Transport Bill*, R. Knowles (ed.), 45–98. London: Institute of British Geographers.

Tyson, W. J. 1992. Bus deregulation – five years on. London: Association of Metropolitan Authorities/Passenger Transport Executives' Group.

Virley, S. The effect of fuel price increases on road transport CO_2 emissions. *Transport Policy* **1**(1), 43–8.

White, P. R. 1990. Bus deregulation: a welfare balance sheet. *Journal of Transport Economics and Policy*, 311–32.

— 1993. Road passenger transport and deregulation. *Public Money and Management* **13**(1), 35–9.

— 1994. Public transport: privatization and investment. *Journal of Transport Policy* **1**(3), 184–94.

— & S. Tough 1993. *Alternative tendering systems and deregulation in Britain*. Paper presented at the Third International Conference on Ownership and Regulation in Surface Passenger Transport, Mississauga, Canada, September.

— & R. P. Turner, T. C. Mbara 1992. Cost–benefit analysis of urban minibus operations. *Transportation* **19**, 59–74.

As developments in government policy are subject to rapid change, readers will find it helpful to keep up to date through the technical press. The most useful reference for this purpose is *Local Transport Today*, published fortnightly.

Index